ETHNIC MINORITY MEDIA

COMMUNICATION AND HUMAN VALUES

SERIES EDITORS

Robert A. White, Editor, *The Centre of Interdisciplinary Studies in Communication, The Gregorian University, Rome, Italy*
Michael Traber, Associate Editor, *World Association for Christian Communication, London, UK*

INTERNATIONAL EDITORIAL ADVISORY BOARD

ETHNIC MINORITY MEDIA

An International Perspective

edited by Stephen Harold Riggins

SAGE Publications
International Educational and Professional Publisher
Newbury Park   London   New Delhi

For information address:

 SAGE Publications, Inc.
2455 Teller Road
Newbury Park, California 91320

SAGE Publications Ltd.
6 Bonhill Street
London EC2A 4PU
United Kingdom

SAGE Publications India Pvt. Ltd.
M-32 Market
Greater Kailash I
New Delhi 110 048 India

Printed in the United States of America

Library of Congress Cataloging-in-Publication Data

Main entry under title:
  Ethnic minority media: an international perspective / Stephen Harold
    Riggins, editor.
        p. cm.—(Communication and human values)
    Includes bibliographical references and index.
    ISBN 0-8039-4723-2. —ISBN 0-8039-4724-0 (pbk.)
    1. Ethnic mass media. II. Riggins, Stephen Harold, 1946-   .
    II. Series: Communication and human values (Newbury Park, Calif.)
    P94.5.M55E87   1992
    302.23'089—dc20   92-20794

93 94 95 96 10 9 8 7 6 5 4 3 2

Sage Production Editor: Astrid Virding

Contents

The Media Imperative: Ethnic Minority Survival in the Age
of Mass Communication   1
   Stephen Harold Riggins

Part I: Models of Aboriginal Survival

1. Ethnic Broadcasting in Alaska: The Failure of a
   Participatory Model   23
      Patrick J. Daley and Beverly James

2. Mass Media in Greenland: The Politics of Survival   44
      Marianne A. Stenbaek

3. Communication, Culture, and Technology: Satellites
   and Northern Native Broadcasting in Canada   63
      Gail Valaskakis

4. Broadcasting in Aboriginal Australia: One Mob, One
   Voice, One Land   82
      Michael Meadows

5. Inadvertent Assimilationism in the Canadian
   Native Press   102
      Stephen Harold Riggins

6. A Radio for the Mapuches of Chile: From Popular
   Education to Political Awareness   127
      Raymond Colle

7. Flaws in the Melting Pot: Hawaiian Media   149
      John Henningham

Part II: The Quest for Media Space by Immigrants and Indigenous, Integrated Minorities

8. Local Radio and Regional Languages in
    Southwestern France   165
    Jean-Jacques Cheval

9. *Revista Mea:* Keeping Alive the Romanian
    Community in Israel   196
    Gabriel Bar-Haïm

10. Minority-Language Broadcasting and the
    Continuation of Celtic Culture in Wales and Ireland   217
    W. J. Howell, Jr.

11. The Postcolonial Policy of Algerian Broadcasting
    in Kabyle   243
    Zahir Ihaddaden

12. Spanish-Language Media in the Greater New York
    Region During the 1980s   256
    John D. H. Downing

The Promise and Limits of Ethnic Minority Media   276
    Stephen Harold Riggins

Name Index   289

Subject Index   294

About the Editor   297

About the Contributors   298

The Media Imperative:
Ethnic Minority Survival
in the Age of Mass Communication

STEPHEN HAROLD RIGGINS

Introduction

This book focuses on the topic of ethnic survival and examines the role that ethnic mass media play in this process. Its aim is to provide a broad international sampling of case studies spanning a variety of ethnic minorities and countries, each presenting a different set of cultural, political, and economic conditions. Historically, the ethnic diversity of most pluralistic societies is due to military conquest. Part I is thus concerned with societies which at the time of conquest were composed of groups that were small, stateless, hunters and gatherers or horticulturalists: Aborigines in Australia, Inuit in Greenland, Native Americans in the United States and Canada, and Mapuches in Chile. Part II addresses the case of immigrant minorities, so-called voluntary minorities, and groups that historically were more closely integrated into the surrounding dominant society and for the most part composed of settled, agrarian populations. Their struggle for regional identity and linguistic survival is obviously occurring in a different sociopolitical context and raises its own type of problems. Groups discussed in part two include the Welsh, Irish, Basques, Occitans, Romanians, Kabyles, and Hispanics.

The term *ethnicity* has been defined in a variety of ways, but there is general agreement that it refers to people who perceive themselves as constituting a community because of common culture, ancestry, language, history, religion, or customs. It is unlikely that a group will perceive itself to be unique in all of these respects, and one or two characteristics may be chosen as most symbolic of collective identity.

1

It has been suggested that *ethno-racial-religious group* might be a more accurate term than *ethnic group* (Herberg, 1989). But for the sake of simplicity the latter continues to be used. *Ethnic group* is not a synonym for *minority*. In the words of Everett Hughes, "we are all ethnic" (cited in Tonkin, McDonald, & Chapman, 1989, p. 16). Nor should it be assumed that only minority identity is fragile. Majority identities are also poorly defined, ambiguous, and are no doubt composed of conflicting values (Forsythe, 1989).

The average person is likely to think of ethnicity as an unalterable fact of life determined at birth. However, modern research tends to conceptualize ethnicity as a social construction, a matter of negotiated self-identity and "imagined communities" (Anderson, 1983, p. 15). Although ethnic identity to some extent obviously consists of ascribed characteristics, that is statuses determined at birth, it is also in part an achievement at both an individual and group level. Far from being an unproblematic primordial given, ethnicity can be "rediscovered" or "reclaimed." Moreover, not only do groups disappear through assimilation and acculturation but new ethnic groups are continually forming. Ethnicity is consequently a dynamic process (Staino, 1980), requiring at least two groups in interaction because social isolation tends to hinder people from perceiving their commonality (Lieberson, 1985). Ethnicity involves an individual's *choice* to identify with a group and the *reaction* to that group by outsiders. "Ethnicity is not a constant or uniform social experience either for individuals or for groups. Rather, it is a variant, processual, and emergent phenomenon and will therefore reveal itself in different forms and with varying degrees of intensity in different social settings" (Marger & Obermiller, 1987, p. 2).

The mass media play a key role in this dynamic process by defining, preserving, or weakening ethnic (and national) identities. All mass media content could be analyzed from the perspective of what is revealed about ethnicity. The *New York Times,* for example, could be read as an ethnic newspaper, although it is not explicitly or self-consciously ethnic. The focus of this book, however, is more narrow because the contributors write about ethnic *minority* media. They thus deal with two related but distinguishable concepts: ethnicity and minority-majority relationships.

The mainstream mass media have tended to ignore ethnic minorities or to present them essentially in terms of the social problems they create for the majority. The assimilationist influences that mainstream media exert on ethnic minorities have been amply documented (e.g., Abu-Laban,

1980; Greenberg et al., 1983; Khaki & Prasad, 1988; LaRuffa, 1982; Lee, 1981; Martindale, 1986; Murphy & Murphy, 1981; White & White, 1983; Wilson & Gutiérrez, 1985). Even apparently neutral news items have been shown to convey deeply rooted prejudices that have far-reaching consequences (e.g., Van Dijk, 1988). To cite the remarks of a minority journalist, the Inuit broadcaster Rosemarie Kuptana has compared mainstream television to the neutron bomb:

> We might liken the onslaught of southern [Canadian] television and the absence of native television to the neutron bomb. This is the bomb that kills the people but leaves the buildings standing. Neutron bomb television is the kind of television that destroys the soul of a people but leaves the shell of a people walking around. This is television in which the traditions, the skills, the culture, the language count for nothing. The pressure, especially on our children, to join the invading culture and language and leave behind a language and culture that count for nothing is explosively powerful. (cited in Brisebois, 1983, p. 107)

The social influence of ethnic minority media is not well understood because the topic has been relatively neglected. There are several reasons for this. Investigating ethnic minority journalism generally requires that a researcher be bilingual and many journalism scholars are not fluent in two languages. Studies of ethnic minority literature, which are considerable in number, typically exclude popular journalism or cover the topic superficially (e.g., Petrone, 1990). In addition, sociologists share some of the blame for the paucity of research, because their preference for quantifiable information has resulted in their ignoring most literary or journalistic sources (Padolsky, 1990).

Obviously, if minority media did not contribute to ethnic cohesion and cultural maintenance to some extent, there would be little justification for their existence except as a marketing tool and an instrument of social control. What better strategy could there be for ensuring minority survival than the development by minorities of their own media conveying their own point of view in their own language? In this manner, steps can be taken to guarantee that cultural traditions are not reduced to the level of folklore and that languages evolve in a manner adaptive to the requirements of modern societies. This might be referred to as the *media imperative* of modern life, a fact recognized by minorities throughout the world who have lobbied for greater access to the means of media production.

On the other hand, ethnic minority media may also unintentionally encourage the assimilation of their audiences to mainstream values (Black & Leithner, 1987; Hardt, 1989; Subervi-Vélez, 1986; Wilson & Gutiérrez, 1985; Zubrzycki, 1958). Assimilation has been defined as a type of "ethnic change in which people become similar, and contrasted with differentiation in which groups stress their distinctiveness, for example by observing food taboos or displaying distinctive signs and symbols" (Cashmore, 1988, p. 26). Many early 20th-century sociologists who studied the immigrant press in the United States concluded that it did promote assimilation because it was one of the major means by which immigrants informed themselves about the dominant social values of their host society (Park, 1922; Bogardus, 1933).

Rather than choosing between these two opposing tendencies, it might be more realistic to assume that ethnic media fulfill both functions. Subervi-Vélez (1986) calls this the "dual role" of ethnic media. The contributors to this volume may not actually use this term in the following chapters, but it is nonetheless obvious from their research that the dual role is an accurate description of the media content they examine in their case studies. Viewing ethnic media as fulfilling a dual role raises many questions. The following questions are some of the most important ones relevant to the problems addressed by the chapters in this volume. Does the balance of assimilationist-pluralist functions vary over time? To what extent is the balance influenced by the group being indigenous or immigrant, modern or traditional? How much assimilationist content could be avoided by changing the education of journalists or the organizational structure of minority media? Is it possible that ethnic media promote assimilation in terms of some core values but in other respects preserve group uniqueness? Do ethnic media have the same influence when diffused in minority and majority languages?

Historical Experiences of
Ethnic Minority Groups

One way of comparing ethnic minority populations is on the basis of their values and geographical origins. This would be the question of whether their values are traditional or modern and their origins indigenous or foreign. *Traditional* refers to the values of hunters and gatherers or pastoralists that are difficult to reconcile with industrialism and capitalism. *Modern* is understood here as values consistent with capitalism or industrialism and the bureaucratic structures both require. *Modern* and *traditional* should not be equated with *progress* and *backwardness*. As Smolicz (1988) writes:

> It is erroneous to regard tradition as invariably hindering social change since, in a society with a long established civilization, resilience depends on new developments being incorporated into traditional values. At the same time, a tradition can only survive the vicissitudes of time and continue to flourish if it accommodates itself to the present. (p. 388)

One category of ethnic minority consists of *indigenous* people who remain committed to *traditional* values. In this volume that includes all of the studies in Part I. Such people have a political advantage in that as indigenous residents their claims for language and cultural protection are likely to be seen by others as more legitimate than the claims of immigrants. This is important because the long-term survival of minority media requires a supportive attitude from the majority population.

A second category of minorities consists of *indigenous* people whose *modern* values appear to be primarily a subcultural variation of the dominant values in their country. This would include several groups studied in Part II of this book: the Welsh, Irish, Kabyles, Occitans, and Basques. Language retention rather than cultural values tends to be the main concern of activists in this category.

A third category is formed by the so-called voluntary minorities, *immigrants* with *modern* values who choose to move usually for economic or political reasons. In Part II this includes Hispanics in the United States and Eastern-European Jews in Israel. These people belong to large linguistic communities whose survival is not threatened, and as voluntary immigrants they are perceived in the host country as having few rights to demand cultural protection. Indeed, their continuing attachment to their countries of origin may be resented by the host country.

The relatively rare fourth category of an *immigrant* group with *traditional* values is not investigated in this volume nor is the informational situation of refugees and migrant workers, a topic that would justify another volume of similar case studies (see Hujanen, 1984, 1989).

In traditional societies the introduction of any form of modern communication, including print media, may be rife with paradoxes involving questions resolved long ago in other groups. Russel Means, one of the founders of the American Indian Movement, believes that the acquisition of literacy is self-defeating in an oral society. Means (n.d.) has said:

> I detest writing. The process itself epitomizes the European concept of "legitimate" thinking; what is written has an importance that is denied the spoken. My culture, the Lakota culture, has an oral tradition and so I ordinarily reject writing. It is one of the white world's ways of destroying the cultures of non-European peoples; the imposing of an abstraction over the spoken relationship of a people. (p. 19)

Means has intuitively understood the basic idea of *medium theory:* A society's preferred medium of communication can be related to its cultural characteristics. (Meyrowitz, 1985, provides a good summary of medium theory and uses it to explain the social influence of television in contemporary North America.) Although none of the contributors to this book takes a position as radical as that of Means, all would undoubtedly agree that some amount of cultural change does result from the introduction of print and broadcast media.

Means's argument, however, should be qualified by pointing out that some compromise, some degree of acculturation, is inevitable—perhaps even desirable—when modern mass media are used in more traditional cultures. As Michael Meadows reports in Chapter 4, Australian Aborigines transform to a significant extent the stories and events that are reported on mainstream television in agreement with their own immemorial traditions. This demonstrates at least the relative plasticity of the electronic media. If Means's position were taken literally, the surest method of protecting the "purity" of a society's culture would be through social isolation. But few societies today are in a position to promote social isolation without incurring devastating consequences. Superficially, broadcast media appear to convey information in a manner consistent with an oral culture, but this overlooks the fact that television and radio contribute as profoundly to cultural change because they are so intrusive within the home and, therefore, influence infants at a crucial stage in their psychological development. Furthermore, few minority groups have the financial possibilities of creating all of the programming they broadcast and are bound to include content produced by outsiders. The result is the multicultural mix (for example, the television program *Sesame Street* broadcast in the Greenlandic language) that characterizes most ethnic minority broadcasting today.

Russel Means would appear to be a *technopessimist* because he foresees only detrimental consequences from new communications technologies. Marianne Stenbaek's research about Greenland rejects most strongly this view (Chapter 2). Stenbaek emphasizes the advantages for minorities of receiving news in their own language about foreign countries. The content of modern mass media can be situated by minorities within the context of their own values and historic experiences, however different they may be from the media's explicit messages. Audiences are not just passive recipients of mass media messages; they are also active interpreters (Fiske, 1987; Gailey, 1989). The research of Granzberg, Steinbring, & Hamer (1977) is one of the best illustrations of this idea as it relates to native North Americans. Using participant observation methods and surveys, Granzberg et al. studied the introduction of television in a remote Canadian Cree community. They found that the Canadian Cree related television to traditional ideas about dreaming and to ceremonies in which "spirits" communicate with participants. The magic of television, that is its reception of sights and sounds over long distances, reminded the Cree of their shaking tent ceremony in which participants communicate with distant spirits. Consequently, the Cree gave television the name of the shaking tent ceremony, *Koosabachigan*. Just as these spirits were assumed to communicate truthfully, the content of television was generally assumed to be truthful. Young boys tended to identify strongly with television heroes, perhaps the way earlier generations would have identified with friendly spirits. Adult Cree also sometimes looked to television programs for omens concerning their own future as one might search for omens in dreams. Nonetheless, the researchers found that it was often the most traditional Cree who were most critical of the content of television, especially its effect on children. In the past, shamans were supposed to protect the young from evil, but in a modern society, they believed, no one successfully protected them from televised violence and sex. Granzberg et al. (1977) concluded:

> Traditional conceptions of communication influence the ways new media are perceived and used. The traditional conceptions seem to cause the Cree to be very susceptible to TV, to take it literally and seriously, to idolize the superhero characters, to read special messages into it concerning behavior requirements, and to be especially concerned about its potential harm to children. . . . We cannot consider TV to be a uniform phenomenon cross-culturally: TV is a different thing to different people and its impact varies according to cultural traditions that surround it. (p. 157)

External Structural Support:
The State

Media organizations are not socially autonomous entities but are integrated in larger socioeconomic systems. They are affected most obviously by the state through policies of subsidization, regulation, and legislation. The state makes possible the technological and economic transfers that permit minorities to assume the means of media production, even though success may ultimately depend most on actions undertaken by minority communities themselves. The boundaries of nation states and linguistic groups rarely, if ever, coincide. Although about 180 nations are presently members of the United Nations, it is estimated that there are between 3,000 and 4,000 languages throughout the world (Srivastava, 1990). Half of the spoken languages are expected to disappear within a century (Ross, 1991). The multicultural, multilingual character of the nations discussed in this volume has been recognized to varying degrees by their respective governments. Genuine multiculturalism requires multilingualism, but in many nations multicultural policies are established within the framework of official unilingualism or bilingualism. This restriction of languages favors the cultural practices, institutions, and history of one or two dominant groups to the disadvantage of the others.

Because allocating money, time, or broadcast space to minorities reduces the available resources, it should not be assumed that technological and economic transfers are spontaneous gestures of goodwill. Instead, they would appear to be decisions made according to state objectives, which may not be fully articulated in public or necessarily identical with the objectives of minorities themselves. Minority journalism carries the threat of promoting national disintegration. Consequently, it is not surprising that a state might have inconsistent policies, promoting minority media while simultaneously following policies of containment and repression. The state's multicultural strategies, on which the development of ethnic minority media depends, might be conceptualized in terms of the following five models that are examined or implied by the papers in this volume.

The Integrationist Model
It might be assumed by state authorities that subsidizing minority media would not fragment the state but better integrate minorities into national life, because such policies would encourage them to perceive

the state as a benevolent institution. At the same time the state would be able to monitor minorities more easily and, if necessary, curtail trends toward political independence. It could also be assumed that through minority media state control would reach those who had not achieved functional bilingualism or fluency in the majority language. This model has been explicitly applied to Australia (Husband, 1986). It also seems to be a factor in all of the countries examined in this book.

The Economic Model

Due to their economic deprivation and often high rates of illiteracy, ethnic minorities are likely to be engaged in unskilled manual labor. However, as societies modernize, the percentage of the population holding such occupations declines and more people are required who can work in positions necessitating higher levels of education and professional training. The state may view multiculturalism as educationally beneficial because it helps to develop literacy and to ensure that primary and secondary schools are more effective in reaching minority students. Thus the state's commitment may not be to multiculturalism per se but to the economic advantages that are perceived as being one of its consequences. That multicultural policies are ineffective from the point of view of long-term preservation of a culture or language may be of little concern to the state because that was never the real motivating factor.

The economic and integrationist models are compatible. Both models presuppose a state superficially committed to multiculturalism. In both cases state officials may publicly proclaim faith in multiculturalism but assume that it is a transitional phase that will not modify their country's core values. Such policies might be referred to as the *new assimilationism,* because they are assimilationist policies disguised as multiculturalism. An analogy is made here with the subtle racism that is sometimes called *the new racism* (Van Dijk, 1987).

A case in point is Canada where English Canadians have tended to define their country in opposition to the United States, contrasting Canadian tolerance of multiculturalism with American pressures to assimilate immigrants (Burnet, 1987; Weinfeld, 1985). The Canadian state has devoted considerable resources to multicuturalism since the 1970s, including publishing and broadcasting. As documented by Gail Valaskakis (Chapter 3), the Canadian government has assisted the creation of one of the most active native television networks in North America. This is the Inuit Broadcasting Corporation, which has been producing about 5 hours of television programming a week. Considering that the Inuit population of Canada is approximately 25,000, this amount of programming is quite an achievement. (In 1992, Canadians launched Television Northern Canada, the largest aboriginal television network in the world and one that will broadcast in 15 native languages, Platiel, 1992.) Comparing Valaskakis's research with Patrick Daley and Beverly James's on Alaska (Chapter 1) and with John Henningham's on Hawaii (Chapter 7), it is clear that in terms of multicultural policies there are real differences between Canada and the United States. In Alaska, preference was given to technological efficiency in establishing a state television network, a pattern that muted citizen participation of all types including native programming preferences. The last Hawaiian-language newspaper ceased publication in 1948. At present, an estimated 30 children under the age of 5 speak Hawaiian as their first language. Nonetheless, the Inuit Broadcasting Corporation in Canada remains fragile, dependent on the goodwill of nonnative politicians, bureaucrats, and broadcasters. No formal government definition of *fair access* to distribution systems, such as satellites, has been made. Therefore, Canada illustrates shallow rather than genuine multiculturalism.

The Divisive Model

The state can also use ethnicity to maintain or create some levels of tension and rivalry in a country to further its own objective of social control either in the context of colonialism or geopolitical order. This model would apply to the Kabyles in Algeria during the colonial era. Zahir Ihaddaden shows that Algeria inherited a Kabyle radio channel devised by French authorities as part of a plan to foster disunity in the colonized country by encouraging ethnic rivalry (Chapter 11). Not surprisingly, this created great ambivalence when Algeria became independent, and the role of the channel had to be reconsidered. Authorities could not abandon the channel because they needed to communicate with a largely illiterate population, but they did not see the Kabyle dialect as the heritage of the whole Algerian people. Now that the government is committed to Arabization, half-hearted support is being given to the Kabyle channel.

The Preemptive Model

It is not unusual for the state to establish its own minority media to preempt minorities from founding organizations which would be independent of the state. This is discussed by Jean-Jacques Cheval in his study of radio stations in southern France (Chapter 8). He writes about a situation in which public and private local radio stations were in competition for the same small ethnic minority audience. State policy seems to have allowed the private stations to drop their commitment to regional languages and evolve in a commercial direction, reducing their potential threat to the status quo. Consequently, state-operated public stations presently remain the ones most committed to regional languages.

The Proselytism Model

The state or a transnational organization may explicitly attempt to promote values through the mass media and thus devise appropriate means for reaching minority audiences in their own language. The proselytism model could be used to interpret Raymond Colle's study of a radio station for the Mapuches of Chile (Chapter 6). The Mapuches transmit cultural programs by means of a station that was created by the Catholic church for social and religious purposes. The preservation of the local language and culture was not the original aim of the station. The Mapuches themselves opportunistically oriented part of the programming in that direction although the station retains its original aims.

These models are not meant to define rigid categories of policies, but rather set forth some significant features of the political and economic motivations that constrain the emergence of ethnic minority media (see also Gordon, 1978; Herberg, 1989). Although fundamental, the state's influence is only one type of control. Naturally, all constraints limit the power of ethnic media to effect change.

External Structural Support:
Social Movements

The ethnic groups that compose multicultural societies are in competition for desired goods: prestige, wealth, land, and so on. Conflicts are unavoidable, in the opinion of some authors, although this is not to say that a high level of violent conflict is necessarily inevitable. All of the ethnic groups examined in this book are populations that, for a variety of reasons, have been relatively unsuccessful competitors and are thus poor, alienated, and marginalized to some degree. In each case a reformative collective or social movement, generated from within or promoted from outside, has endeavored to restore the group to a position of equality. Consequently, ethnic minority mass media need to be conceptualized as part of the larger framework of social movements.

A social movement is defined as "shared activities and beliefs directed toward the demand for change in some aspect of the social order" (Gusfield, 1970, p. 2). A minimal level of organization is required for collective activities to qualify as a social movement. By definition, social movements lack many normal channels for effecting change. They do not have legislative or enforcement powers; they lack money and have few ways of rewarding and punishing adherents. Stewart, Smith, and Denton (1984) write in their book on social movements and persuasion:

> The [mainstream] mass media are rarely favorable toward social movements (unless success appears to be near), are rarely controlled in any manner by social movements, and provide exposure at great monetary expense or when a social movement does something spectacular or stupid. Persuasion is the sole means available to most social movements for accomplishing such functions as transforming perceptions of society, prescribing courses of action, and mobilizing the movement. (p. 5)

Thus mass media affiliated with social movements are essential for creating and sustaining beliefs in collective goals. The life cycle of social movements and media organizations are intertwined. Media have an impact on a movement's progression through its life cycle; in turn the stage of the life cycle influences media viability. The fate of minority media is linked to the perception and success of social movements in the nation as a whole because they are the source of audiences and volunteer workers. Social movements also influence concepts of communication ethics. In a paper on the social and political factors related to different communication ethics, Robert A. White (1989) contrasts the conventional idealization of professionalism in mainstream commercial media with its rejection by minority media. Because the latter is more concerned with journalists' responsibility to a community or movement, there may be an active rejection of autonomous professionals whose standards are set internally in favor of a participatory approach to communication that welcomes citizen input. The result may not necessarily be the most objective reporting of events.

The linguistic activists who belong to social movements may have disagreements about the best strategy for language preservation. This theme is discussed by W. J. Howell, Jr., in his study of broadcasting in

Irish and Welsh (Chapter 10). Howell refers to two rival concepts of language held by activists: *language as a means of communication* and *language as an expression of cultural identity and heritage.* Such rivalries can only interfere with the policy of survival through minority media. In Howell's opinion, the Welsh activists who have a flexible attitude toward collaboration with commercial broadcasters have achieved the most in terms of minority-language production. The inflexibility of competing ethnic organizations, which is by no means unusual and can trap journalists as well as researchers, is documented by Maryon McDonald (1987) in a study reflecting on her fieldwork experiences in the French province of Britanny.

Some of the authors in this volume tend to conceptualize ethnic minorities primarily in terms of their culture, whereas other authors place more emphasis on the class position of the minority. John Downing argues in his study of Hispanic media in New York City that an ethnic group should be conceptualized in terms of both culture and class (Chapter 12). To use minority media for the purpose of assimilating American Hispanics, who are largely of working-class origin, may help to solve problems of social inequality, but then the community disappears; alternatively, to emphasize cultural retention, which would preserve the community, may do little to resolve inequality. It is clear from such considerations that the effectiveness of media empowerment depends partly on social and cultural factors independent of the state. They have to be taken into consideration when assessing the emergence, evolution, and eventual success or failure of minority media.

Internal Structural Support

It is likely that some of the erosion of linguistic and cultural diversity that has occurred in the past decades is not due to mass media per se, but to an organizational framework based on commercial values. An interesting example of how commercial values can distort the filmed version of minority stories and mythology is provided by Fienup-Riordan (1988) in a discussion of an Alaskan native film that was supposed to star the white actor Robert Redford. For the screenplay, the site of the story was changed; a wife and grandchildren were invented for the hero who was childless and unmarried in the traditional stories; his attitudes toward violence were altered; distinct social roles of warrior, hunter, and shaman were collapsed into one role; native concepts of space, time, and personhood were ignored; and so forth. Mundane questions about how film production companies, radio stations, and newspapers pay their bills are not insignificant because the level and origin of funding affect the type and quality of the product presented to the public. The internal operation of media organizations establish the context within which news is gathered and processed and events defined as worthy of public attention. Important components of the internal structural support of ethnic minority media are the organization of communications societies, the goals of associations that sponsor ethnic media, and the available human resources (Gallagher, 1982).

Few of the organizations examined in this book are operated as profit-making enterprises. The exception is some Hispanic media in the United States, which generate profits at a level attractive to major American corporations because of the sheer number of members of this minority and advertiser interest in it. Otherwise, ethnic minority media organizations are typically structured as informal associations rather than formal bureaucracies. Their organization is similar to many noncommercial alternative media. Much of the work at all levels is done on a volunteer basis or by underpaid, part-time staff. Roles and regulations are often quite flexible, and there is likely to be little task specialization. Individuals hired to fill one role may find themselves working at a variety of functions. Indeed, from the point of view of personal satisfaction, this is one of the advantages of minority journalism. It is not unusual for cooperative agreements concerning advertising, articles, or personnel to be made among the media of an ethnic group to reduce costs. A formal statement of organizational goals may be produced, but it is probably written in vague, idealistic terms and rarely used by the staff except in exceptional circumstances. An editor may report to a board of volunteer directors that has the formal authority to determine content. However, the board may allocate responsibility for most managerial decisions to the editor.

Many of the organizations studied in this book are unstable and may prove to be short lived. Only one has an impressively long history, the Greenlandic newspaper *Atuagagdliutit,* which was established in 1861 and still survives, although in a bilingual format. Poor funding would appear to be the major reason for the chronic instability. A balance between private and public sources of funding—a pattern that might maximize freedom of expression—is difficult for many organizations to maintain (Rada, 1979). Ethnic media have small audiences or low circulations and are often poorly distributed. Audiences may be too small, too poor, or too scattered to have much appeal for advertisers. Key people in fund-raising activities are frequently ethnic politicians, who may be quite ambivalent about their own media. Although they would like to see thriving ethnic minority media, they may also fear its potential to criticize. The result may be highly supportive verbal statements, but parsimonious funding (Riggins, 1983).

In some countries the easy solution—at least until the fiscal conservatism of the 1980s and 1990s—was to solicit government funding either through direct grants or through public service announcements. But these are likely to be comparatively small and changes in governmental policy are unpredictable. This instability and poor funding restrict the critical potential of ethnic minority media. Another common solution is to have the media formally affiliated with a more secure association such as a community center or a church. The umbrella organization may be the actual source of funding or it may allocate funds from a global budget originating elsewhere, perhaps from the government. The sponsor not only typically exerts influence on editorial policy and hiring but this type of organization also causes confusion in the public's mind about whether the media are serving the sponsor or the whole ethnic community.

Despite amateur backgrounds in journalism, it is not unusual for ethnic minority journalists, both volunteers and paid employees, to be better educated than their target audience and differ in personal interests and linguistic skills. With the best of intentions, the content they produce may not appeal to the audience as much as mainstream commercial programs.

A cursory examination of ethnic minority media makes a reader or viewer aware of the sustained attention they give a wide range of issues related to their audience. Mainstream media, in contrast, tend either to ignore minorities or treat them as social problems. The ideology of most of the programs and publications the contributors discuss would seem to be centrist or even conservative. There appears to be little radical, oppositional content. This may in fact be a general characteristic of ethnic minority media rather than a bias of the researchers who chose to study less controversial media. Although it is conceivable that the employees or the audiences prefer this type of content, alternatives are also hindered by the organizational structure within which this content is produced (see, e.g., Veciana-Suarez, 1990).

Conclusions

Students of ethnic minority media as well as policymakers and community leaders should keep in mind the system of variables that conditions the emergence and evolution of modern media as a tool for minority empowerment or domination. First, it is important to take into consideration the characteristics of ethnic minorities: the absolute and relative numbers of the ethnic minority population, the degree of homogeneity and self-organization, whether it is a literate or oral culture, the degree of assimilation and integration that the minority has achieved or the repression and persecution it has experienced, the degree of self-sufficiency or dependence on external assistance, and the degree of self-reliance with respect to financing, administering, and handling the technological component of the media.

Second, researchers must take into account the political structure and prevailing ideology of the state within which the process of empowerment or domination takes place. This includes ideologies varying from authoritarian centralism to constitutional pluralism and from coercive assimilation to a relative tolerance of diversity. The current capacity of the state to implement its policies should also be considered because this will either enhance or weaken the bureaucratic interface with ethnic minorities. The economy is an important variable for the process of empowerment. This applies not only to the economic system that prevails (that is a market economy, socialist economy, or various blends of the two) but also to the particular economic situation of a country.

A third set of variables pertains to the international context and includes such factors as whether there is an international consensus on the historical legitimacy of the minority's claims for empowerment, whether or not members of the same ethnic minority group form the dominant majority of other countries, whether as a result of history or recent immigration the minority forms a sizable or influential part of the population of another country, and the extent to which the political and economic interests of other countries happen to coincide with those of the ethnic minority.

As the case studies presented in this volume show, the presence or absence of some of these variables command a range of strategies of empowerment that may result in reliance on both internal and external resources. The former would include persuasion or negotiation, legal or illegal confrontation, and piggybacking; the latter would include the external help of another state in terms of money, equipment, technology, or international pressure on the diplomatic front and the outcome of hostile international confrontations. It is no less important to keep in mind that the very notion of ethnic minority survival is rife with social and ethical dilemmas. The concept of ethnic identity elicits such a range of passionate opinions that the topic is not unlike the projective ink blots of a Rorschach test. Ethnicity is for some people an indicator of a premodern identity and the ethnic revival of the 20th century, an inhumane retreat to "tribal caves wired for sight and sound" (Isaacs, 1975, p. 2). But others have seen in ethnicity an effective way of framing issues of social inequality in societies whose political elite feel less threatened by ethnic-based social movements than by those based more explicitly on class. Ethnic identity has been welcomed as a possible antidote to the excessive individualism of modern societies and its ironical consequence: uniformity. However one conceives of ethnicity, the current geopolitical situation proves that ethnic minority identity is going to remain a lively issue for a long time and increasingly to involve the mass media, particularly broadcasting.

As is suggested by the contributors to this volume, minority media entail unexpected paradoxes. Minority empowerment is in itself paradoxical. On one hand, the unique group identity of a relatively marginal population is revitalized from within and the politics of multiculturalism are advanced. But on the other hand, at the same time, the minority is likely to become more integrated into national life, because short of reaching total political independence, a high level of assimilation seems to be a prerequisite for achieving empowerment. The control of one's own media in the context of civil peace requires voluntary outside intervention, professional training, and efficient communication channels with the state and the population at large. In addition, effective minority media require that the group already possess the attributes of empowerment, such as high levels of education, status, and wealth.

All of the chapters forming this book are examples of various efforts to break this vicious circle. The circumstances vary, as do the results; the consequences may be unclear even when some level of empowerment is achieved. Hence the ambiguity that underlies the whole process of ethnic journalism. If cultural assertion and revitalization emerge from these chapters as more complex social processes than initially imagined, this is not to say that such efforts are necessarily doomed to fail. In fact, an understanding of the scholarly literature on ethnic media would seem to increase their likelihood of success.

References

Abu-Laban, B. (1980). *An olive branch on the family tree: The Arabs in Canada.* Toronto: McClelland & Stewart.

Anderson, B. (1983). *Imagined communities: Reflections on the origin and spread of nationalism.* London: Verso.

Black, J. H., & Leithner, C. (1987). Patterns of ethnic media consumption: A comparative examination of ethnic groupings in Toronto. *Canadian Ethnic Studies, 19*(1), 21-41.

Bogardus, E. S. (1933). The Filipino press in the U.S. *Sociology/Social Research, 28,* 581-585.

Brisebois, D. (1983). The Inuit Broadcasting Corporation. *Anthropologica, 25*(1), 107-115.

Burnet, J. (1987). Multiculturalism in Canada. In L. Driedger (Ed.), *Ethnic Canada: Identities and inequalities* (pp. 65-80). Toronto: Copp Clark Pitman Ltd.

Cashmore, E. E. (Ed.). (1988). *Dictionary of race and ethnic relations* (2nd ed.). London: Routledge.

Fienup-Riordan, A. (1988). Robert Redford, Apanuugpak, and the invention of tradition. *American Ethnologist 15*(3), 442-455.

Fiske, J. (1987). *Television culture.* London: Meuthen.

Forsythe, D. (1989). German identity and the problem of history. In E. Tonkin, M. McDonald, & M. Chapman (Eds.), *History and ethnicity* (pp. 137-156). London: Routledge.

Gailey, C. W. (1989). "Rambo" in Tonga: Video films and cultural resistance in the Tongan Islands (South Pacific). *Culture, 9*(1), 21-31.

Gallagher, M. (1982). Negotiation of control in media organizations and occupations. In M. Gurevitch, T. Bennett, J. Curran, & K. Woolacott (Eds.), *Culture, society and the media* (pp. 151-173). London: Methuen.

Gordon, M. (1978). *Human nature, class and ethnicity.* New York: Oxford University Press.

Granzberg, G., Steinbring, J., & Hamer, J. (1977). New magic for old: TV in Cree culture. *Journal of Communication, 27*(4), 154-157.

Greenberg, B. S., Burgoon, M., Burgoon, J., & Korzenny, F. (1983). *Mexican Americans and the mass media.* Norwood, NJ: Ablex.

Gusfield, J. R. (Ed.). (1970). *Protest, reform, and revolt: A reader in social movements.* New York: John Wiley.

Hardt, H. (1989). The foreign-language press in American press history. *Journal of Communication, 39*(2), 114-131.

Herberg, E. N. (1989). *Ethnic groups in Canada: Adaptations and transitions.* Toronto: Nelson.

Hujanen, T. (Ed.). (1984). *The role of information in the realization of the human rights of migrant workers.* Unpublished manuscript, Publications Series B, University of Tempere, Department of Journalism and Mass Communication, Tempere, Finland.

Hujanen, T. (Ed.). (1989). *Information, communication and the human rights of migrants.* Lausanne, Switzerland: Philip Morris Europe.

Husband, C. (1986). Mass media, communication policy and ethnic minorities: An appraisal of current theory and practice. In *Mass media and the minorities* (pp. 1-38). *RUSHSAP Series of Occasional Monographs and Papers, 17.*

Isaacs, H. R. (1975). *Idols of the tribe: Group identity and political change.* New York: Harper.

Khaki, A., & Prasad, K. (1988). *Depiction and perception: Native Indians and visible minorities in the media.* Vancouver: Ad Hoc Committee for Better Race Relations.

LaRuffa, A. (1982). Media portrayals of Italian Americans. *Ethnic Groups, 4,* 191-206.

Lee, A. M. (1981). Mass media mythmaking in the United Kingdom's interethnic struggles. *Ethnicity, 8,* 18-30.

Lieberson, S. (1985). Unhyphenated whites in the United States. *Ethnic and Racial Studies, 8*(1), 159-180.

Marger, M. N., & Obermiller, P. J. (1987). Emergent ethnicity among internal migrants: The case of Maritimers in Toronto. *Ethnic Groups, 7*(1), 1-17.

Martindale, C. (1986). *The white press and black America.* Westport, CT: Greenwood Press.

McDonald, M. (1987). The politics of fieldwork in Brittany. In A. Jackson (Ed.), *Anthropology at home* (pp. 120-138). London: Tavistock.

Means, R. (n.d.). The same old song. In W. Churchill (Ed.), *Marxism and native Americans* (pp. 19-34). Boston: South End Press.

Meyrowitz, J. (1985). *No sense of place: The impact of electronic media on social behavior.* New York: Oxford University Press.

Murphy, J. E., & Murphy, S. M. (1981). *Let my people know: American Indian journalism, 1828-1978.* Norman: University of Oklahoma Press.

Padolsky, E. (1990). Establishing the two-way street: Literary criticism and ethnic studies. *Canadian Ethnic Studies, 22*(1), 22-37.

Park, R. E. (1922). *The immigrant press and its control.* New York: Harper & Brothers.

Petrone, P. (1990). *Native literature in Canada.* Toronto: Oxford University Press.

Platiel, R. (1992, January 18). North channels own resources into primetime. *The (Toronto) Globe and Mail,* A7.

Rada, S. E. (1978). Ramah Navajo radio and cultural preservation. *Journal of Broadcasting, 22,* 361-372.

Riggins, S. H. (1983). The organizational structure of the *Toronto Native Times* (1968-1981). *Anthropologica, 25*(1), 37-52.

Ross, P. (1991, August). Hard words. *Scientific American,* 138-147.

Smolicz, J. J. (1988). Tradition, core values and intercultural development in plural societies. *Ethnic and Racial Studies, 11*(4), 387-410.

Srivastava, A. K. (1990). Multilingualism and school education in India: Special features, problems and prospects. In D. P. Pattanayak (Ed.), *Multilingualism in India* (pp. 37-53). Clevedon, Avon: Multilingual Matters Ltd.

Staino, K. V. (1980). Ethnicity as process. *Ethnicity, 7,* 27-33.

Stewart, C. J., Smith, C. A., & Denton, R. E., Jr. (1984). *Persuasion and social movements.* Prospect Heights, IL: Waveland Press.

Subervi-Vélez, F. A. (1986). The mass media and ethnic assimilation and pluralism: A review and research proposal with special focus on Hispanics. *Communication Research, 13*(1), 71-96.

Tonkin, E., McDonald, M., & Chapman, M. (Eds.). (1989). *History and ethnicity.* London: Routledge.

Van Dijk, T. (1987). *Communicating racism: Ethnic prejudice in thought and talk.* Newbury Park, CA: Sage.

Van Dijk, T. (1988). *News analysis: Case studies of international and national news in the press.* Hillsdale, NJ: Lawrence Erlbaum.

Veciana-Suarez, A. (1990). *Hispanic media: Impact and influence.* Washington, DC: The Media Institute.

Weinfeld, M. (1985). Myth and reality in the Canadian mosaic: °Affective ethnicty." In R. Bienvenue & J. Goldstein (Eds.), *Ethnicity and ethnic relations in Canada: A book of readings* (2nd ed., pp. 65-86). Toronto: Butterworth.

White, N. R., & White, P. B. (1983). Evaluating the immigrant presence: Press reporting of immigrants to Australia, 1935-1977. *Ethnic and Racial Studies, 6*(3), 284-307.

White, R. A. (1989). Social and political factors in the development of communication ethics. In T. W. Cooper, C. G. Christians, F. F. Plude, & R. A. White (Eds.), *Communication ethics and global change* (pp. 40-65). White Plains, NY: Longman.

Wilson, C. II, & Gutiérrez, F. (1985). *Minorities and the media: Diversity and the end of mass communications.* Beverly Hills, CA: Sage.

Zubrzycki, J. (1958). The role of the foreign language press in immigrant integration. *Population Studies, 12,* 73-82.

PART I

Models of Aboriginal Survival

1

Ethnic Broadcasting in Alaska:
The Failure of a Participatory Model

PATRICK J. DALEY
BEVERLY JAMES

Introduction

In recent years, native Alaskans living in the state's rural areas have suddenly been exposed to commercial, entertainment television. Along with other culturally disruptive innovations, television has had a profound influence on native patterns of life. The imposition of television follows a long-standing policy in the United States of welcoming national, ethnic, and racial minorities into the mainstream cultural melting pot. But although the policy of assimilation has worked reasonably well in the case of immigrants who share the dominant culture's European heritage, it has often had tragic consequences for native Americans.

Barrow native Charles Edwardsen, Jr., describes the effects of Western culture, including the mass media, on the cultural identity of Inupiats:

The "assimilated" Native places very little value on himself or his culture. He sees himself as he has been taught to see himself: inferior to the white man. The hostility and hate he may show for white society are as nothing compared to the tortured view he has of his own. The tragedy is not that he has been taught that he is worthless; the tragedy is that he believes it. . . . From papers, movies, television in the cities, from boarding school and books, he has come to know much about the clean, white, electric comforts of America and of the dirty, poor, muddy, sloppy village in which he was raised and in which he lives and in which he will die. (Gallagher, 1974, p. 80)

The sudden appearance of television in rural Alaska is not unlike its introduction in other isolated regions of the world. Indeed, Alaska has been likened in both popular (Fallows, 1984) and scholarly literature (Madigan & Peterson, 1977) to a developing country with substandard communication and transportation systems. Klausner and Foulks (1982) employ Wallerstein's concept of world systems as composed of core and peripheral societies to describe Alaska as peripheral to the United States, and native Alaskans as living at the periphery of the periphery.

Until the mid-1970s, the dominant paradigm for studying the process of modernization in underdeveloped regions was Everett Rogers's diffusion of innovations model. As Rogers (1976) describes it, the classic development model emphasized economic growth through industrialization and urbanization, based on the importation of capital-intensive technology. Neither distribution of wealth nor quality of life indicators were considered important; it was assumed that material comforts and mental well-being would trickle down to the poor. A major assumption was that patterns of development in North American and Western European nations could serve as blueprints for other regions.

In the postcolonial world of the 1960s, the model was widely used in programs aimed at assisting the developing nations of Africa, Asia, and Latin America. However, as Rogers (1976) himself later noted, the results of these programs were discouraging. Nations that received aid based on the dominant paradigm suffered increased economic stagnation, greater polarization of wealth and power, high unemployment, and food shortages. At the same time, the paradigm came under increasing attack for its paternalism and imperialistic overtones by critical scholars in the Third World (Fanon, 1965; Freire, 1970) as well as the West (Schiller, 1969).

By 1976, Rogers acknowledged the passing of the dominant paradigm and the emergence of alternative ways of conceptualizing the development process by diffusion scholars. He noted that the emerging paradigms have certain elements in common: They agree that there is no one "correct" path to development, but they share a set of practical and moral assumptions about the process of development. Among these assumptions is the belief that people must be allowed to assume greater responsibility for self-development. Diffusion scholars agree that development activities should be decentralized as much as possible, so that popular participation at the village level can take place (Rogers, 1976).

The development of telecommunications policy in Alaska was guided by these emerging notions of development as a participatory process.

With the exception of some minimal local public involvement in cable television programming, grass-roots participation in determining telecommunications policy is an alien practice in the United States. Rural Alaska is an exception for a couple of reasons. First, a modern communications system was erected almost overnight. In 1970, a large majority of communities in the state had no phone, radio, or television service. Today, almost all communities receive these basic services, and many locations are also integrated in electronic mail systems, teleconference networks, and computer-assisted instructional facilities.[1] The virtual absence of preexisting communication systems meant that planners could start with a fresh slate and attempt to draw users into the process of designing, implementing, and operating technically sophisticated systems.

Second, the economics of telecommunications in Alaska deviates from the usual private, commercial pattern found in the United States. Because of the state's extremely low population density, commercial television is unprofitable outside a handful of cities. Television was introduced to the bush through a series of experimental projects by the state in providing satellite-based telecommunications services to all villages with a population of at least 25. As a public service supported by state monies, television in rural Alaska was to be accountable to the public it served. Provisions were built into the experiments to allow village residents, mainly native Alaskans, to have a voice in programming decisions.[2]

This chapter argues that the ideal of development as a participatory process was doomed from the start because telecommunications policies in Alaska arose within an ideology that systematically mutes the public voice. Before examining the diffusion of television and efforts to institute consumer participation in programming decisions, we will suggest an alternative framework for understanding the process of modernization. This perspective is informed by Marx's concept of ideology as reformulated by the German critical theorist Jürgen Habermas to account for the depoliticized nature of contemporary Western societies.

Technology as Ideology

Marx's sketchy writings on ideology appear in his efforts to develop a materialist theory of history. For Marx, the starting point of human history is humanity's struggle with nature and the transformation of the conditions of our existence. In the course of producing the means of subsistence, humanity also produces ideas, language, and consciousness.

These find concrete expression in the institutions we construct, such as laws, political systems, and religions. This mental production is shaped by the material conditions and material activities in which we are engaged. Thus consciousness grows out of our material existence as real, physical human beings. Furthermore, ideas, language, and consciousness are social products. They arise only as individuals begin to modify nature through their productive activities, and thus see themselves as apart and separate from their natural surroundings, including other people (Marx & Engels, 1970).

At some point in the historical struggle with nature, the techniques of survival are advanced to the degree that individuals produce more than they consume. At that point, conflicts arise as to how to distribute the excess production. Situations develop in which some people appropriate the fruits of other people's labor, and a class society arises. The various forms this appropriation takes determine the forms of political life and consciousness, that is, how people understand their own existence.

In a key passage of *The German Ideology,* Marx and Engels (1970) write that the class that is the ruling material force is also the ruling intellectual force. The ruling ideas are the expression of the dominant material relations. The ruling class controls the production and distribution of the ideas of their age, and these ideas take on the character of eternal law. In the bourgeois era in which Marx was writing, control over the production and distribution of ideas was concentrated in the hands of capitalist owners of the means of production. As a result of this control, their views and accounts of the world dominated the thinking of subordinate groups. The prevailing ideology, which served to maintain class inequalities, was one of just exchange and equality of the market.

Habermas believes Marx's analysis was correct, but that a reformulation is called for, because over the last century, industrialization has radically altered the productive process. He agrees that in Marx's time the chief source of surplus value was the labor power of workers, and that the dominant ideology that served to mask this fact was the notion of equal exchange. But in advanced industrial society, technology and science have become the leading productive forces and have given rise to a new ideology, a technocratic consciousness, in which political decisions are justified in terms of technical questions (Habermas, 1970). Following Marcuse, Habermas (1970) argues that because technical rationality "extends to the correct choice among strategies, the appropriate application of technologies, and the efficient establishment of systems (with *presupposed* aims in *given* situations), it removes the total social framework of interests in which strategies are chosen, technologies applied, and systems established, from the scope of reflection and rational reconstructions" (p. 82).

In other words, the public is no longer capable of participating in social, political, and economic affairs, as administrators and experts are increasingly called on to make decisions based on technocratic criteria of efficiency and economy. The progress of science and technology appears to follow an immanent law of objective exigencies that must be obeyed. But when this appearance has taken root, Habermas (1970) writes, "then propaganda can refer to the role of technology and science in order to explain and legitimate why in modern societies the process of democratic decision making about practical problems loses its function and 'must' be replaced by plebiscitary decisions about alternative sets of leaders of administrative personnel" (p. 105).

As we will see, Habermas's (1970) description of technocracy as a "background ideology that penetrates into the consciousness of the depoliticized mass of the population" (p. 105) pertains to the politics of electronic communication in Alaska. Our research shows that despite apparently good intentions state planners only gave fleeting attention to communication as interaction and focused their attention on communications hardware as if it were the solution to modernization and education. The reification of communication as object, together with the diffusion of the means of monologic communication without regard for the cultural context of the recipients, resulted in the imposition of a technocratic and consumer consciousness that threatens the survival of traditional native Alaskan culture and identities.

Low-Power Television Stations

The first serious consideration of satellite communications in Alaska began in 1970 with a joint UNESCO-National Education Association investigation into the feasibility of using satellite technology to alleviate the state's educational problems (Governor's Office of Telecommunications [Governor's Office], 1975). At the same time, the Alaska Educational Broadcasting Commission was exploring the possibility of low-power VHF television transmission of videotaped programming in remote communities. In 1971, the Corporation for Public Broadcasting granted the Alaska Educational Broadcasting Commission funds for a pilot project involving three communities, Angoon, Togiak, and Fort Yukon. The objective was explained by the project director, C. M. Northrip: "There was no organized program, just random choice programming. The whole idea was to demonstrate the technical feasibility of low-power transmission" (personal communication, August 29, 1985). Based on technical criteria, the project was a success: The equipment functioned perfectly in two of the three sites.

By 1972, the Alaska Educational Broadcasting Commission was moving ahead on two fronts. In March, it submitted a plan to the U.S. Department of Health, Education, and Welfare for use of the National Aeronautics and Space Administration's (NASA's) proposed Applied Technology Satellite-6 (ATS-6) to explore health and educational communications in rural Alaska (Governor's Office, 1975). And in the fall, it sought funds from the Corporation for Public Broadcasting for establishing a rural network of low-power television stations, using bicycled videotapes of public television programs. Its stated purpose was to gain necessary information for the eventual establishment of delivering public television to all remote areas (Anthropos, 1974). The Corporation for Public Broadcasting awarded the commission $30,000 to cover the purchase of cassette tapes and equipment, the duplication of tapes, and the necessary travel for project support. The first programs hit the airwaves in January 1974 in the widely separated communities of Fort Yukon, St. Paul, and Unalaska (Alaska Educational Broadcasting Commission [AEBC], 1974).[3]

As with the 1971 pilot project, the primary objective in establishing this rural network was to answer technical questions—mainly whether it would be possible to extend the system to all remote areas. Implicit in both objectives is the idea that the right to communicate is understood as a right to access information, hardware, and software facilities. This conception of communication ignores altogether the notion of interaction. In a Habermasian sense, communication involves at least two acting subjects, and its purpose is to come to an agreement "that terminates in the intersubjective mutuality of reciprocal understanding, shared knowledge, mutual trust, and accord with one another" (Habermas, 1979, p. 3). Habermas (1970) contrasts communication as symbolic interaction with communication as purposive-rational action, that is, communication oriented toward the solution of technical problems and the achievement of administratively determined ends. This distinction helps us understand the politics of defining communication in technical terms in the early experiments with low-power television. Habermas

(1970) writes, "The solution of technical problems is not dependent on public discussion. Rather, public discussion could render problematic the framework within which the tasks of government action present themselves as technical ones" (p. 103). The ideology of technological expertise thus presents a plausible justification for the depoliticization of the public.

The structure of a 1974 progress report by the Alaska Educational Broadcasting Commission to the Corporation for Public Broadcasting provides evidence of the priority placed on operational capabilities. Its preliminary findings were divided into eight categories, only two of which dealt with program content or audiences. The first six categories reported problems on progress in such areas as equipment ("Except for a blown fuse on one transmitter, there have been no problems with the equipment," p. 6), videocassette distribution, Federal Communications Commission (FCC) licensing requirements for operators, and the durability of shipping containers. The last two categories dealt with programming and use. The first noted that each station supplemented the network's offerings with its own collection of cassettes or dubs of television programs obtained from other sources. And the concluding preliminary finding noted the origin of local programming:

> Perhaps the most notable accomplishment of the mini-TV licensees is their wide-ranging utilization of their recorders to originate programming important to the communities they serve. At Unalaska, for instance, fifty-seven hours of broadcast time in January had been locally originated. Activities in English and history classrooms, instruction in pottery-making and fishing and presentations of the Unalaska band and chorus have been recorded and broadcast. Weekly basketball games are also recorded and when broadcast, contribute to the instruction of the Unalaska basketball team. News, weather, and local announcements are also broadcast by the school's class of video students. (AEBC, 1974, pp. 6-7)

However, according to a report by Anthropos, a private, Anchorage-based firm hired by the state to evaluate the program, the opportunity for programming that would enhance the local cultures went largely unfulfilled in two of the three villages. These evaluators traced the problem in part to the stations' differing managerial structures. In Fort Yukon and St. Paul, the city held the license. City managers determined policy, and station managers made programming decisions. In each case, programming was considered a routine matter. The evaluators contended that the people may be "happy with what they get" but that this "neglects the potential each community has for establishing criteria by which to determine its values and priorities" (Anthropos, 1974, p. 17). To use Habermasian language, the concern with technical virtuosity was enshrined by instrumental reason at the expense of practical reason embodied in communicative interaction. Unalaska presented a different case. There, the local school district held the license, and the station was physically located in the school—a center of community activity. Although the school superintendent was responsible for the station, he shared power with a media committee representing a cross-section of the Aleutian village's 500 residents. According to Anthropos, the committee took its responsibilities seriously. At the very least, Anthropos (1974) reports, this arrangement acknowledges:

> that public interest is best served where there is opportunity provided for initiatives and reaction. Where community representatives use their intelligence and creativity in such a forum, and station management is responsive, much can be done to serve the best interests of the people. (pp. 17-19)

The major technical difficulty of this pilot project was the erratic distribution of the videocassettes. The tapes were dubbed at a public television station in Bethel and then mailed 800 miles to Fort Yukon using three different aircraft. From there, the tapes were sent to Unalaska, roughly 1,200 miles away. This leg also involved three aircraft. Finally, the tapes were sent to St. Paul, a 400 mile hop out into the Bering Sea. These distances, coupled with unreliable mail schedules, made for erratic and often unsequential programming. These difficulties in the mail distribution of videocassettes heightened the Alaska Educational Broadcasting Commission's interest in satellite delivery of television programming to the state's rural areas (AEBC, 1974). The implicit definition of communication in these technical problems is that of transportation and transmission. In discussing controversy over the shifting meanings of the word *communication,* Raymond Williams (1983) writes that "it is often useful to recall the unresolved range of the original noun of action, represented at its extremes by *transmit,* a one-way process, and *share,* a common or mutual process" (pp. 72-73). Participation is inherent in the latter and manipulation and control are highly probable in the former. The ATS-6 Satellite Demonstration Project showed how these definitions could be contested and played out in concrete conditions.

ATS-6 Satellite Demonstration Project

Alaska was selected for inclusion in NASA's ATS-6 experiments and conducted a year-long series of medical and educational projects in conjunction with the U.S. Public Health Service in 1974-1975. The ATS-6 satellite footprint covered only the southeastern, southcentral, and interior areas of the state, reaching few Eskimo communities, even though Eskimos comprise the state's largest minority group. The footprint did include 5 of the 10 Athabascan languages and five Tlingit-speaking communities. Of the state's approximately 270 communities, 63 fell within the footprints; of these potential sites, 19 were selected to participate. A main criterion for selection was the remoteness of the community and the anticipated benefits of satellite technology in meeting the community's needs. Most of the villages chosen had populations between 150 and 250 (Governor's Office, 1975). This represented the first satellite transmission of visual images in rural Alaska.[4]

The primary objective of the ATS-6 project was to install and operate experimental satellite equipment to give the state technical experience from which to plan permanent systems. The Governor's Office of Telecommunications (1975), which served as the point of contact between the state and NASA, described this goal in its final report: "The state's objective was not to determine if a satellite could be useful, but how to most effectively use it" (Sum. Vol., p. 4). In other words, as far as the state was concerned, the usefulness of the satellite was a given. The only matter that remained was to gauge the efficiency with which the state could use it. Any consideration of the cultural dynamics and efficaciousness of the communication process for the recipients was, at best, ancillary to the technical imperatives. The overemphasis on communication as hardware is a classic case of technological reification. In discussing the rhetoric that reifies communication machines in general, Finlay-Pelinski (1983) argues that

the insistence upon access to hardware (objects) is accompanied by an acceptance of the discursive procedures of exchange at both commercial and social levels. What has not been considered in the identification of, possession of, or access to, communicational object referents with participation, creation and democracy is precisely the difference between: 1. participation and interaction as dynamic acts and events, 2. communication-objects as reified referents. (p. 15)

The ATS-6 project illustrates the domination of the second point over the first, even when project planners showed some awareness of the importance of participation and interaction. With this disjunction in mind, ATS-6 was important in two respects. First, the Governor's Office of Telecommunications made a last-minute decision to supplement educational programming with a general audience program called *Alaska Native Magazine*. And second, the Governor's Office of Telecommunications established *consumer committees* of village representatives for both educational series and the general audience program in an attempt to ensure relevancy and cultural authenticity.

For purposes of our analysis, the most important aspect of the ATS-6 project was its establishment of these consumer committees. As we have already pointed out, for the state's purposes, the most important objective was technical. The second objective for the state was education, although its thrust is somewhat curious and merely reiterates the primacy of the first objective. The Goveror's Office of Telecommunications (1975) explains that "Alaska's primary interest was not precisely measuring the instructional efficiency of various programming and dissemination techniques. Rather the state was exploring effective ways of utilizing the technological resource at hand" (Sum. Vol., p. 9). The third objective was to involve users in all phases of the communication process. With ambiguous logic, the report elaborates on this final objective: "No one else, regardless of knowledge, experience or authority can accurately predict what users will want. Until users obtain experience with a service they cannot accurately define their needs" (Governor's Office, 1975, Vol. 1, p. 15). Although this appears to provide an opening wedge for creativity and participation, it does so only after experience has been obtained, instead of allowing for them right from the beginning. As we shall see, the door closed quickly, but not before state bureaucrats had entered to assume control over the communication process. It is instructive at this point to recall that the residents of Unalaska had shown that creativity need not be unduly hampered by technological naïveté.

Bureaucratic control over the ATS-6 Alaska Education Experiment rested in two state agencies, the Governor's Office of Telecommunications and the Alaska Department of Education. These agencies were responsible for instructional programming decision making, including the incorporation of village representatives into the process. Some 10 months before broadcasting actually began, the Governor's Office of Telecommunications and the Department of Education set up the requisite consumer committees, drawing representatives from the participating villages (Governor's Office, 1975). Although it is perhaps inevitable that state agencies were charged with setting the committees in motion, their subsequent infringement on the scope and autonomy of the consumer committee is harder to justify. As the following account demonstrates, the Governor's Office of Telecommunications and the Department of Education were firmly in control of the educational experiment, and consumer committees functioned mainly as technical advisers on often fairly trivial details.

As a first step in organizing the committees, the Governor's Office of Telecommunications's utilization manager contacted participating villages and asked them to select, by whatever means they felt appropriate, a resident to represent them on consumer committees for three instructional series on health education, basic oral language development, and early childhood education. Requests for representatives were also made to the Alaska Division of Public Health, the Alaska State Operated School System, the Alaska Federation of Natives, and the Tlingit and Haida community councils (Governor's Office, 1975). Curriculum development and program design had already been contracted out to the Northwest Regional Educational Laboratory, a Portland, Oregon-based education design company (Governor's Office, 1975). Before the consumer committees met, the Governor's Office of Telecommunications collaborated with the Northwest Regional Educational Laboratory to establish guidelines for the functioning of the consumer committees. A formal charter for committee policies was drawn up among the Governor's Office of Telecommunications, the Northwest Regional Educational Laboratory, and KUAC-TV—a Fairbanks public television station that had been awarded the production contract (Governor's Office, 1975).

The first consumer committee meetings were held in Juneau in February 1974 to acquaint the representatives on the three committees with the project. Several structural points about these and other consumer committee meetings are noteworthy. All meetings were under the auspices of the Governor's Office of Telecommunications, which set the agendas and paid the expenses. In most cases, "outsiders" outnumbered village representatives. These outsiders included staffers from the Governor's Office of Telecommunications and the Department of Education, consultants from the Northwest Regional Educational Laboratory, KUAC-TV producers and technicians, and various support personnel.

Tellingly, the first action of the consumer committees was a vote to ratify their subordinate status with regard to their roles and responsibilities as previously defined by the Northwest Regional Educational Laboratory (Governor's Office, 1975). In the course of the meetings, a few committee members expressed some skepticism about their roles. As one member put it, "Not until I see the implementation of the goals and objectives and am able to see the advice we give being properly carried out over the TV satellite screen will I believe we are . . . involved in a productive workshop committee" (Governor's Office, 1975, Vol. 1, p. 82). Personnel from the Governor's Office of Telecommunications attributed this attitude to the villagers' previous experiences with numerous governmental projects: During the early stages of each new experiment, rural natives adopted a wait-and-see attitude toward the project and its alleged benefits. The Governor's Office of Telecommunications (1975) was confident that in this case the state could avoid raising false expectations by allowing specific programming goals to come from the consumer committees themselves.

Instructional consumer committee meetings were held throughout the summer and fall of 1974, although they suffered from poor attendance and a lack of continuity among representatives. During one of the early basic language meetings, one of the committee members complained that the programs were too commercial and not sufficiently relevant culturally. According to the minutes of the meeting, however, the committee as a whole "decided that trying to put in too much so called cultural relevancy would alter the basic design and destroy its effectiveness" (Governor's Office, 1975, Vol. 3, App. h.9, p. 43). From the very beginning, it had been the practice of the Northwest Regional Educational Laboratory to present alternative designs from which the consumer committees could choose. This truncated form of decision making allowed the programs to be bicultural only in a restricted sense. The committees served mainly to guard against cultural incongruities, and their actions were largely cosmetic. For example, the language committee's major modification to the six program designs presented at the second meeting consisted of changing a scene in which characters wore hats, substituting the more familiar beaver and spruce hats for cowboy and fireman hats (Governor's Office, 1975).

A fourth series of programs, the aforementioned *Alaska Native Magazine,* was added at the suggestion of the Governor's Office of Telecommunications utilization manager in a January 1974 meeting with the executives of the Alaska Federation of Natives, a statewide organization of the native regional corporations.[5] At least on the surface, this fourth series appears to be an anomaly. In the case of the three educational series, the Governor's Office of Telecommunications had clearly stated that the idea was to involve users in program design. However, the name given to the fourth experimental category casts doubt on the state's expectations for the instructional programs. The fourth category was called Viewer Defined Programming. The Governor's Office of Telecommunications never explained what seemed to be an obvious discrepancy: If the fourth series was viewer defined, what were the other three series?

In any event, at that January meeting, executives from the Alaska Federation of Natives recommended that representatives for the content selection committee be drawn from the four native regional corporations within the satellite footprint. The utilization manager followed through on the recommendation and assembled a consumer committee for the *Alaska Native Magazine* comprising members of the Chugach and Cook Inlet native associations, the Calista and Sealaska corporations, and two noncorporate organizations, the Tanana Chiefs Conference and Alaska Federation of Natives (Governor's Office, 1975).[6]

The first *Alaska Native Magazine* consumer committee meeting took place in July 1974, a scant 3 months before the program went on the air. According to the minutes of the meeting, the program's philosophy was described to the committee as an effort "to get ideas from people as to what they want to see and develop programming accordingly" (Governor's Office, 1975, Vol. 3, App. h, p. 129). State planners suggested a format for reports on salient topics by the program's host, followed by audio interaction between people in the studio and the villages. Committee members expressed reservations about this format and the possibility that villagers would find the medium alienating. They suggested that care be taken to avoid overslick formats and bureaucratic language. Finally, the committee agreed on a list of program topics, including civil rights, native land claims, environmental protection, education, native culture, and profiles of prominent natives (Governor's Office, 1975).

These consumer committee meetings also suffered from poor attendance and a lack of continuity among representatives. But an even more troubling matter had become apparent to the Governor's Office of Telecommunications by late 1974. Although the experiment was designed to deliver programming to rural areas, the consumer committee was made up mainly of urban natives who did not regularly watch *Alaska Native Magazine*. This problem became obvious in committee meetings when it was necessary to review programs that had already been telecast in the bush before planning future programs (Governor's Office, 1975). By designating native corporations as the vehicles for selecting consumer committee representatives, the Governor's Office of Telecommunications had effectively chosen the wrong sample: urban, corporate leaders who move comfortably in the white people's world, rather than rural villagers who retain traditional values and cultural patterns. Although these individuals had once led the political and economic battle for the control of their own destiny with the core society, they were now members of a native elite who served equally as agents for the core society, sometimes at variance with their own cultures (see Klausner & Foulks, 1982).

Apparently, administrators were less concerned with whether committee members actually represented rural audiences than with the time wasted in reviewing past programming. The situation reflects what Habermas (1970) sees as the central problematic of industrial society: the relationship between technology and democracy. He understands technology as "scientifically rationalized control of objectified processes . . . coupled with feedback from the economy and administration," and democracy as "the institutionally secured forms of general and public communication that deal with the practical question of how men can and want to live under the objective conditions of their ever-expanding power of control" (Habermas, 1970, p. 57). As Habermas poses it, the problem is "How can the power of technical control be brought within the range of the consensus of acting and transacting citizens?"

For Habermas, the answer has to do with the political mediation of technical progress. He writes that the "challenge of technology cannot be met with technology alone. It is rather a question of setting into motion a politically effective discussion that rationally brings the social potential constituted by technical knowledge and ability into a defined and controlled relation to our practical knowledge and will" (Habermas, 1970, p. 61). But in Alaska, there was no time for politically effective discussion. Although there was certainly a desire to involve consumers in planning and decision making, there was a characteristic technocratic frustration with the inherent inefficiency of democratic participation. The problem was exacerbated by the technical constraints of an exceptionally tight production schedule. In a letter dated December 17, 1974, the third utilization manager in a year responded to suggestions by the program's producer for streamlining the system. He wrote:

I donnot [*sic*] feel that the committee can pick 14 topics in the short time allotted to them at this meeting and effectively plan program content, objectives, etc. The proposals in your letter, in my opinion, would result in a token committee. Rather than have that happen I would disband the committee, if they didn't quit first, and chalk up the native involvement as another one of those nice but meaningless phrases that are put into project summaries. (Governor's Office, 1975, Vol. 3, App. g, p. 14)

Cinematographer Mark O. Badger identified a couple of administrative design flaws that surfaced in the production of the *Alaska Native Magazine* (personal communication, September 20, 1985). First, when Badger went into the villages, he was surprised at how little attention had been given to involving local people in the process of planning the programs. The consumer committee served as a formal representative structure, but there was not actually a process for involving villagers. In practice, Badger claimed, it was up to the production crew to find out what villagers thought of the project and whether it met their needs. Second, he claimed that the tight schedule "was a meat grinder." The project involved a delicate and critical intrusion into another culture, and he believed the production crew should have been given much more time to work with and learn from villagers.

The ATS-6 educational broadcasting experiment came to an end in May 1975, just a little more than 7 months after its first broadcast. Technically, the project was quite successful. In less than a year, 100 hours of original television programming had been designed, produced, and broadcast. Instructional programming had been made available to 1,200 rural schoolchildren and 150 rural educators, and the *Alaska Native Magazine* had been offered to 9,000 villagers and the 50,000 urban residents of Fairbanks (Governor's Office, 1975).

In the case of the experiment's subsidiary goal of involving users in the communication process, success or failure is not so easily quantified. Technical and instrumental imperatives interfered with the participatory process, in spite of the planners' best efforts to avoid this trap. A major problem was the selection of consumer committee members who did not truly represent the villages. The Governor's Office of Telecommunications apparently recognized this mistake. In assessing the project, administrators acknowledged that "Native input will be of the utmost value if future representatives are those who work with the villagers on a one-to-one basis, rather than Native leaders at the regional policy making level" (Governor's Office, 1975, Vol. 1, pp. 225-226). All too soon, however, the enthusiasm of the Governor's Office of Telecommunications over another project clouded this lesson.

The Establishment of
the State Television Project

The experiment with low-power television transmissions and the ATS-6 project conclusively demonstrated the technical feasibility of television delivery in the bush. The state made a major commitment to satellite communications in 1975, when it appropriated $5 million for the construction of small, two-way earth stations in 100 villages. Originally, the earth stations were used for providing telephone service. Their success in that arena set the stage for demands that television be added as a service to the state's rural areas (Dowling, 1982).

In December 1975, a legislative subcommittee on telecommunications held an informal meeting to discuss the distribution of television programming in Alaska. Various interests were present: commercial and public broadcasters, cable operators, the Alaska Public Utilities Commission, the Alaska Educational Broadcasting Commission, the State Division of Communication, and the Governor's Office of Telecommunications. An ad hoc television advisory group comprising mainly commercial broadcasters was organized to look into problems with financing and programming (Governor's Office, 1978). The two groups met again in February 1976, and the discussion revolved around the issue of whether entertainment television ought to be developed by private enterprise or the state government. Despite opposition from commercial broadcasters, the legislature passed a bill that spring that provided $1.5 million for a 1-year Satellite Television Demonstration Project in 24 communities (Governor's Office, 1978).

Wary of concerns from the private sector, the Governor's Office of Telecommunications, as project director, steadfastly maintained its position as merely a coordinator for program requirements. The Governor's Office of Telecommunications contracted with the Alaska Public Broadcasting Commission (until 1976 the Alaska Educational Broadcasting Commission) to operate a tape-delay center in Anchorage, where programs were dubbed from the three commercial networks and the Public Broadcasting Service and transmitted via satellite to rural receivers.[7] Responsibility for the selection of programs was placed in the hands of the Alaska Federation of Natives's telecommunications committee, formed in the fall of 1975 in anticipation of the project. The committee was composed of representatives from each of the 12 native regional corporations (Governor's Office of Telecommunications, 1978). The state's final report on the project contained evidence that the committee and some of the audience members it represented held reservations about participating in the experiment within the framework of mainstream television fare. The committee specifically asked the Governor's Office of Telecommunications about the availability of programs produced in Alaska and Canada that would be relevant to northern life. As Finlay-Pelinski (1983) notes, Canada has a reasonably good record in situating communications technology within its social context. The possibility of this kind of programming was discussed in passing in the experiment's final report, but the idea was questioned on the grounds of quality control, capital and operating costs, broadcast right restrictions, and lack of interest (Governor's Office, 1978). The autonomy of cultural and democratic values could not hold their own in a battle with technological autonomy and capital considerations.

Guests present at some of the early meetings also expressed alarm over the potentially harmful effects of televised sex and violence on bush committees. They argued that programs with a local emphasis, depicting village life, might enhance the villagers' awareness of themselves and their surroundings. As the final report noted, the Alaska Federation of Natives committee "was acutely aware of the vast cultural and educational differences in their regions and of the harmful effects that commercial television could have" (Governor's Office, 1978, Vol. 1, Sec. 12, p. 36).

Although the actual experiment ended after 1 year, the Television Demonstration Project has been continued to the present with annual appropriations by the state legislature. Over the years, the system has been expanded, and today the state-sponsored entertainment channel reaches some 227 communities (Alaska Department of Administration, 1986). Programming is selected by the Rural Alaska Television Network Council, which includes two appointees of the governor as well as representatives for each native regional corporation. Officially, the council encourages providing audiences with Alaskan-produced programs (Rural Alaska Television Network Council, 1981). However, according to project director Tony Ramirez (personal communication, March 28, 1986), there is very little locally produced programming available, and the council's choices are confined to programs offered by affiliates of the American Broadcasting Company (ABC), Columbia Broadcasting System (CBS), National Broadcasting Company (NBC), and Public Broadcasting Service (PBS).

Conclusion

Although efforts were made to construct a television system in rural Alaska based on a participatory model of development, local participation was blunted by a technocratic consciousness that enshrined efficiency, technique, and speed as imperatives that overrode serious consideration of cultural values. Once the decision to concentrate on instrumental technological values was made, there was no turning back. The opportunity for alternative programming congruent with native cultures was lost. In keeping with Alaska's frontier spirit, the communications system was erected with an uncritical optimism over humankind's ability to conquer nature's limits through technology. Ironically, Habermas's suggestion that we seek a fraternal rather than an exploitative relationship with nature reminds us of the traditional bonds of native Alaskans to the land. Habermas (1970) writes, "At the level of an as yet incomplete intersubjectivity we can impute subjectivity to animals and plants, even to minerals, and try to communicate with nature instead of merely processing her under conditions of severed communication" (p. 88). The enchained subjectivity of nature can only be unbound when human communication is free of domination. He continues: "Only if men could communicate without compulsion and each could recognize himself in the other, could mankind possibly recognize nature as another subject: not, as idealism would have it, as its Other, but as a subject of which mankind itself is the Other" (p. 88).

Looking back over the development of communications in Alaska, Robert Walp, former head of the Governor's Office of Telecommunications, writes, "Where progress has been made in Alaska we have generally erred on the side of *doing,* rather than *planning,* largely because of impatience to meet sharply felt needs and also because the funds were quickly appropriated" (p. vi). Walp (1982) adds that although a great deal of effort was put into involving users in the planning process it was "often on a crash basis due to the small amount of time available" (p. vi).

The planners' haste perhaps obscured a fundamental conflict between the model of participation and the diffusion of this particular innovation—

that is, the inherently centralizing tendencies of satellite-based communication. Scholars have long noted the social and cultural influences of media technology on traditional peoples. Employing the work of Harold Adams Innis, James Carey and John Quirk (1970) warn of the imperialistic dangers of modern electronic media, which "widen the range of reception while narrowing the range of distribution. Large audiences receive but are unable to make direct response or participate otherwise in vigorous discussion." One result of the centralizing tendencies of the technology was the introduction of mainstream television content in rural Alaska. Because entertainment television is replete with Western industrial values, it is only logical to question whether that broadcasting model was an appropriate one for Alaskan natives as they struggled to cope with threats to their cultural integrity.

Notes

1. The Alaskan economy suffered severely in 1986 from a sharp decline in oil prices, and state-supported telecommunications services did not escape the legislature's budget-reduction measures. In the summer of 1986, LearnAlaska, the state's satellite-based instructional network, was dissolved. The television component of LearnAlaska was transferred to Anchorage Community College, Division of Instructional Communication. Instructional television programming, which once reached 250 communities via satellite, is now offered only to the Anchorage area over the cable system. Louise Fowler, instructional television coordinator, explained that the state has begun to send some instructional material to rural areas over the rural entertainment channel. However, she noted that because of a lack of planning, not much use is made of it presently by rural educators (personal communication, November 14, 1986).

2. *Native Alaskans* is a term used to refer collectively to several racially, linguistically, and culturally distinct groups inhabiting different regions of the state. In 1970, the population of native Alaskans was 50,605, which represented 17% of the state's total population of 302,173. The population figures for the three major native groups were as follows: Eskimos (including Inupiaq and Yupik), 28,233; Indians (including Athabascan, Tlingit, and Haida), 16,080; and Aleuts, 6,292 (U.S. Department of Commerce, 1974). In 1980, the U.S. Census Bureau began designating rural communities with 25 or more native residents as *Alaska native villages*. Of the state's 64,103 natives, 39,301 lived in 209 native villages. The total population of Alaska native villages was 49,653, which means that 79.2% of that population was native (U.S. Department of Commerce, 1984).

3. Other villages were gradually added to the system. By 1976, some 41 communities were equipped with low-power transmitters.

4. Alaska participated in NASA's first applied technology satellite (ATS-1) experiments in satellite-delivered audio in 1971.

5. Regional and village native corporations were set up for dispensing entitlements awarded in the 1971 Alaska Native Claims Settlement Act, which granted natives 44 million acres of land and $1 billion compensation for lost lands.

6. The original utilization manager (there were three during the short life of the project) was himself an Athabascan. He left the Governor's Office of Telecommunications in March 1974 and was appointed to the *Alaska Native Magazine* consumer committee as the Tanana Chiefs Conference's representative.

7. A. G. Hiebert, who represented the state's commercial broadcasters in negotiations among the state, the networks, and the FCC, reported that the arrangement benefited all parties. As an incentive for cooperation by the networks and commercial broadcasting, the state provided use of its leased satellite transponder for live delivery of news and sports to the urban audiences of commercial broadcasters. In turn, affiliates in Anchorage fed programs to the rural network's tape-delay center. Hiebert reported that the FCC also supported the project, although "it took a lot of explaining and proving that the public service aspects outweighed the fact that it had never been done before" (personal communication, November 13, 1986).

References

Alaska Department of Administration. (1986). *Inventory of communication facilities serving Alaska communities*. Juneau: Alaska State House of Representatives Research Agency.

Alaska Educational Broadcasting Commission. (1974). *Pilot system of mini-TV transmitters to provide public television to rural Alaska* (2nd progress report). Juneau: Alaska Department of Administration.

Anthropos. (1974). *Evaluation of the impact of mini TV stations upon three remote communities in Alaska*. Unpublished manuscript, University of Alaska, Center for Cross-Cultural Studies, Fairbanks.

Carey, J. W., & Quirk, J. J. (1970). The mythos of the electronic revolution. *The American Scholar, 39*(2, 3), 219-241, 395-424.

Dowling, R. P. (1982). The Alaska small earth station program: Mitigating isolation through technology. In R. M. Walp (Ed.), *Telecommunications in Alaska* (pp. 31-35). Honolulu: Pacific Telecommunications Council.

Fallows, J. M. (1984, August). Nigeria of the north. *The Atlantic, 254,* 18-22.

Fanon, F. (1965). *The wretched of the earth*. New York: Grove Press.

Finlay-Pelinski, M. (1983). *Technologies of technology: A critique of power and social control in discourses on new communications technology* (Graduate Communications Program Working Paper Series). Montreal: McGill University.

Freire, P. (1970). *Pedagogy of the oppressed*. New York: Herder & Herder.

Gallagher, H. G. (1974). *Etok: A story of Eskimo power*. New York: G. P. Putnam's Sons.

Governor's Office of Telecommunications. (1975). *ATS-6 health/education telecommunications experiment, Alaska education experiment summary final report* (3 vols., summary vol.). Juneau.

Governor's Office of Telecommunications. (1978). *Satellite television demonstration project (SATVDP), final report* (2 vols.). Juneau.

Habermas, J. (1970). *Toward a rational society*. Boston: Beacon Press.

Habermas, J. (1979). *Communication and the evolution of society*. Boston: Beacon Press.

Klausner, S. Z., & Foulks, E. F. (1982). *Eskimo capitalists: Oil, politics, and alcohol.* Totowa, NJ: Allanheld, Osmun.

Madigan, R. J., & Peterson, W. J. (1977). Television on the Bering Strait. *Journal of Communication, 27,* 183-187.

Marx, K., & Engels, F. (1970). *The German ideology.* New York: International.

Rogers, E. M. (1976). Communication and development: The passing of a dominant paradigm. *Communication Research, 3,* 213-240.

Rural Alaska Television Network Council. (1981). *Policy guidelines regarding the use of the state of Alaska satellite television project.* Adopted December 3, 1981; amended February 17, 1984 and June 14, 1984.

Schiller, H. I. (1969). *Mass communications and American empire.* New York: Kelley.

United States Department of Commerce, Bureau of the Census. (1974). *Native population of Alaska by race: 1970* (Report No. PC[SI]-64, suppl. to *1970 census of population*). Washington, DC: Government Printing Office.

United States Department of Commerce, Bureau of the Census. (1984). *American Indian areas and Alaska native villages: 1980* (Report No. PC80-SI-13, suppl. to *1980 census of population*). Washington, DC: Government Printing Office.

Walp, R. M. (Ed.). (1982). *Telecommunications in Alaska.* Honolulu: Pacific Telecommunications Council.

Williams, R. (1983). *Keywords: A vocabulary of culture and society.* New York: Oxford University Press.

2

Mass Media in Greenland:
The Politics of Survival

MARIANNE A. STENBAEK

Introduction

The development of the mass media in Greenland is intimately connected to the evolution of the country's political institutions over the past 125 years. The Greenlandic mass media have been one of the main catalysts for the political and cultural changes that have consistently moved Greenland toward home rule. So profound has this influence been that self-government probably would not have been attained without the lively public forum provided by the media. As Greenlanders have assumed greater control of the media in Greenland, so have they assumed greater control over their political lives.

Greenland (*Kalaallit Nunaat* in the Greenlandic language) was almost totally isolated until 1953 because of its geography as well as its colonial status. It is the world's largest island (extending more than 840,000 mi^2, or 2,175,600 km^2), but it is mostly covered by ice. It has been compared to a giant bowl filled with frozen water that has a rim around it, referring to the mountainous regions on the west and east coasts, where the settlements and towns are located. The icecap covering the middle of Greenland is estimated to be several thousand years old and is up to 10,000 ft (3,000 m) thick. The island's 52,000 inhabitants live mainly on the west coast and in a few settlements on the east coast. Of these, 42,000 are *Greenlanders* (i.e., of primarily Inuit or Eskimo ancestry) and 10,000 are non-Inuit, most often referred to as *Danes,* although by nationality all inhabitants are Danes. The capital and largest city Nuuk (formerly Godthaab) has a population of only about 12,000. (For historical and geographical information on Greenland, see Erngaard, 1972; Gad, 1970, 1973, 1982; Rink, 1877/1975; Smiley, 1988).

The towns and settlements are distant and isolated. Until the advent of airplanes, travel was possible only by dog sled, kayak, or other forms of boats. These means of transportation are still in use, although most traffic is now by helicopter or airplane. There are many cars in the towns, but it is not possible to drive from town to town because there are no roads over the mountains, which are often, in any case, cut by fjords or bays. The longest paved road in 1990 was 13 km. Thus transportation has always been a major obstacle for the circulation of print media. The west coast is isolated from the east, and all of Greenland is remote from the rest of Denmark. The geographical isolation has resulted in the growth of a variety of local dialects and cultures over the approximately 4,000 years it has been inhabited (Maxwell, 1985).

The Vikings settled parts of Greenland around the 10th century and stayed for 5 centuries; it has never been fully determined why the Vikings disappeared from Greenland. In 1721, Hans Egede, a Danish-Norwegian Lutheran minister, arrived in Greenland, and with him came the modern introduction of Danes that ultimately led to Greenland becoming part of the Danish kingdom (Garnett, 1968). Pastor Hans Egede traveled to Greenland to minister to the Vikings, whom he mistakenly believed still inhabited the island, but found instead that it was inhabited solely by Inuit. He tried to convert them to the Lutheran faith and in so doing made one of the fundamentally important decisions for the later evolution of the mass media and the preservation of the island's indigenous culture. He learned Greenlandic. The Lutheran church was the first colonial institution to put Inuit in positions of authority and trust as well as the first to set up a rudimentary school system. All of this contributed to the establishment of Greenlandic as a language of instruction and communication. The first books printed on the island were in Greenlandic as was the first formal academic instruction. By the mid-19th century, in most settlements, a local Greenlander was the one who was the catechist responsible for many church services as well as the local one-room school. Two Greenlandic teachers colleges were also founded in 1847. Thus a tradition of literacy in Greenlandic was established by the settlers early on, a situation that contrasts sharply with many other colonies around the world where the colonial powers insisted on using their own language. However, in the early process of colonization some aspects of the Greenlandic culture were destroyed by missionaries and settlers—for example, much of the drum music and dancing was eradicated—and Greenland became politically and economically a colony.

The Print Media and the Rise of Greenlandic Nationalism

In a way, Greenlanders have a long history of mass media (or shared media), because like all Inuit they have a long oral/aural history. Greenlanders have always been known for their story telling and their singing debates, which can be classified as mass media although not in the modern sense. Modern mass media in Greenland started in 1861 with the founding of the newspaper *Atuagagdliutit* (*Something Offered for Reading*) by the Danish geologist and then district commissioner for southern Greenland Hinrich Johannes Rink. This is one of the oldest, continuously published newspapers in Europe and the first anywhere in the Arctic to publish original literature and art by the Inuit (Fleisher, 1980). The publication of *Atuagagdliutit* really marked a new era in Greenland, because the newspaper has been immensely important for the modernization of the country.

Atuagagdliutit was started at a crucial moment, a time when many important cultural and economic issues were being debated. By 1861 Greenlanders had almost lost their first battle for cultural identity and integrity as an increasing number of Europeans were arriving. The introduction of Danish tools and food was starting to disrupt their age-old subsistence economy. On the positive side, Rink proposed to set up municipal councils, the embryonic beginnings of self-government, as a way of giving more responsibility to Greenlanders. The councils constituted a forum not only for dealing with many local concerns but also for raising ultimately the whole question of Greenland's relationship with Denmark. It is in this context that Rink—with the linguist and grammarian Samuel Kleinschmidt and the director of the teachers college in Nuuk, Professor Janssen—decided to publish a newspaper that would give Greenlanders a chance for active cultural participation and debate as well as some responsibility for their own development.

An important characteristic of *Atuagagdliutit* is that first and foremost it was published in the Greenlandic language. The newspaper helped to make Greenlanders literate in their own language and to ensure that Greenlandic was not perceived as old-fashioned or folkloric but as the language of everyday life, business, and politics. One of the newspaper's main functions over the years was to constantly update the local language and to reaffirm it as a living and evolving means of communication. Younger generations were thus encouraged to use it creatively. It can be claimed (e.g., Prattis & Chartrand, 1983) that language is the single most important factor that contributes to the survival of a people as a distinct entity, because it empowers them with a positive self-image, the psychological foundation for successful self-government, and a unique linguistic/cultural identity.

Atuagagdliutit is remarkable in several other respects. It was conceived in the old tradition of the newspaper as a debating forum, and it fostered national debates in the form of letters and articles written by readers from across the country. For instance, hunters and fishermen wrote accounts of their hunting trips, old legends, and reports on local events. Much of the culture was saved in this way. Early volumes of the newspapers were recently reprinted because they shed much light on the traditional culture.

From its beginning in 1861, the newspaper had a Greenlandic editor and co-publisher. The Inuk Arqaluk (Lars) Møller, who was also manager of Sydgrønlands Bogtrykkeri, the main publishing house and printing press in Greenland, became editor in 1873 and remained in charge until 1926. The first editor (1861-1873) was Rasmus Berthelsen, but his name never appeared on the masthead because of his modesty. The masthead simply read, "Printed by Lars Møller."[1] Although *Atuagagdliutit* had a great deal of regional content—Greenlandic material written by Greenlanders for Greenlanders, informing them about what went on in other parts of their vast country—it was also in many ways an international organ.

Rink was a visionary who had focused the paper on local content. Although continuing this policy, Møller also wanted to break the isolation that Greenlanders lived in and tried to open the newspaper to the world by printing excerpts from world literature and articles about Europe and other international matters. A unique feature in the early issues was the insertion of beautifully hand-colored illustrations depicting life in Greenland and in other countries. This included, for instance, drawings from North Africa and Europe and pictures of camels, elephants, Russian soldiers, the Eiffel Tower, and other wonders of the world. It should also be noted that Sydgrønlands Bogtrykkeri (the first publishing house in Greenland) was created by Rink. This is where some of the earliest known Greenlandic lithographs and pictures, especially by

the Inuit seal hunter Aron and later by Møller himself, were printed.
They are now considered national treasures (see, e.g., Erngarrd, 1972;
Rink 1877/1975).

In the early days, the whole process of publishing the newspaper was
done almost entirely by Møller who wrote the content; set the type; and
looked after the printing, binding, and circulation. Møller was not only
an efficient printer and publisher but he was also an artist. From Danish
officials and traders, he obtained illustrations depicting European and
Asian scenes as well as Greenlandic, which he reproduced in etchings,
sometimes in soot, lithographic stone, and even stiffened syrup. Once
printed, he colored them quite exquisitely by hand. These were distributed free of charge with *Atuagagdliutit*.

Atuagagdliutit had a much smaller format than today's newspapers
and had a press run of only a few hundred copies. It was distributed free
of charge in bound volumes. Once a year the bound volumes were sent
by boat along the eastern and western coasts. Copies were delivered to
the municipal councils who then circulated them so that every family could
read the paper even if they had to take turns. In 1874, *Atuagagdliutit*
became a monthly publication and remained so for 58 years, but the
newspaper continued to be distributed in bound volumes only once a
year along the coastal areas. In 1932 it became a bimonthly publication.
In the 1930s the newspaper's content changed. It became more oriented
toward social problems and started to include a cartoon section, the first
one in Greenland.

For more than 90 years, *Atuagagdliutit* was a purely Greenlandic
newspaper, written, published, and paid for by Greenlanders. A certain
percentage of the hunters' income was deposited in a public purse from
which the paper, among other things, was financed. At the beginning,
the newspaper had to be submitted to the censorship of the Royal Danish
Inspector who read all manuscripts in translation before they could be
printed. Ironically, this state of affairs came to an end in 1927, when
the state ensured the newspaper's financing.

**Evolution of the Print Media,
1952-1990**

Atuagagdliutit remained a unilingual Greenlandic newspaper until
1952 when it merged with the *Grønlandsposten,* a Danish-language
newspaper that had been created during World War II by the zoologist

Christian Vibe. When this happened, *Atuagagdliutit-Grønlandsposten* (*A/G*) ceased being free of charge (it cost 35 ore, approximately $0.05 US), and it also started to carry advertising. In 1974 it was transformed into a weekly newspaper and one year later became an independent institution with its own governing board. In 1989 the Danish journalist Philip Lauritzen was appointed the editor. Under Lauritzen, the paper has changed radically. It remains a forum for debate, but caters much more to the tastes of modern Greenlanders, having evolved toward a tabloid format with an emphasis on fashion, sports, and international news. Nonetheless, it still sometimes features highly controversial articles on Greenlandic politics and society. *A/G* is now published three times a week.

Greenland has another national newspaper, *Sermitsiak,* as well as many local and special interest papers. *Sermitsiak* is independent from special political and economic interests. It was created in 1958 as a Greenlandic-language paper, but a few months later merged with the Danish-language paper *Kamikken* and since then has been bilingual. For its first 15 years, it was essentially published as a labor of love by nonprofessional volunteer journalists and editors, both Danish and Greenlandic. Danish engineer Per Danker, who served as editor during the 1970s, made it into a substantial paper. He also created the well-known *kamiknisser,* a series of Inuit political cartoons. As *Kamikken* had to rely on a volunteer staff, its rhythm of publication was sporadic. However, since the first professional journalist was hired in 1973 it has been published on schedule with a paid staff. Many now consider it to be the more serious and weighty of the two national newspapers.

Sermitsiak is published weekly in an edition of approximately 5,500 to 6,000 copies (a circulation that is close to that of *A/G*). Originally it was a local Nuuk newspaper but has now acquired a national dimension, and its distribution outside Nuuk is as great as within. In the late 1980s, it took over many of the previous functions of A/G as that paper moved toward the tabloid format in terms of both form and content. *Sermitsiak* has become a more politically oriented organ with many background and in-depth stories. At the beginning, it was principally an alternative newspaper, often funny and a little irreverent. Now it has become the more serious, solid newspaper.

Greenland also has a large number of local newspapers, often published in settlements by municipal councils or by volunteer groups. Each political party and several associations—for example, hunters', trappers', and women's associations—publish their own bulletins. Local newspapers vary in number but there are more than 20 such newspapers in the country. They appear every 2 weeks or less frequently; some are quite sporadic. Usually they are more oriented toward local issues than toward general news and background information. Some are bilingual; some are unilingual. Their readership is mainly the inhabitants of the village or region in which they are published, although there is a weekly time slot on the radio for summaries of stories from the local press. Most of them have very few pages and are often mimeographed or printed on simple home presses.

The Greenlandic government's information service, *Tusarliivik,* held a conference in 1982 to discuss the future of local newspapers. The conference concluded that it was imperative for the local and national governments to secure better and more uniform conditions for their publication. The present state of the print media was described as follows in a working document prepared for a media conference in Nuuk:

> Some local papers have modern equipment, some have to make do with old mimeographs. Some local papers have good revenue from ads, others have none. Some local papers get by with only volunteers, others operate with paid help. Some local papers get small or large municipal grants, others get none. Some have a relatively large circulation, others have a very small one. Some are published quite regularly, others sporadically.

In other words, local newspapers differ widely, but they have in common the focus on local stories and they are not self-supporting, let alone profit-making ventures. (Lokalbladskonference, 1987)

The Greenlandic press is thriving, although its standards in terms of reporting and distribution do not equal those of the European or North American press. Nonetheless, if one considers the Greenlandic press in the context of the limited resources of the country's 52,000 inhabitants and the difficult conditions of distribution, it is a fair assessment to say that the Greenlandic press is healthy. The main problem of the press, and this applies to the electronic media as well, is that it often lacks a critical edge. The media in Greenland may be the societal watch dog, but sometimes the treatment of news stories is tempered by financial considerations, although this is less often true now because most media are becoming financially independent from government subsidies. It must also be kept in mind that Greenland is a small country in which "everybody knows everybody." The editor or journalist who sharply attacks a politician may very well bump into him or her an hour later in the local supermarket; the smallness and interrelatedness of the society itself sometimes makes strong investigative reporting difficult. But nonetheless, it should be noted that some of the local newspapers are quite critical and are looked on as being more critical than the two national papers. (Additional information on the Inuit press in Greenland, Alaska, and Canada can be found in Stenbaek, 1983).

Greenlandic Radio and the Resistance to Assimilation

The first radio programs in Greenlandic and Danish went on the air in 1926, due to the efforts of telegraph operator Holten Moller. Radio news was broadcast somewhat irregularly until 1942, when Danish administrator Eske Brun began broadcasting a regular *radioavis* ("evening news") as well as other radio programs. During World War II, when Greenland was administratively cut off from Denmark, the United States (and to a lesser extent Canada) assumed the protection and supply of Greenland. One of the first major purchases made in the United States was a new radio transmitter with the power of 1 kW, which was erected on the Kook Islands just outside Nuuk. Radio broadcasts were still somewhat sporadic, although daily, and could be heard by most of the inhabited west coast and sometimes in northern Quebec, because of favorable geographical conditions. Radio broadcasts, even shortwave broadcasts, to the east coast were generally impossible and at best very difficult, because it appears that the properties of the icecap interfere with the transmission of radio waves.

The increased contact with countries such as the United States and Canada, the material progress with its many new and exciting consumer goods—Greenlanders were then introduced to the Sears catalog—and the shift toward a money economy resulted in a feeling that it was possible to live well without the tight administration of the Danish government. Following the United Nations declaration on decolonization, Denmark adopted in 1953 a new constitution that made Greenland an integral part of the Danish kingdom. Greenlanders consequently received the same rights and privileges as other Danes. Two Greenlanders were elected to the *Folketing,* the Danish parliament, thereby ensuring Greenland's representation in national politics.

To some Danes, the designation of Greenland as an equal and integral region of Denmark meant that Greenlanders (or "northern" Danes as they were sometimes called) should be assimilated, i.e., modeled on the image of "southern" Danes, and that a blueprint of Danish society—its institutions, its architecture, its educational system—should be used to develop Greenlandic society. These trends peaked in 1964 in the controversial Bill G-60, which consisted of a 10-year plan for social and economic development and led to the administrative integration of settlements and outposts into larger units and to the centralization of social and health services. Bill G-60 included the *foedestedskriterie* ("the birthplace criterion"), which made a person's place of residence a major criterion for the determination of salaries. Greenlanders with the same education as Danes would thereby get a smaller salary even if their jobs were identical. This was one of the regulations that caused resentment among Greenlanders due to its inherent discrimination and became a catalyst for political and cultural changes. As early as 1958, a new school law had created an educational system in which the standard for success was how well a student learned Danish, because the brightest students were sent to Denmark for further education. Bill G-60 solidified the establishment of a new Greenlandic elite, but it was precisely among members of this new, well-educated elite that discontent started.

Partly as a reaction to the school law of 1958 and Bill G-60, the *Unge Grønlaenders Raad* ("Young Greenlanders Council") was formed among Greenlandic students in Copenhagen in 1963. Their goal was to obtain a much stronger voice for Greenlanders in the island's political, economic, and cultural future. Among its members were several students who are now prominent Greenland politicians, such as Prime Minister Jonathan Motzfeldt.

An example of major social change caused by the interaction of economic, political, and cultural forces was the closing of the mining town of Qutdligssat in 1972. It was a Danish bureaucratic decision that made eminent sense when laid out on a government desk in Copenhagen, but was the sort of measure that fed revolutionary cultural movements in Greenland. Qutdligssat was a coal mining town in Disko Bay. The coal mine was closed because it was no longer profitable; its inhabitants were moved in a negligent manner to larger towns on the west coast. To many Greenlanders, this forced relocation meant unemployment, despair, and the destruction of families and led to an increase in suicide and alcoholism. The process was documented in the first modern Greenlandic feature-length film (which was made by Aqqaluk Lynge, a former minister for social affairs in the home-rule government).[2] The film and its highly political songs depicting the tragedy of Qutdligssat had a stunning impact on many Greenlanders and resulted in the determination that this should never happen again. The film's most visible and influential result was the reestablishment in 1976 of the old Inuit custom of summer camps. The Aasivik camps became an institution devoted to the preservation of traditional Inuit values. They became a place for the discussion of political, social, and cultural events; the teaching of Inuit history and traditional Inuit songs and dances; and the creation of modern Inuit music and literature. The Aasivik camps have become a major cultural force in Greenland and are still held each summer (each year in a different settlement), drawing up to 2,000 people from all over Greenland, northern Canada, Alaska, and Siberia. The Aasivik camps have been influential in the formation of the Inuit Atagatigiit party, which puts a strong emphasis on Greenlandic identity and independence. Members of the party have occupied several ministerial posts in the home-rule parliament, and the party has held the balance of power in the government.

After World War II and the profound changes brought about in the 1950s and 1960s in the educational system and administration of Greenland, the country was launched into the modern world. It was a time when change came extraordinarily rapidly, moving from a traditional hunting society (which had hardly changed since 1721) to a modern Inuit-Northern European society based on the Scandinavian model, which combines state and private enterprise. There was a negative side to these changes, such as the destruction of old settlements, the disruption of traditional family patterns, and an increase in suicide and alcoholism. But there was also a positive side—a twofold increase in the population since 1950 as a result of better health care, better education, closer contacts with the rest of the world, and an unequivocal move toward self-government. Despite the drawbacks of the centralization policy introduced by the Danes, it also created more contact and interaction between the local settlements and improved social services.

Atuagagdliutit contributed to this rapid political evolution by its serious editorial and in-depth articles on many of these issues. As it was then published only once a week, it dealt less with the news, a role that the radio had taken over, and concentrated on providing background information. It developed a readership accustomed to reviews and insightful analysis of issues that were important for political independence. But the radio played the major role because of its immediacy. In 1956, the fledgling radio station in Nuuk became the broadcasting corporation *Kalaallit Nunaata Radioa* (KNR), or Greenland Radio. It broke the isolation of Greenlanders by providing daily news and access on the air to the various political groups and other associations and organizations. Peter Frederik Rosing, former director of KNR, explained in an interview how important the radio had been for the development of modern Greenland:

> The radio has been able to gather this very scattered population together and to give it the feeling of being one people. Because of strong local pride, there had not been a common feeling that we are in fact the same people with the same language and history, only with some small regional differences. (personal communication, June 1989)

> But the new media, the radio, could be heard with a little bit of luck by almost everyone in the fifties and sixties. It gave people the feeling, "Yes, we are the same people. We really are one people." It means much for the creation of a national identity. If there is a gathering force, the radio has been of immense importance in this respect. (personal communication, 1987)

An important result of the radio has been to make people in Greenland, and Inuit in particular, capable of understanding one dialect, the one that might be called the *western Greenland-Nuuk dialect;* perhaps more than anything else, that has unified the country. The radio, being more immediate than the press, has indeed been a catalyst in the emancipation process by providing a focus for national debates. Although the print media did not lose their influence, they remained handicapped because of the transportation difficulties that prevailed in Greenland: it still sometimes took 2, 3, or even 4 weeks after a newspaper was published for it to reach a settlement. The radio, however, was instantaneous every day.

In Greenland, the radio is a monopoly. There is still only one radio station. Although it used to broadcast only a few hours a day, KNR now broadcasts approximately 18 hours a day, 7 days a week. It is divided into two main sections: a news and current affairs section and a culture and entertainment section. The director of KNR has always been a native Greenlander. This has been one way of ensuring a specific Greenlandic direction. As KNR has a monopoly on radio transmission, it has to be bilingual; approximately 75% of its programs are in Greenlandic and 25% are in Danish. Of the present 100 employees, approximately 80% are Greenlanders. Again, because of its monopoly status, it must strictly adhere to an *alsidighedskriterie,* which roughly translates as "equal access." This means that KNR has an obligation to reflect all opinions and all tastes of the island's society. KNR's mandate and by-laws stipulate that the station has to be exceptionally scrupulous in giving equal time to every political party. KNR is required to reflect the characteristics of its audience and their special interests. For example, more than 50% of the Greenland population is under 18 years of age, thus a large number of programs are geared to the young and to education. KNR also has an obligation to reflect diverse tastes. Therefore, it has programming that ranges from current literature to language courses, from rock music to opera. The programs were recently described by KNR:

> Besides the daily news programs, KNR also has 4 background programs on current affairs; 2 in Greenlandic and 2 in Danish.
>
> KNR has scores of entertainment programs such as interviews with popular personalities, and every week KNR has a direct talk-show with music lasting 2 hours.
>
> KNR has a children's program every morning—15 minutes in Greenlandic and 15 minutes in Danish. There is also a weekly program geared towards young people with 1 hour dedicated to Greenlandic, and 1 hour to Danish.
>
> There are numerable cultural programs with differing titles. Most of the programs showcase storytelling, programs about the Greenlandic language, and others on art and music.
>
> KNR does not operate with the traditional "locked in" program. Its schedule is flexible and covers all areas of interest. Besides news, weather reports, "locked in" music programs, and religious services, all other programs are put in the program schedule with reference to the main aim of KNR—to serve the people of Greenland according to the languages used—80% Greenlandic and 20% Danish. The weekly schedule of radio and television programs is distributed to the whole of Greenland through their weekly newspapers, and is announced on radio and television on a regular basis. (Murin, 1987)

KNR's most important function is to produce daily news coverage of Greenland and the rest of the world. The noteworthy aspect of the Greenlandic news coverage is that it presents the news as seen and filtered through Inuit eyes. As in most other cultures, what is news in one culture is not necessarily news in another, so it is important to present events with a Greenlandic perspective (Stenbaek, 1988). It is essential also that KNR maintain an office in Copenhagen with both a

Danish and a Greenlandic journalist. This gives the station direct access to Danish and other European news and allows Greenlanders in Denmark, as well as Danes, to hear Greenlandic news every day, because there is 5 minutes of Greenlandic news in Danish and 5 minutes in Greenlandic daily on the Danish broadcasting system. This has made Danes generally more aware of political events on the island.

Apart from the news office in Denmark, KNR has two other regional studios. The first was established in Ilulissat in 1981 and, later, another was created in southern Greenland at Qaqortoq. Both of these regional offices are staffed by a journalist and a technician. They provide news input every day to the main radio station in Nuuk as well as occasionally longer feature stories. Because KNR was deemed to be of paramount importance to Greenlandic society, it was one of the first institutions to be handed over fully to Greenlanders after the advent of home-rule government in 1979. KNR also maintains archives containing more than 4,300 tapes of interviews and programs of cultural and historical interest, as well as more than 800 tapes of Greenlandic music. The archive is a unique and invaluable collection of Greenlandic culture.

KNR is governed by the law on radio and television broadcasting in Greenland (*Radioloven*). It operates in close cooperation with the Danish Broadcasting Corporation, although it is administratively completely independent from it. KNR is still financed by the Greenland home-rule government in an arm's-length manner that limits governmental supervision over programming and content. The structure of subsidization for KNR is thus similar to the practices followed in Britain, some Western European countries, and Canada. During the late 1980s its annual broadcasting budget was approximately $10 million US. This also covers television broadcasting. Both the radio and television are still totally noncommercial; no advertisements of any kind are allowed. KNR now broadcasts to all parts of Greenland. The radio signal is distributed by Nunatek (the government agency responsible for communication technologies) along the *radio chain* erected on the west coast. The radio chain is a UHF microwave relay system. Programs are provided to the settlements in east Greenland through the Intelsat satellites as well as by shortwave transmission.

In the 1960s and 1970s, the radio had an interesting consequence. Every morning there were programs called *Skoleradio* ("school radio"), which were educational programs for the primary and secondary grades. Because there was no other radio station, and people had gotten into the habit of listening, most Greenlanders used to listen to the school radio.

Even people who did not have much formal education, whether they were out on fishing boats or working in their kitchens, got quite an education by osmosis so to speak. This has certainly contributed to the fact that Greenlanders are generally as well educated today as Scandinavians. The radio has contributed to the preservation of language and to the education of Greenlanders and has served to provide a modern and competent understanding of national issues. It has created a linguistic and cultural identity and a keen political consciousness—the necessary preconditions of self-government.

Developments in Television

Television in Greenland started on January 1, 1970, at the personal initiative of Ole Winstedt, a Danish businessman who wanted to sell television sets in Nuuk. Obviously programs were needed if television sets were to be sold. He set up a private cable association in Nuuk with members who had to pay an annual fee to receive between 3 to 4 hours of television 6 days a week. This marketing device was later imitated in a number of settlements. The early programs were taped from the Danish Broadcasting Corporation on the first videocassette recorder in Denmark and sent by airplane to Greenland where they were broadcast locally, originally only in Nuuk. Within the next 6 years, 17 cable associations were established in various settlements, mainly on the west coast.

The Danish programs were quite limited in scope and content because in those days Danish television broadcast only 3 to 4 hours daily. There was also a language problem because even the Danish programs (understandable only to the Inuit who were bilingual) were not all in Danish but in British or American English, French, and Italian. Greenlanders received programs in all kinds of languages that had Danish subtitles that many could not read. In fact, an audience survey from 1973 showed that many Greenlanders watched television with the sound turned off, but with the radio playing. So questions of language and culture were obviously quite critical.

Another major problem was that it was illegal to tape programs off the air and rebroadcast them, especially when the Danish Broadcasting Corporation had turned down an official request to share these programs. There was the strong possibility of prosecution for copyright violations, because the programs were rebroadcast for financial gain by the various cable associations. Despite being illegal, everyone cooperated in this venture. Many bureaucrats as well as officials of the Danish Broadcasting Corporation pretended not to know anything about it, although almost everyone was in fact quite helpful behind the scenes. The cable associations did their own scheduling, as each settlement would receive copies of tapes either from Denmark or the other cable associations. Some of the associations then started to do local programming. At the beginning these were very simple programs, usually 15 minutes long, done with portable video cameras. Sports and political events were the most common topics. These amateurish programs were very important because they marked the beginning of indigenous television. Producers, camera operators, and on-the-air personalities learned as they went along. Some large cable associations, such as the one in Nuuk, employed a few Danish technicians and producers who were able to do local programs, and some Greenlanders, who had learned film and video techniques in Denmark. But the whole operation was very much "learn-as-you-go" and depended on private enterprise and people's goodwill, both in Denmark and Greenland.

As it became increasingly apparent that television was a very powerful medium, people wanted more local programming in Greenlandic. There was also concern that television had to become legal. Therefore, it was decided that Greenland should have a centralized television corporation operated by Kalaallit Nunaata Radioa. The new television corporation, KNR-TV, centralized production in Nuuk, although it maintained some local studios. Unlike earlier, when tapes were sent by airplane to each cable association, the programs were broadcast from Nuuk to the settlements or cable associations via the radio chain. Greenland is covered by the Intelsat satellites, but the price of satellite time was too high for KNR. The existing microwave chain operated by Nunatek was an economical solution. Only a very few settlements on the east coast are still served by tapes sent by plane and occasionally also by satellite. KNR-TV now sends a centralized feed, but there are allowances for brief local feeds.

On November 1, 1982, the first national television programs were broadcast from the newly built studio in Nuuk. KNR-TV now produces a wide variety of programs: children's programs, musical programs, political programs, dramas, news magazines, and features on family life. KNR-TV airs 2,000 hours of television broadcasts annually. Like its radio broadcasts, it follows a flexible schedule except for its children's programs and news programs, which are always broadcast at fixed times. Most programs are still in Danish or other foreign languages with Danish subtitles. Only about 5% of the broadcasts are in Greenlandic or with Greenlandic subtitles.

Some authorities claim that it was the KNR's programs in Greenlandic that were heard by Canadian Inuit on their transistor radios when they camped in northern Quebec that originally gave them the impetus to press for programs in their own language in Canada. It is a measure of the importance that the Inuit across the Arctic attach to television as a medium of cultural survival that since 1980 they have engaged in discussions about panarctic television and have now signed exchange agreements concerning television programs under the auspices of the Inuit Circumpolar Conference. Since 1986, the Inuit Broadcasting Corporation (IBC) in Canada has each week shown a Greenlandic-language television program, and KNR has shown an IBC program in Inuktitut. At the beginning of the exchange, the programs (which are broadcast in their original versions) were either introduced by a short summary in Inuktitut or Greenlandic or had occasional voice-overs explaining the program to the viewers. However, this practice has been discontinued because it is believed by both IBC and KNR that the ears of the Greenlanders and the Canadian Eastern Arctic Inuit have become attuned enough to each other's dialects that a Canadian Inuit can comprehend enough of the Greenlandic language and vice versa to understand these programs. Television has now furthered this common cultural and linguistic ground and has made it possible, although on a modest scale, for Inuit to understand each other once again.

Rosing, who directed the introduction of the national television services in Greenland, remarked:

> I don't think that television will come in and change us all into Americans or Europeans. Of course, it has an entertainment value and will, at the same time, give people some ideas that it is cool to be a European or an American. We have our increased consciousness of being our own people, a special people who are able to make it on our own, even as a small country. We have our own special characteristics and our own special culture. I don't think that television or video can really destroy that consciousness. The worst thing that can happen is that a child might not use his time to finish his homework or get enough sleep, but in the overall picture, those are small things and are not enough to destroy a complete culture. If it were like that, then foreign literature would have spoilt us too, some time ago.

There are so many other things that are coming into our country to distract us from being ourselves and being Greenlanders. There is not that much any more in Greenland that is purely Greenlandic except possibly our temperament and personality, but that is not a result of television. It is something that is in our souls.

The growing concern for cultural independence and political autonomy and our basic Inuit personality is not something that media can alter. (personal communication, 1987)

Television and radio have an important positive influence in other ways. There are no daily newspapers anywhere in the Arctic in the Inuit languages. In Greenland only the largest settlements receive Danish daily newspapers, and even they are usually a day or two late. Only radio and television are capable of bringing news and information on a daily basis and in the Greenlanders' own language. In a period of such rapid social and economic dislocation—with its attendant cultural change—up-to-date, accessible information is a necessity for cultural and political survival.

The growing concern for cultural independence and political autonomy led to the negotiations and referendum that established home rule in Greenland on May 1, 1979 (Lynge, 1976, 1977). Greenland now has its own home-rule government that step by step has taken over the responsibility for all areas of jurisdiction from the Danish government, except defense and foreign affairs. The last area of jurisdiction, the health sector, will be turned over to Greenlandic authority in 1993. It is indicative of the impact that Greenlanders thought the media would have on their independence that the media were the first areas of jurisdiction (together with the schools and the church) to be taken over by the home-rule government. Greenland remains a part of the Danish kingdom; however, it presently has its own flag and Greenlandic is its official language. As a part of Denmark, Greenland became a member of the European Economic Community in 1972, even though 70% of Greenlanders voted against entry. It is a mark of the new Greenlandic self-confidence that Greenland held another referendum in 1982 and voted to withdraw from the European Economic Community in 1985, because it no longer wanted its cultural and economic future dependent on decisions taken by foreign powers.

Technopessimists have forecast dire consequences as a result of the introduction of television in indigenous societies, predicting that it would completely destroy their cultures. This, however, has not happened; in fact, television has had many positive effects. It has helped to teach people Danish and to a lesser extent English, and whatever one may say about the negative influence on native languages, it should not be forgotten that it is, of course, imperative for Greenlanders to know Danish (and English) to deal with the modern world and to play an active role in it. Maybe more important, television showed the Inuit that other minority groups in the world were able to survive. For example, in Alaska, where native groups received television before Greenlanders, images of the U.S. black civil rights movement were particularly powerful in this respect and were a serious factor in the rising native consciousness in Alaska in the 1970s.

In Greenland, television ended the physical and psychological isolation of the Inuit and made them identify with the rest of the world. Television introduced new ideas to them in many spheres and gave them a more comprehensive introduction to the European and North American political systems that had been enigmas to them before but in which, of course, they have to live. One can argue that watching the *Muppet Show* in Greenlandic is a cultural mishmash, but it does link people to the rest of the world and provides an understanding of what the world is doing. That can never be a bad thing.

Notes

1. A printing press existed in Greenland earlier than 1861. One of the Moravian missionaries set up a small handpress in 1790, which produced a hymnal, the first book printed in Greenland.
2. Some films and coproductions have been made by Greenlanders, and many more films about the country have been produced by outsiders. The first Greenlandic feature-length film was *Paolo's Wedding* made in 1939 by the Greenlandic explorer Knud Rasmussen and a Danish film company. Greenland also has an active national literature encompassing novels, poetry, short stories, essays and dramas. On average, 50 new titles are published annually.

References

Erngaard, E. (1972). *Greenland, then and now*. Copenhagen: Lademann.
Fleisher, J. (Ed.). (1980). *Et Grønlandsk blad Atuagagdliutit—120 aar*. Nuuk: Det Grønlandske Forlag.
Gad, F. (1970). *The history of Greenland, earliest times to 1700* (Vol. 1). London: Hurst.
Gad, F. (1973). *The history of Greenland, 1700-1782* (Vol. 2). London: Hurst.
Gad, F. (1982). *The history of Greenland, 1782-1808* (Vol. 3). Copenhagen: NYT Nordisk Forlag Arnold Busck.

Garnett, E. (1968). *To Greenland's icy mountains: The story of Hans Egede, explorer, coloniser, missionary.* London: Heinemann.

Lokalbladskonference: Mange problemer. (1987). Unpublished manuscript.

Lynge, F. (1976). *The relevance of native culture to northern development: The Greenland case.* Kingston, Ont.: Queen's University, Centre for International Relations.

Lynge, F. (1977). A vision of a future home rule cultural policy for Greenland. In P. J. Amaria (Ed.), *Arctic systems* (pp. 307-314). New York: Plenum Press.

Maxwell, M. S. (1985). *Prehistory of the eastern Arctic.* Orlando, FL: Academic Press.

Murin, D. L. (Ed.). (1987). *The northern native broadcast directory.* Montreal: Runge Press.

Prattis, I., & Chartrand, J. (1983). Inuktitut-English bilingualism in the Northwest Territories of Canada. *Anthropologica, 25*(1), 85-105.

Rink, H. J. (1975). *Danish Greenland, 1877: Its people and its products.* New York: AMS Press. (Original work published in 1977.)

Smiley, J. (1988). *The Greenlanders.* New York: Knopf.

Stenbaek, M. (Ed.). (1983). *Inuit media directory.* Montreal: Centre for Northern Studies and Research.

Stenbaek, M. (1988). Politics of cultural survival: Towards a model of indigenous television. *American Review of Canadian Studies, 18*(3), 331-340.

3

Communication, Culture, and Technology: Satellites and Northern Native Broadcasting in Canada

GAIL VALASKAKIS

Introduction

On September 20, 1990, the Canadian Radio-Television and Telecommunications Commission (CRTC) issued the Northern Broadcasting Policy (NBP), a revised version of its 1983 policy. The new policy is an expanded recognition and definition of aboriginal broadcasting. Even within the current context of extensive government reductions in the subsidies for native communications, this policy statement is a landmark in the development of northern communications. In addressing issues of native language and culture related to broadcasting access and distribution, the Native Broadcasting Policy is the symbol and focus of a Canadian social process that has spanned two decades. This process reflects Canada's long-standing interest in issues of culture and in communications technologies. But the development of native communications "from smoke signals to satellites" (Valaskakis, 1987, p. 5) is in equal measure the result of the insight and determination of aboriginal peoples themselves.

Communications technologies have been increasingly recognized as agents of economic centralization, cultural fragmentation and political control. Within this context of persuasive critical analysis relating communications to cultural imperialism and economic domination (e.g., Schiller, 1976), aboriginal peoples across Canada have demanded access to media in an effort to support native culture and identity and to build native community and institutions. This is evident in the far north, where Inuit and other aboriginal nations have used media in attempting to combat and even reverse the cultural impact of compelling, new communications technologies. As in other countries, "The demand for local programming, and even more, for local programming rooted in tradition . . . is a question of whether one wants one's culture to be overwhelmed and homogenized" (Katz, 1977, p. 116).

Technology and Change: Historical Trends

In the far north, technology and cultural change have been interrelated throughout the 400-year contact period. The Inuit experience in eastern Canada suggests definite patterns of control related to technological access, including media access and participation (Valaskakis, 1979). More recently, questions of indigenous language and culture have been raised in relation to native broadcasting. These questions arise in the context of native social change and cultural incorporation, processes that, in the far north, are closely associated with the availability of technology.

Northern social history is, at the most significant level, an analysis of the relationship between native and nonnative peoples. This relationship has been defined and cemented through technology and the conditions of its access and transfer from a dominant to a marginal people. Historically, technology has been provided to native people on a limited and directed basis. The earliest and most continuous form of interaction between Inuit and nonnatives took the form of trading. At first, bells, mirrors, and beads were traded for skins, food, and tools. But when whalers and traders realized the potential of a native labor force for resource extraction, European technology became important as a motivating force. Knives, guns, traps, and boats were exchanged for Inuit goods and services. The influence of this early transfer of technology led to clear patterns of social and cultural change in Inuit communities.

A knowledge of three major trends is important to understand the relationship between current communications technology and Inuit culture in modern northern communities. First, nonnatives gained overriding authority through mere possession of technology and control over its distribution. Inuit responded to the functional superiority of metal knives, guns, and wooden boats. In the eastern Arctic, the authority this conferred on all nonnatives was reinforced by European navigational skills, the impact of the English language and Christian religion, and a seemingly endless supply of trade goods.

Second, through the directed transfer of technology, nonnatives initiated pluralism and new criteria for leadership in Inuit society. As the first nonnative agents of change in the far north, whalers acted on the motives and mandate of an outside institution in designating *whaling bosses* as contact agents, Inuit who directed native activity to serve the economic needs of nonnative institutions. Whaling bosses were the captain's "voices" (Fleming, 1956, p. 75) who engaged Inuit hunters, guides, and other personnel necessary to the whale hunt. They were rewarded for their efforts with technology—guns, ammunition, and boats—which, in turn, secured their positions of status in the Inuit community.

Whalers worked within a social unit that was hierarchically structured. This social structure was altered as European technology was introduced. As Inuit with wooded boats decided where and when to travel and Inuit with guns provided more food for their extended families, leadership began a rudimentary shift toward people with access to nonnative technology and authority. Social and cultural change was not extensive during the seasonal activity of the whaling period because Inuit leaders such as shaman or *angakok* (respected healers in Inuit society) could easily take on the new role of whaling boss. But this system of contact became the modus operandi used by all the nonnative institutions that penetrated the north. Missionaries established *lay readers* or *catechists* who assisted ministers or themselves propagated the faith. Inuit who became *Christian bosses* could be young or even women but, for obvious reasons, could not be shaman or angakok. Native catechists tended to spread Christian and southern culture and to undermine the most powerful Inuit leaders at the turn of the 20th century, when institutionalized trading entered the north.

Trading companies brought new technology and trade goods. The processes of trapping meant new hunting techniques and residence patterns; the processes of trading reinforced nonnative authority and hierarchical interaction. Traders established both camp and district *trading bosses,* Inuit who, like *leading Indians* in the fur trade empire to the south, organized native trading on a local level. They gained their positions on the basis of being able to obtain furs, a criterion that could exclude older and less robust hunters, and their status was enhanced by their knowledge of the new technology and trade goods. Post trading eventually established Inuit families who remained in the employ of traders as *post servants* and, as missionaries and traders were joined by police, settlements began to develop in the far north. The Royal Canadian Mounted Police (RCMP) also engaged *contact agents:* Inuit guides and providers who eventually took on the role of special constables, employees outside the normal ranks of the force.

With the formation of small northern settlements, the role of contact agent led to new activities and functions that demanded new skills: interaction skills. These were acquired, used, and diffused through families whose access to authority established "the forerunners of new groups for Eskimo society" (Vallee, 1967, p. 110). *People of the land* could be distinguished from *people of the whites* (p. 140), who had adopted more Euro-Canadian customs and languages through their association with nonnative institutions. With several institutions in the north, conflicting authority figures became absorbed in a new, plural society that distinguished between those who were contact agents and those who were not. This distinction "was instrumental in eroding or eliminating the process of local decision-making, except in those matters well outside the white man's interest" (Phillips, 1967, p. 80). At the same time, pluralism began to fragment the consensual basis of Inuit cultural and social action.

A third aspect of technology is related to contact. Beginning with the 16th-century explorer Martin Frobisher, nonnatives traded goods for certain Inuit information. This exchange was formalized through the broad authority of the nonnative institutions that moved north. As new technologies became essential to Inuit life-style, information became a commodity that, like skills and products, Inuit exchanged for material goods. The importance that information acquired is related in Archibald Fleming's (1956) account of a contact agent for an American whaler who was killed by other Inuit for revealing how many pelts they intended to trade with a second whaler (pp. 153-154). Information about the Inuit was used to control residence, credit, and trading. The police joined the missionaries and traders in establishing social order in the north. The integrating role of messages in Inuit society was redefined, and Inuit found it more difficult to withhold information from the researchers and agency personnel who followed. At the same time, Inuit access to information was restricted through the introduction of Inuit literacy, a process that reinforced the development of two, separate, and noncomplementary communication systems: one within the Inuit community and the other within the nonnative community.

Missionaries introduced syllabic and Roman orthography systems for writing the native languages in the late 1800s. By 1910, probably 98% of Inuit in the eastern Arctic were literate in Inuktitut (Graburn, 1969). But three different orthographies in Canada and six across the greater north maintained dialect differences and regionalization among Inuit whose languages were basically similar. Because Inuit did not become functionally literate in English, written information did not allow native adaptation of their own institutions or participation in those brought north. Before 1972, only nine secular books and four periodicals had been published in Inuktitut and, according to Jennes, oral tradition in the form of story telling was no longer evident by 1924 (Mayes, 1972). Information between Inuit and nonnatives passed through contact agents or community go-betweens.

As a result of this historical process, technology and communication during the first half of the 20th century played a vital role in Inuit cultural and social change. This process contributed to the economic and political dependency of Inuit people. It was equally important in supporting the acculturation of Inuit within a model that can best be described as *cultural replacement.* Inuit culture became associated with the communication medium over which Inuit maintained control: syllabic writing. Because this technique for writing the Inuit language was limited largely to Christian communication, secular documents of Inuit culture and society did not appear in the postcontact period. Inuit wrote no historical documents, no community policies, no precedents in law, and no educational material. In Harold Innis's (1950) terminology, nonnatives established an English-language "monopoly of knowledge" as they moved southern institutions to the north. Nonnative authority defined public process in northern communities; nonnative control of information and technology excluded Inuit from participating in the cultural and social change fundamental to adaptation and development. Southern institutions stood at the political center of northern settlements (Brody, 1975).

> Most of the important sources of messages are not natives of the Arctic, and . . . most messages flow into the region from outside. . . . The political and social position of the senders determines their authority. . . . Decision-makers of the most important channels of information are almost exclusively white, and located outside the Arctic. (Mayes, 1972, p. 84)

During the past two decades, Inuit participation in northern social and cultural adaptation has changed considerably, primarily as a result of the organization and action of native people themselves.

Early Communications Technology

Native people began establishing aboriginal organizations across Canada on regional and national bases in the late 1960s and early 1970s, a period when the federal government's interest in communications extended to issues of northern development and native acculturation. Satellite programs illustrate "the degree to which Canadian experience has been shaped by the spread of communication technologies" (Kroker, 1984, p. 9). At the same time, the Inuit experience bears out contentions drawn from Innis (1950; 1951) and James Carey (1967) that important changes in communication take place historically over lengthy periods of contact and incorporation. In the early 1970s, Inuit became increasingly aware of the role early media played in reinforcing, even expanding the southern cultural values and the economic and political control initiated by earlier technologies.

Radio was established in the far north in the late 1920s, just as airplanes began to provide easy access to the Arctic. In the eastern Arctic, radio reception was often poor, but agencies were still quick to recognize the advantage of shortwave for communication over distance. By the early 1930s, trading posts, missions, and police posts were equipped with high-frequency radios. Small radio networks were established, primarily to communicate the directives of southern agencies. New interaction patterns removed much of the localized authority of post managers and, as Innis (1950, 1951) suspects, placed Inuit under the increasing control of southern bureaucracies.

The role that radio played in the development of the RCMP suggests the relationship between early communications technologies and the increasing marginalization of the Inuit people. In 1927, three radio stations were established in the eastern Arctic, to which RCMP constables were attached in an advisory capacity (Steele, 1936). For the following 3 years, RCMP annual reports included a discussion of "wireless and radio telegraph communication" within the section titled "Control of the North." In 1934, after he had toured the Arctic posts by airplane, the commissioner of the RCMP restructured the agency and centralized the control of Arctic detachments "for greater administrative convenience" (Kelly & Kelly, 1973, p. 171). Beore 1934, the Mackenzie and western Arctic posts were controlled from Edmonton, detachments on the west side of Hudson Bay reported to Winnipeg, and the eastern Arctic posts were under the jurisdiction of Montreal. With increased access by air and communication through radio, all the Arctic detachments were integrated into G Division, with headquarters in Ottawa. And although high-frequency radio solidified the interests of southern institutions, broadcast radio, which was appreciated by nonnative northerners by the mid-1930s, provided little information for the Inuit. The first Inuktitut program was broadcast in 1960, two years after the formation of the Canadian Broadcasting Company (CBC) Northern Service. In 1972, most Inuit did not speak English; and only 17% of CBC's shortwave service was broadcast in the Inuit language (Mayes, 1972). And beyond that, Canadian broadcasting was limited in the eastern Arctic before the introduction of satellites. Nigel Wilford (1986) describes listening to radio in Pengnirtung, Baffin Island:

> I remember listening to Radio Moscow, Radio Peking, Voice of America, the B.B.C. and sometimes on a clear night if the wind was blowing in the right direction, the Northern Service of the C.B.C.

When television was introduced in the north, Inuit were not consulted. They were equally removed from decisions on television availability or programming. In 1967, Frontier Package television began in the first of 18, largely western Arctic communities. These 4-hour videotape packages of southern programming were sent north primarily for the transient, nonnative population. Relayed videotapes contained no native-language programming, a pattern that extended into the 1970s.

The modern era of aboriginal communications really began in Canada in 1969, when Jean Chretien, then minister of Indian affairs, released a white paper on Indian policy. In its intention to change the status of Indian people, this governmental position paper ushered in a new era of native action. As they united against the paper's assimilationist implications, aboriginal nations realized that they lacked communication channels to inform or receive feedback from their people. In the west, work had begun in communications with the formation of the Alberta Native Communications Society (ANCS), which received federal funding as early as 1970. With the white paper, several provincial native organizations began communication branches. Some of these became native communications societies when the program of the Department of Secretary of State was established in the mid-1970s. The far north was also drawn into communications issues in 1969. In that year, the Telesat Canada Bill proposed the first geostationary satellite system in the world as a "Northern vision for the 1970s" (Kenny, 1971, Pt. 1, p. 20). Although the Anik system was clearly a welcome response to the conditions of northern distance and isolation, it was a mixed blessing for native northerners. Inuit, who were never consulted in the discussions that led to the satellite program, knew that the introduction of earlier media played a forceful role in maintaining the authority of nonnative institutions and in restricting native access to information in their communities. Satellite television posed new threats to their language and culture "by parachuting telephone, radio and live television simultaneously into a region that is culturally different from that of the producers of both the technology hardware and software" (Roth, 1982, p. 3). And the south-north structure of the broadcasting system threatened to increase southern domination, making native northerners even more marginal to the political and economic reality of southern Canada. This prospect seemed all the more probable when the Canadian Cabinet refused the CBC's 1969 request for a northern programming budget, the first of CBC Northern Service's many attempts to meet the media needs of native northerners. At the same time, the communication needs of native northerners—expressed in the words of Peter Inukshuk of Inukjuaq, northern Quebec, were widely recognized among the Inuit:

> We need information, masses of it. We need it in our own language. . . . We need to have that information spread throughout our communities. . . . This has to happen fast. If it doesn't, we will vanish as a people. Our future is at stake. (Northern Quebec Inuit Association [NQIA], 1974, p. 112)

In 1971, the first government-sponsored communication project took place in the north, and it involved both Indian and Inuit communities. The federal Department of Communications sponsored the 3-year Northern Pilot Project in community radio in Big Trout Lake, Ontario, and the Keewatin community Baker Lake. This was the forerunner of Wawata Native Communications Society in northern Ontario and, in some ways, of the Baker Lake Production Centre of the Inuit Broadcasting Corporation. In 1971, a community video project was mounted in La Ronge, Saskatchewan. This project reinforced the National Film

Board's interest in the relationship between film and video and social change. Applied on a small-scale basis, these media could provide regional communication to increase Inuit participation in northern communities. At the same time, Inuit films could be televised, allowing Inuit the first opportunity to see themselves on broadcast media. In 1972, the National Film Board began the Cape Dorset film workshop in Baffin Island. This led to the Iqualiut film workshop that, begun in 1974, became Nunatsiakmiut a year later.

A second phase of native communications developments began in 1973. In that year, the Anik satellite system became operational and the Cabinet approved funding for CBC's Accelerated Coverage Plan (ACP), providing radio and television to all Canadian communities with populations of 500 or more. Monies were allocated for hardware but not for production; little of the programming available through the ACP was relevant to northern people:

> The Accelerated Coverage Plan was originally intended to provide intra-provincial distribution of services, but many of the transmitters installed relayed local and regional news programming which is not relevant to the viewers in the area. For instance, viewers in Baker Lake receive the volleyball scores from the Avelon Peninsula [in Newfoundland], viewers in Dryden, Ontario, hear about municipal gatherings in Winnipeg [Manitoba], and viewers in Old Crow in the Yukon watch the crocuses blooming in Vancouver [British Columbia] in mid-winter. (Canada, Ministry of Communications, 1983, p. 15)

In 1973, the Cabinet approved funding for the Native Communications Program (NCP). But as the first communication societies incorporated in Alberta, Nova Scotia, Ontario, and elsewhere, Inuit in northern Quebec protested the CBC's plan to extend television service to the north without Inuktitut programming or even relevant northern programming. This position was strongly supported by Inuit Tapirisat of Canada, the national Inuit organization.

Thus by the mid-1970s the players in the development of native communications were all in place: politicized native organizations, a framework and funding for native communications societies, government-sponsored local media projects, initial northern broadcasting policy statements, and evaluation to provide information and data on the ongoing process.

With the establishment of native communication societies, several groups began developing media programming, broadcasting agreements, and newspapers. In British Columbia, Ontario, and northern Quebec, media priorities included community radio and *trail radio,* communication for people traveling on the land to hunt, fish, or camp. As communication societies continued to develop in response to regional needs, satellite experiments became a new focus of aboriginal action. In 1975, ANCS mounted the Hermes satellite project called Ironstar, and in 1977 Taqramiut Nipingat Inc. (TNI) began the Naalakvik I project, which linked the Hermes and Anik A satellites to produce an interactive, or two-way, radio network in eight northern Quebec communities. Between 1978 and 1981, TNI and Inuit Tapirisat of Canada participated in Anik B satellite experiments, using interactive audio and direct video, which included the first direct, north-to-north television programming through satellite uplinks. These efforts led to the formation of the Inuit Broadcasting Corporation (IBC), the first native-language television network in North America, in 1981. In the same year, the CRTC expanded the availability of native broadcasting by licensing undertakings of Indian communication societies in the western Northwest Territories and the Yukon. But native communities contended with an increasing array of southern media. Canadian Satellite Communications Inc. (CanCom), a pay television package of U.S. and Canadian television and radio stations, was also licensed in 1981. In addition, commercial television became widely available across the north on an off-satellite basis. And as more native communities received southern television on satellite dishes that they purchased, video playback units became common in native homes. Within this context of diverse and competing media, the Inuit Broadcasting Corporation has become a flagship of northern native television.

The Development of Inuit Broadcasting

Inuit television is the result of northern native peoples' resolve to participate in the social transformation of their world. Inuit acted to gain access to this compelling and pervasive medium "to strengthen the social, cultural, and linguistic fabric of Inuit life" (Inuit Broadcasting Corporation [IBC], 1982, p. ii). Amid commercial television spanning the range of programming from *All in the Family* to *Cheers, Sesame Street,* and the national news—which Rosemarie Kuptana (1982, p. 5), then president of IBC, labeled a "cultural assault" because it reflects southern interests and values—Inuit television represents

> a means of cultural expression through drama, documentary, current affairs, news entertainment, and the arts. . . . We want to preserve part of ourselves—our language, our social habits, our survival skills. And we want to do it in the context that is most comfortable for us: an Inuit system which can link the old and new Inuit. (pp. vi-v)

The opportunity to develop such a system was forged through satellite-access experiments and smaller-scale communications projects. The most important of these in regard to television were the Inukshuk and the Naalakvik II experimental satellite projects.

The 3-year Inukshuk Project used the Anik B communications program to experiment with Inuktitut television broadcasting in the Baffin, Keewatin, and central Arctic regions of the Northwest Territories. This project linked six communities in regions with different time zones and dialects through one-way video transmission from Iqaliut and two-way audio among all six communities. The project established regional production facilities and trained staff, and for 8 months during 1980 to 1981, it broadcast Inuktitut television on both local and network bases. A significant amount of the 323.7 hours of network programming broadcast during the experiment was devoted to public affairs, current issues, and education, areas of particular relevance to Inuit cultural stability and social participation (Valaskakis, Robbins, & Wilson, 1984). In northern Quebec, where TNI operated a similar Anik B experiment linking five communities, Inuit broadcasting expanded with production facilities, training, and regional television broadcasting. By the time the two Anik B projects led to the formation of the Inuit Broadcasting Corporation, Inuit broadcasting had attained considerable experience, expertise, and credibility. At the same time, Canadian communications policy reflected increasing concern with issues of national pluralism and cultural sovereignty. Native broadcasting took on new importance as the country became more aware of the threat to Canadian cultural sovereignty posed by U.S. satellites. In the early 1980s, recognition of the relationship between broadcasting and the cultural and linguistic integrity of aboriginal peoples began to be reflected in regulatory policy.

In 1980, the CRTC issued the report of the Therrien Commission on the Extension of Service (Canadian Radio-Television Telecommunications Commission [CRTC], 1980). Reflecting the deliberations of the first CRTC commission to hold northern hearings and to include an Inuk commissioner, the Therrien report asserted that government had a responsibility to ensure broadcasting that supported aboriginal languages and cultures. As native people gained a "special place in cultural policy" (Applebaum & Hébert, 1982, p. 11), the Therrien report became the basis for the federal government's first Northern Broadcasting Policy, issued in 1983. The five basic principles of this policy recognized the communications needs of northerners, especially native northerners, for whom it specified widespread participation in all aspects of media programming, regulatory decision making, and broadcasting distribution on the basis of fair access and consultation (Canada, Federal Government News Release, 1983).

The implementation of these principles led to the Northern Native Broadcast Access Program (NNBAP), begun in 1983. The program originally provided $13.4 million a year to subsidize the productions of 13 regionally based northern native communication societies. Funding for the NNBAP was cut to $11.1 million in 1990-1991; funding for the Native Communications Program, which sponsored native newspapers and radio among southern groups and for the National Aboriginal Communications Society was eliminated altogether. The Inuit Broadcasting Corporation and the 12 other northern production groups are working to raise monies from other sources. But given the limited resources of native people themselves, the NNBAP will remain the primary funding source for the production and distribution of northern native media. The elimination of the Native Communications Program and the reduction of funding for the Northern Native Broadcast Access Program are severe setbacks for all native media. However, native communication societies continue to play central roles in defining the nature and extent of native broadcasting, a process that has had important implications for the very definition of aboriginal cultures.

Issues of Native Culture and Language

The NNBAP was approved as a vehicle to promote aboriginal cultures and languages. This is reflected in the production guidelines for the program, which target 5 hours of television and 20 hours of radio per week. An Irish study on broadcasting and the "lesser used languages of the European community" (Alcock & O'Brien, 1980) suggested that this amount of programming was the minimum exposure needed to maintain a minority language. Drawing direct parallels with this study raises problems of European application and Canadian distribution. On a broader level, the Irish study points toward the more basic and highly politicized issues of what is meant by *native cultures,* what is recognized as *native languages,* and how these assumptions relate to the values and codes that are instrumental in the daily lives of native peoples today. These issues raise questions about the notion of *culture* itself and the role of media in cultural expression.

> Culture is individuality and collectivity. It is an expression of being, of vitality, of assertiveness, of confidence and of pride in a way of life. Culture grows by the vitality and dynamism of society. Cultural industries grow, not only from commercial viability, but because of their ability to express the cultural goods of the societies in which they emanate. (Bergman, 1985, p. 9)

Culture is, at the most basic level, a patterned response to environment based on selected values. It is rooted in shared social practices and experiences—the context of social relations—which are maintained through communication. For Inuit, the dynamic nature of culture and the process of northern social history have contributed to a redefinition of *traditional* culture. Hugh Brody (1975) writes that eastern Arctic Inuit consider square dancing, the mouth harp and the accordion, trapping, the Christian church, syllabic writing, and other aspects of culture that they have incorporated since European contact to be *traditional.* These activities and even the institution of the church can be considered part of the culture of the *Inummariit,* or "real Inuit" (p. 144), largely older Inuit who demonstrate skill and control on the land, where they continue to hunt and trap on a regular basis. Based on his fieldwork in a northern Quebec community, Nathan Elberg (1984) observed that the concept of *real Inuit* is causing problems for the identity and self-esteem of younger Inuit, who are far less adept at hunting and trapping and far less knowledgeable about the land. Elberg (1984) suggests that the stories of urban difficulties told by young Inuit are "as significant in understanding the life of contemporary Inuit as some of the older stories about cold and anguish collected in earlier decades are to an understanding of the culture of those times" (p. 6). He believes that "it is time that the people in southern Canada stopped evaluating the authenticity of contemporary Inuit according to the standards (should I say cliches) for previous generations of Inuit" (p. 9). Elberg (1984) concludes with a comment from a young Inuk (singular for Inuit):

> It's like if you have Inuit as primitive people of the past, cavemen sort of deal. . . . That can be one definition of Inuk. . . . The definition of Inuit today should be an Inuk with a Honda, living in a house designed by a non-Inuk. But the Inuit of today is obviously not the same as quallunaak culture. . . . We are aware of people going to the moon and we're using speedboats and things like that but still we are saying, "We are Inuit." And some people are saying that we are too much of space men, not enough stone-age men. In that way, mixed up. (pp. 9-10)

As nonnatives associate traditional Inuit activities with precontact behavior, young Inuit experience the cultural struggle related to the concepts of *traditional* and *real Inuit*. At the same time, assimilation characterized by the control patterns of earlier Euro-Canadian contact have been encouraged by satellite access to southern broadcasting. Cultural incorporation and adaptation are important factors in defining the native cultures and languages that are basic to daily life in contemporary native communities. These processes also relate to the media products that reinforce native languages and cultures. Recognizing this has challenged broadcasting policy and programs to defer to native nations in determining the cultural or linguistic definition and relevance of indigenous media products.

Inuit broadcasting spans a range that is similar to southern programming: public affairs, documentaries, news, drama, and children's programming. But local broadcasting may also reflect the communality of radio or television Bingo, the creativity of local rock bands, or the social involvement of municipal elections. And on both local and regional levels, Inuit programming goes far beyond traditional cultural content, which can reflect the "quaintness of culture: the preservation of native traits, colorful customs, folk-dances and songs" (Bergman, 1985, p. 9). The difference between southern network programming and Inuit television is suggested in the following discussion of *Qagik*, IBC's regular current events/news program:

> *Qagik* may look western. It even adheres to several characteristics applied to southern news. But it does it on its own terms. Its programs focus on items of geographic or psychological proximity to its audience (the Inuit and issues important to them). It is concerned with timeliness (but that can mean something that happens within weeks, not minutes and hours).

Significance plays a major role in the *Qagik*'s staff story selection (but what is significant can range from the rescue of a snowy owl, and an examination of an eight-legged caribou fetus, as well as the Nunavut Constitutional forums discussing the possibility of quasi-independence within Canada, and alcoholism and environmental issues). Visuals are important (to) *Qagik* (but the visual style is different). (Madden, 1990, p. 14)

Inuit resisted the communication policy and program guidelines that framed the provision of services within the boundaries of traditional culture rather than the broader context of access to native information. Narrowly defined, cultural broadcasting runs the risk of becoming a vehicle for the continued marginalization of native people themselves. In the words of George Henry of Northern Native Broadcasting Yukon, "Media consumption without the ability to answer back is the most colonized situation possible" (cited in National Aboriginal Communication Society, 1987). There can be little doubt about the increased tendency of native people to answer back. At the same time, research indicates that aboriginal people are listening to and watching native broadcasting and that aboriginal languages are a vital but not exclusive feature of native programs.

Perspectives on Media Impact

Considerable research has been done on the impact of southern broadcast media in northern native communities. Even before satellite television was pervasive, Coldevin (1977) began collecting data on the attitudes of Inuit adolescent viewers. His hard data approach differed from the longitudinal fieldwork of Granzberg, Steinbring, and Hamer (1977) on the cultural role of television among the northern Cree. But both studies documented native cultural dislocation resulting from the prevalence of southern television viewing.

The interpretative framework for these studies and the many that followed focused on the relationship between television images and information, and native cultures. Television was understood not as a force for successful native modernization, but as "an alien socialization agent" (Coldevin, 1977), carrying disruptive cultural images (Caron, 1977; Granzberg, 1982; O'Connell, 1977; Wilson, 1981). The benefits of electronic media were associated with community-level communication (Dicks, 1977; Hudson, 1977; Salter, 1976) rather than attitude change, motivation, and skills to encourage acculturation. Analysis emphasized the historical role of earlier agents of change in native communities and the expansion of media as a factor in southern control of the north (Mayes, 1972; Valaskakis, 1979). More recent studies have considered the longer-term impact of southern media (Coldevin & Wilson, 1984) and the role of native communications projects in northern participatory development (Roth, 1982; Roth & Valaskakis, 1989). No long-term, research has been conducted on the impact of native media in native communities. But Madden (1990) has begun to analyze Inuit cultural expression in IBC programming, and native communication societies under the NNBAP have surveyed audience viewing patterns and preferences. This research indicates that in many northern areas, native-language use is widespread, especially among the old who often do not speak or understand a second language. As a result, "A high percentage of respondents from all regions tend to listen to or watch native language and native-oriented programming when it is available" (Hudson, 1985, p. 4). The surveys also suggest a strong interest in extending native-language programming, and in providing programming that will reach the young, the majority population in most native communities. This is consistent with the decade-long Inuit lobby to add aboriginal language broadcasting rights to the English and French rights entrenched in the Broadcasting Act.

But equally important to our understanding of native nations today, language is intimately but not uniquely associated with culture. In some northern regions like the eastern Arctic, 95.2% of the Inuit population speak Inuktitut (Valaskakis & Wilson, 1985). On the other hand, a large percentage of Inuit in Labrador and Indians in the Yukon and British Columbia do not speak their native language on a regular and daily basis. An analysis of the 1981 census data indicates that English is replacing aboriginal languages in southern regions, especially among the young. The study found that the retention rate for native languages is higher for native people the further north they live and the older they are but concludes that, in general, the retention rate of native languages is decreasing (Jarvin, n.d.). This suggests a special role for native media. Working to increase the interest and ability of young native speakers, broadcasters may help to slow the growing generation gap between young and old, and the relative isolation of unilingual elders. But at the same time, native media must respond to the changing cultural and linguistic realities of northern communities, and they must compete with southern media programming. Native cultural products need not be produced exclusively in native languages. Their importance lies in the reflection of native perspectives and the extension of community achieved in shared expression, shared information. This position is recognized in the 1990 Native Broadcasting Policy, which defines a native undertaking not in relation to "the preservation of aboriginal languages and cultures" as proposed by commercial broadcasters but in relation to native ownership and control, native target audience, and native-oriented programming (CRTC, 1990, pp. 6-7).

Conclusions

During the past two decades as native communications have developed, satellites have become a critical force in Canadian broadcasting, and they have been joined by fiber optics in the development of telephone and data transmission. Newer satellites have greatly enlarged capacities, and current regulatory policy allows Telesat Canada to distribute communications services directly rather than through common carriers. These developments play important roles in the continuing strength of the Canadian cable industry and the trends toward competition, privatization, and integration of telecommunication services. Debate continues over the definition, role, and mandate of public broadcasting and narrowcast, or specialty, broadcasting services in Canada. And as telecommunications encourage shifts in interaction, control, and culture, aboriginal broadcasting increases in both vulnerability and importance.

The Native Broadcasting Policy and the Northern Native Broadcast Access Program represent a framework for the development of northern communications in Canada. Ironically, in the 1990s this framework is being both strengthened through the provision of a dedicated satellite channel to extend distribution and weakened through cutbacks to production funding for native broadcasting. At the same time, native northerners have demonstrated the efficacy of their position as a first service and full partner in the regional broadcasting system. The communication services that native media provide are basic to aboriginal access and participation in the cultural and political realities of northern life. Native northerners will continue to struggle with marginality and unsettling notions of culture and language related to historical patterns of control and the changing nature of native communities. Native broadcasting will play an increasingly important role in the far north as Canada responds to the threats and promises of new communications technologies.

References

Alcock, A., & O'Brien, T. (1980). *Policies to support radio and television broadcasting in the lesser used languages of the European Community.* Northern Ireland: University of Ulster.

Applebaum, L., & Hebert, J. (Federal Cultural Policy Review Committee, Department of Communications). (1982) *Summary of briefs and hearings.* Ottawa: Minister of Supply and Services.

Bear, J. (Director). (1987). *Sharing a dream* [video]. National Aboriginal Communication Society

Bergman, M. (1985). The impact of free trade on Canadian cultural industries. *Cinema Canada,* 8-9.

Brody, H. (1975). *The people's land: Eskimos and whites in the eastern Arctic.* Harmondsworth, UK: Penguin.

Canada, Federal Government News Release. (1983). *The northern broadcasting policy.* Ottawa.

Canada, Ministry of Communications (Minister of Indian and Northern Affairs, Secretary of State). (1983, February 18). *Discussion paper: Northern broadcasting.* Ottawa.

Canadian Radio-Television Telecommunications Commission. (1980). *The 1980's—a decade of diversity: Broadcasting satellites and pay-TV* (Report of the Committee on Extension of Service to Northern and Remote Communities). Ottawa: Canadian Government Publishing House.

Canadian Radio-Television Telecommunications Commission. (1990). *Native Broadcasting Policy.* Ottawa: Canadian Government Publishing House.

Carey, J. W. (1967). Harold Adams Innis and Marshall McLuhan. *The Antioch Review, 26.*

Caron, A. (1977, June). The impact of television on Inuit children's cultural "images." Paper presented at the annual meeting of the International Communications Association, Berlin.

Coldevin, G. O. (1977). Anik I and isolation: Television in the lives of Canadian Eskimos. *Journal of Communication, 27*(4), 143-153.

Dicks, D. J. (1977). From dog sled to dial phone. *Journal of Communication, 27*(4), 120-129.

Elberg, N. (1984). *In search of real Inuit.* Paper presented at the Fourth Etudes Inuit Studies Conference, Concordia University, Montreal.

Fleming, A. L. (1956). *Archibald the Arctic.* New York: Appleton-Century-Crofts.

Graburn, N. H. (1969). *Eskimos without igloos.* Boston: Little, Brown.

Granzberg, G. (1982). Television as storyteller: The Algonkion Indians of central Canada. *Journal of Communication, 32*(1), 43-52.

Granzberg, G., Steinbring, J., & Hamer, J. (1977). New magic for old: TV in Cree culture. *Journal of Communication, 27*(4), 154-157.

Hudson, H. (1977). *Northern airwaves: A study of the CBC Northern Service.* Ottawa: Keewatin Communications Studies Institute.

Hudson, H. (1985). *The need for native broadcasting in northern Canada: A review of research.* Ottawa: Department of Secretary of State.

Innis, H. A. (1950). *Empire and communications.* Toronto: University of Toronto Press.

Innis, H. A. (1951). *The bias of communications.* Toronto: University of Toronto Press.

Inuit Broadcasting Corporation. (1982). *Position on northern broadcasting.* Ottawa: Inuit Broadcasting Corporation.

Jarvin, G. K. (n.d.). *Changes in language use among native peoples of Canada.* Ottawa: Department of Secretary of State.

Katz, E. (1977). Can authentic cultures survive new media? *Journal of Communication, 27*(2), 119-120.

Kelly, N., & Kelly, W. (1973). *The Royal Canadian Mounted Police: A century of history.* Edmonton: Hurtig.

Kenny, G. I. (1971). *Communications study: Man in the North Project* (2 parts). Montreal: The Arctic Institute of North America.

Kroker, A. (1984). *Technology and the Canadian mind.* Montreal: New World Perspectives.

Kuptana, R. (1982, November 30). *Brief to the CRTC.* Ottawa: Inuit Broadcasting Corporation.

Madden, K. (1990). *Inuit Broadcasting Corporation.* Paper delivered at International Communications Association meetings. Dublin.

Mayes, R. G. (1972). *Mass communication and Eskimo adaptation in the Canadian Arctic.* Unpublished masters thesis, McGill University, Montreal.

Northern Quebec Inuit Association (1974). *The Northerners.* La Macaza, Que.: (Taqramiut) Les Septentroinaux.

O'Connell, S. (1977). Television and the Canadian Eskimo: The human perspective. *Journal of Communication, 27*(4), 140-144.

Phillips, R. A. (1967). *Canada's north.* Toronto: Macmillan.

Roth, L., & Valaskakis, G. (1989). Aboriginal broadcasting in Canada: A case study in media democratization. In M. Raboy & P. Bruck (Eds.), *Communication for and against democracy* (pp. 221-234). Montreal: Black Rose Books.

Roth, L. F. (1982). *The role of communication projects and Inuit participation in the formation of a communication policy for the north.* Unpublished masters thesis, McGill University, Montreal.

Salter, L. (1976, August 12). *Community radio—five years later—concept and development in review.* Speech given at the Canadian Broadcasting League Conference, St. Mary's University, Halifax.

Schiller, H. I. (1976). *Communication and cultural domination.* White Plains, NY: M. E. Sharpe.

Steele, H. (1936). *Policing the north: The story of the conquest of the Arctic by the Royal Canadian (formerly North-West) Mounted Police.* London: Jarrolds.

Valaskakis, G. (1979). *A communication analysis of interaction patterns: Southern Baffin, eastern Arctic.* Unpublished doctoral dissertation, McGill University, Montreal.

Valaskakis, G. (1987). From smoke signals to satellite. *The native Canadian.* Vancouver: Native Canadian Media.

Valaskakis, G., Robbins, R., & Wilson, T. (1984). *The Inukshuk Anik B Project: An assessment.* Ottawa: Inuit Tapirisat of Canada.

Valaskakis, G., & Wilson, T. (1985). *The Inuit Broadcasting Corporation: A survey of viewing behavior and audience preferences among the Inuit of seven communities in the Baffin and Keewatin regions of the Northwest Territories.* Montreal: Concordia University.

Vallee, F. G. (1967). *Kabloona and Eskimo in the central Keewatin.* Ottawa: St. Paul University.

Wilford, N. (1986). Exhibition. Northwest Territories Pavilion. Vancouver: Expo 86.

Wilson, T. C. (1981). *The role of television in the eastern Arctic: An educational perspective.* Unpublished masters thesis, Concordia University, Montreal.

4

Broadcasting in Aboriginal Australia: One Mob, One Voice, One Land

MICHAEL MEADOWS

Introduction

Aboriginal broadcasting in Australia is at a stage that is exciting because of its potentially unique expression but at the same time frustrating because of its uncertain future. The aim of this chapter is to provide an overview of these ambiguous developments by examining the organizational structure and context of Aboriginal media. The research on the interpretation and use of film and television by Aborigines, undertaken by the late Eric Michaels, will be discussed in detail, because it is revealing of the different ways information is conveyed in modern and in technologically older societies. These differences create cultural conflicts when film and television are introduced in Aboriginal or native societies. The subtitle of this chapter—one mob, one voice, one land—comes from a headline used by the award-winning Aboriginal newspaper *Land Rights News*. The word *mob* is used extensively by Aborigines and generally does not have negative connotations. While the diversity of Aboriginal societies guarantees that there will be a multiplicity of perspectives on the airwaves, the subtitle symbolizes the underlying need for unity.

Unlike indigenous people in many other countries, Aborigines have never been offered a treaty or even government recognition of their occupation of the Australian continent for thousands of years before the British invasion that began in 1788. Presently, people of Aboriginal ancestry constitute less than 2% of the national population. Between 14% and 30% live in remote inland areas; about 50% live more than

100 km from the coastal urban fringe. Lack of control over decisions that affect their lives has left them in a seriously disadvantaged position, especially in the socially important areas of health, education, and housing (Department of Aboriginal Affairs [DAA], 1984). Years of government inaction and paternalism have merely exacerbated problems. Before European settlement two centuries ago, more than 200 Aboriginal languages were spoken. It is now estimated that 50 of these are extinct, about 100 have very small speech communities, and perhaps 50 are likely to survive for another generation (Walsh, 1981). Among those still in a relatively healthy state, several are used for communication in both print and broadcast media.

Many Aborigines have a negative perception of the mainstream media's coverage of Aboriginal issues. They are critical of the media's quest for sensationalism and appear to have turned their backs on any hope of gaining what they perceive to be fair and accurate coverage (Meadows, 1987). For example, about half of the Koories who were surveyed thought the newspapers they read did not print enough news about Aboriginal topics (Snow & Noble, 1986).[1] About one third of the interviewees thought Aboriginal perspectives were slighted in news stories about them. Most preferred to get Aboriginal news from other Koories.

The Australian Journalists' Association (AJA) has no special guidelines for journalists reporting on sensitive racial topics, unlike its British counterpart, the National Union of Journalists, which has had a race relations working party since 1974 (Cohen, 1982). The word *race* is mentioned just once in the AJA's code of ethics—a document rarely, if ever, found in Australian news rooms. Lyle Munro compares the media's portrayal of Aborigines with the treatment given blacks in the U.S. media 20 years ago (Noble, 1980). Aboriginal activist, Sammy Watson, Jr. (1978), described the Australian media's stereotyped images of Aborigines as either that of the "drunken no-hoper" or the "angry young militant" (p. 2). The image of the traditional Aborigine living in a remote community could be added to the list. A former commissioner for community relations, Al Grassby, wrote in 1981 that of the nearly 4,000 complaints about racism made to the commission since 1975, approximately 40% were from Aborigines complaining of either racial discrimination or defamation in the media.

In 1979, the federal government made a decision to launch AUSSAT, Australia's first telecommunications satellite. A fierce debate about the possible impact on remote Aborigines took place before the launch of the satellite. After a 5-month inquiry, the government report, *Out of the Silent Land* (Willmot, 1984), made numerous recommendations, which became the basis for policy. But there was criticism that the government had already determined its policy before the task force completed its report, and accusations—perhaps more serious—that the investigation failed to look closely at the needs of the most remote Aboriginal communities, rather than those of urban and less-isolated communities (Michaels, 1986). Once AUSSAT began operating in late 1985 anyone in the country with the proper equipment could receive at least one Australian Broadcasting Corporation (ABC) television channel and two ABC radio stations (Willmot, 1984).

It has been suggested that choices about new media are really choices about new culture: " 'What kind of media do we use?' is really another way of asking, 'What kind of people do we wish to become?' " (Mackay, 1985, p. 144). How far the approaches I outline in this chapter contribute to counteracting the possible effects of satellite broadcasting is uncertain, but the "sameness" Katz (1977) spoke of in the mainstream style of radio and television presentation does threaten Aboriginal language and culture:

> Cannot Nigerian or Peruvian or Senegalese television be more indigenous, not just in programming, but in style? What is needed are more radical suggestions for making radio and television relevant for traditional peoples who have more important problems than those which can be solved by Chief Ironside. (pp. 119-120)

Mass Media and Social Change
in Oral Cultures

Eric Michaels, an American immigrant to Australia, was influenced by the pioneering studies on film communication undertaken by Sol Worth and John Adair in the 1960s. Worth and Adair (1972) gave film equipment to young Navajo Indians, explaining as unintrusively as possible only how the equipment worked and responding to questions that the students initiated. After closely observing the filming and editing processes, Worth and Adair analyzed the completed films to see if themes and structures differed from the conventions of commercial European and American films. Their book, *Through Navajo Eyes*, is interesting not only for their remarks about the stylistic characteristic of Navajo films but also for the authors' frankness concerning the near impossibility on occasion of following their own research methodology. Despite their intentions, they did sometimes interfere with the filming by obliging unwilling students to shoot content—facial close-ups, for example—that the professionals thought was essential to achieving a good film.

In the early 1980s Michaels undertook experiments with community television in the remote Warlpiri community of Yuendumu near Alice Springs in central Australia. He encouraged the establishment of a "pirate" television station (Yuendumu Warlpiri Media Association, 1985). Michaels showed residents how to operate VHS video cameras and encouraged them to make programs of their own for broadcast to the local community. He also tried to give as little guidance as possible.

Michaels observed the extreme attention Warlpiri accorded the landscape in their videos. The pans were not smooth, but variable and included the unexplained but apparently intentional focusing on details of the landscape. Some films gave as much prominence to the landscape as to the actors. Michaels believed that to most European observers the tapes might appear boring because of this feature. However, when questioned, the camera operator could provide a justification for all of the details:

> What appeared arbitrary, or accidental, and could be dismissed as directorial unsophistication (and thus criticized and trained out) turns out to be an invaluable part of the story and a criterion for legitimacy of the story for the Aboriginal audience. (Michaels, 1984, p. 30)

In Aboriginal societies, information is exchanged through face-to-face interaction. Significantly, Aborigines interpret the landscape as a medium of communication between the living and the supernatural. According to Peterson (1975) Aborigines believe that marks

> left on the landscape are the results of the activities of ancestral heroes. These ancestral heroes emerged from their subterranean world releasing animating life-forces. The heroes led lives similar in many respects to those of the people today, though on a grander scale, and the evidence of their activities can be seen in all named places, the most important of which are known to us as sacred sites. It is from the points where the heroes emerged and re-entered the ground that the present people derive their existence. These points which are the foci of personal identity lie at the heart of the peoples' religious beliefs and of their attachment to the land. (p. 73)

A major theme Michaels pursued in his research was the role of secrecy in structuring the flow of information among the Warlpiris. To what extent this should be allowed to influence modern broadcasting is a subject of debate. Michaels criticized Marshall McLuhan's contention that television functions to create in modern societies an oral culture of shared knowledge and experience similar to the way orality functions in technologically older societies. Michaels argued that McLuhan failed to understand that information is not conveyed freely to everyone in technologically older societies, but is highly structured by gender, age, ritual status, and so forth. The Warlpiris distinguish between the right to tell a story and the right to hear it. A story may be known by many people but cannot be told publicly by the former unless the latter act as an audience authorizing the telling. Otherwise, the story must remain secret. The appropriate audience is usually small, local, and composed of relatives. The relevance of knowledge and kinship ties was graphically illustrated when in response to Michaels's request to make a video the Warlpiris chose to recreate a 1928 massacre. To his surprise, 27 Warlpiri people accompanied him to the location for the filming:

> Each of the people accompanying us was directly accountable in terms of Aboriginal reckoning, for some aspect of the story we were telling. The video could not be made without their presence. The fact that almost all chose not to appear on camera is also formally significant. (Michaels, 1984, p. 30)

There is little recognition by non-Aboriginal journalists of the special informational needs of Aborigines. A dance ceremony, for instance, may be public in one area but secret in another. Consequently, televised images of religious events may bypass the traditional system of information exchange, possibly desacralizing the information. White journalists have a tendency to visit Aboriginal areas and take whatever they want—sacred songs or ceremonies—and then use the material without consultation. Michaels (1983; 1987) cites an example in which the employees of ABC believed that their freedom of editorial opinion was infringed by Aborigines' right to maintain their traditions through their exercising a right of information control. Despite assurances that Aborigines would be involved in the making of a documentary about their community, an ABC documentary film unit showed little interest in attempting either to consult with or involve Aborigines in the film they wanted to make. Aborigines were forced to threaten to take out an injunction to prevent the film from being broadcast because the final cut was deemed by the ABC to be its own editorial property. Aborigines were concerned that the material chosen to appear on ABC might not be publicly accessible to other Aborigines. Legal challenge was threatened on the grounds that the program included videotapes made by the Aborigines themselves. Eventually, the community agreed to forgo the copyright on its tapes if it was allowed to approve the final cut.

Several authors argue that the maintenance of these traditionally elaborate systems of information ownership, exchange, and control are critical for the maintenance of Aboriginality. Once again, these systems are quite foreign to the systems that structure the way information flows through modern mass media. As Michaels (1985) observed, "The Aboriginal societies I encounter in Australia provide no models for progressive global villages [à la Marshall McLuhan]. To the contrary, a future modelled on their information management systems would more closely resemble a vast gerontocratic bureaucracy than a hippie commune writ large" (p. 510).

At Yuendumu, people watched videos in large, kin-based groups. When videos originating outside the community were shown, youngsters sat in front, occasionally interpreting to the elders sitting behind. But when locally made Warlpiri tapes were shown, the situation was reversed. Michaels believed that the foreign videos undermined the authority of the elders, whereas the indigenous ones reinforced it. Douglas Thompson (1984) documented a similar phenomenon in the Northern Territory. A few individuals who owned a video player charged admission to the showings. The video enabled the owners to gain more authority than they would have had otherwise.

Another major problem related to secrecy that affects broadcasting is the taboo surrounding death. To show the face of dead people or to mention their names in most traditional Aboriginal communities is forbidden. Bell (1983) documented elaborate methods used by Aborigines to avoid saying the names of the deceased. For instance, in some Warlpiri areas, teachers' aides allowed the names of the deceased to be used at school in settlements, but then reverted to the taboo, or *kumanjayi,* system in the camps. Michaels was continually visited by people who wanted the segments of films destroyed that included pictures of their recently deceased relatives. He seems to have agreed to their demands or at least did not allow the segments to be shown in the immediate area.

Aborigines use the same word for "story," "dreaming," and "the law." Not surprisingly, Michaels and other researchers have noted that when

Aborigines were first exposed to films they had difficulty distinguishing truth from fiction. In one incident, related by Michaels, Aborigines called out during a film to warn an actor about an impending shark attack. In another, Aborigines warned American Audie Murphy about an imminent Indian attack. Michaels (1986) was asked on several occasions whether film characters were real or not. Thompson (1984) came to similar conclusions. He found that Aboriginal children did not fully understand a lot of what they saw on the screen and had difficulty differentiating between truth and fiction.

In a paper reviewing Michaels's contribution to anthropology and cultural studies, Robert Hodge accused Michaels of *Aboriginalism*. According to Hodge (1990), "the foundation premise of Aboriginalism is the construction of Aboriginals as 'primitive,' in *binary opposition* [italics added] to 'civilised' " (p. 202). Hodge, unlike Michaels, emphasized similarities between Aboriginal and English cultures. The resemblances include somewhat similar notions of how people distinguish between truth and fiction. Michaels's Aboriginalism was revealed in his assumption that Aboriginal interpretations of videos were due solely to cultural uniqueness, not inexperience with the medium. Hodge claimed that some Aboriginal reactions to the fictionalized content of films were similar to those of many people, regardless of their culture, who were unfamiliar with the medium. This obviously complex issue of the meaning of realism in different cultures remains unresolved.

The influence of television on Aboriginal children was investigated by Thompson (1983). He also discovered that Aboriginal children, especially boys, identified strongly with characters in action films such as Bruce Lee and Charles Bronson. In one incident, a group of Aboriginal boys used a method of holdup that they had seen in a film to mug a local. But it should be noted that the influence of television on children is mediated by their peer groups. Harris (1980) found evidence of strong peer pressure among the Yolngu children of Northeast Arnhem Land in the Northern Territory. Habitually, between the ages of 18 months and 5 or 6 years, Yolngu children began to spend most leisure activities with peer groups, a major source of language learning. Harris (1980) suggested that such groups might be a strong source of inspiration for learning, and he also noted that a high level of personal independence and cultural conservatism existed among young Yolngu. He postulated that Yolngu youngsters did not necessarily see as inconsistent the coexistence of two systems of knowledge: the school and traditional culture. Another study, conducted in North Queensland

(Obijiofor, 1988), concluded that 2 years of mainstream television seem to have wrought no remarkable changes in traditional values and life-styles—no changes, that is, that could obviously be attributed to television. Children were affected in that they spent more time indoors, but this was seen as positive by adults, because they believed it helped to keep the young from an early introduction to alcohol. Researchers now understand that the influence media exert on audiences is complex and indirect. Media may exert the greatest impact when they reinforce, rather than change, the opinions of those in the audience (Wilson & Gutiérrez, 1985).

Australian Broadcasting Corporation and Special Broadcasting Service

The Australian Broadcasting Corporation (ABC) is Australia's national broadcaster, operating 280 radio transmitters through a terrestrial and satellite delivery system (ABC, 1988-1989). ABC's involvement with Aboriginal broadcasting is relatively long. In the 1970s the corporation (then a commission) supported the Central Australian Aboriginal Media Association when moves were first made for Aboriginal voices to be heard on Northern Territory airwaves. In the 1980s, ABC established a consultation process with communities to ensure a continuing recognition of the complementary but different roles sought by itself and Aboriginal communities (John Newsom, November 14, 1989, personal communication). Generally, ABC is involved in areas where no local public radio serves the local Aboriginal community. The aim is to help local media associations in remote areas set up their own broadcast stations using ABC transmitters (see Wangkiyuparnanapurru et al., 1989). Several of these communities—Kununurra and Broome—now have their own public radio stations. A number of independent Aboriginal broadcasting organizations are currently funded by Aboriginal and Torres Strait Island-ers Commission (ATSIC), formerly the Department of Aboriginal Affairs, to produce programs for ABC television and public radio. However, in 1990 the future of such funding was unclear.

ABC broadcast each week in 1990 more than 100 hours of Aboriginal and Torres Strait Islander[2] radio programs through its regional trans-mitters in North Queensland, the Torres Strait, South Australia, and throughout Western Australia as well as on shortwave in the Northern Territory through its High-Frequency Inland Radio Service. Programs broadcast through these services are produced by local Aboriginal media associations in their own languages. ABC draws programs from organizations funded by ATSIC and has recruited a number of Aboriginal trainees. In addition, some Aboriginal and Torres Strait Islands media associations broadcast on mainstream ABC radio through *windows* in local programming. The ABC transmitter on Thursday Island, near the tip of North Queensland, broadcasts for more than 10 hours a week in three Islander languages and in English (Meadows, 1989).

ABC was asked by Aboriginal people in the Kimberley area of Western Australia to undertake a study of radio needs in the district in 1988. The resulting report recommended that several special interest public radio licenses be made available in the area and that the federal government examine the creation of a remote area broadcasting service for the Kimberleys. This study is indicative of the specifically local nature of broadcasting desired by Aboriginal groups around the country and goes against former trends toward attempts at national programming.

The corporation has undertaken to train and employ 116 Aborigines and Torres Strait Islanders in all areas of its operation over a 3-year period. The number represents about 1% of the total ABC staff. An ABC Aboriginal program unit recently produced its first regular television program, called *Blackout*. The series included documentaries, studio audience discussions, Aboriginal music and dance, interviews, and news. On ABC national radio, a new weekly program called *Speaking Out* features profiles of prominent Aboriginal members of the community along with Aboriginal music, interviews and news.

The position of the board of ABC on Aboriginal and Torres Strait Islander broadcasting is as follows:

> The ABC recognises that a special need exists for the Aboriginal people to develop their own cultural identity in order to redress the special disadvantages they have suffered. Accordingly, the ABC will encourage community awareness of the Aboriginal people's aspirations in its programs, and it affirms its commitment to providing television and radio programs made by Aboriginal people themselves. (McCarthy, 1985, p. 147)

ABC has been under increasing financial pressure from successive federal governments for the past 12 years or more, during which time it has undergone a decline in real levels of funding leading to cost-cutting measures that have, as of 1990, apparently not affected Aboriginal broadcasting (O'Hara, 1988). The government allocation to ABC of

$450 million is about eight times that of the Special Broadcasting Service (ABC, 1988-1989).

The Special Broadcasting Service (SBC) was set up in 1978 following an amendment to the Broadcasting and Television Act. Its original aim was to create and broadcast programs for immigrant minorities in Australia. Initially, of course, this did not include Aborigines. However, this policy soon changed and the service now regards the production and presentation of Aboriginal radio and television programs as an integral part of its goals (Willmot, 1984; Special Broadcasting Service [SBS], 1988). Indeed, the first broadcast of an Aboriginal radio program on any form of government-backed radio took place in November 1980, on the SBS's Sydney station, 2EA—only 11 months after the first Alice Springs broadcasts by the Central Australian Aboriginal Media Association (CAAMA). The service soon extended to Radio 3EA in Melbourne. In addition, the SBS is obligated to correcting, not fostering, the popular misconception that the British were Australia's first settlers and projecting a 40,000 not 200 year old Australian history (Bostock, 1990, p. 53).

SBS states its intention to pay proper regard to the sensitivities, cultural traditions, and languages of Aboriginal people in producing Aboriginal programs. The service expects to continue with and enhance Aboriginal broadcasting in the future (SBS, 1988). SBS television aired Australia's first prime-time Aboriginal and Torres Strait Islander program in 1989. The half-hour program called *First in Line* was produced entirely by the service's Aboriginal and Torres Strait Islander unit. As of 1990 it is the only mainstream broadcasting organization in Australia that publicly acknowledges the validity of Aboriginal claims for land rights.

The main technical disadvantage of SBS is that it broadcasts solely on the UHF frequency band—the only television network in Australia to do so (apart from some local stations). Its consistently low audience share (around 1% according to traditional methods of rating) is perhaps a reflection of this (Evans, 1987). However, recent studies indicate that the audience may have been underestimated.

The Central Australian Aboriginal Media Association

In the early 1970s, initiatives were undertaken by the federal Department of Aboriginal Affairs to look at ways of giving Aborigines a voice on the airwaves. One government representative examined the Papua New Guinea Government Broadcasting Service and suggested such a system could be set up to serve Aboriginal communities in northern Australia (Lewis, 1974). Recommendations to give Australia's indigenous people air rights surfaced again 3 years later in another study by the Department of Aboriginal Affairs. The document recommended a role for the Australian Broadcasting Corporation and for the planned new public FM radio stations about to be put into operation (Moore, 1976).

Aboriginal initiatives to gain a voice eventually came to fruition in the Central Australian desert. CAAMA is now the major Aboriginal broadcasting agency in Australia. Established in 1980, CAAMA supported moves for a community radio license to operate a new FM station in Alice Springs—8CCC. The following year, broadcasts by CAAMA increased to almost 23 hours a week on the local commercial, public, and ABC stations. CAAMA finally won the right to a license for its own FM public radio station, 8KIN, 4 years after its inception. It is now on air for more than 100 hours each week with 60% of this in the five major central Australian languages (Central Australian Aboriginal Media Association [CAAMA], 1989). It has also become a major production house for audio cassettes and videocassettes for distribution throughout Aboriginal communities. Many of the contemporary Aboriginal country and rock bands record at CAAMA's studios in Alice Springs. Along with Aboriginal radio, Aboriginal music—much of it *in language*—has become the most popular content on Aboriginal radio both in remote and urban areas. All staff, except one training officer, are Aboriginal. CAAMA is seen as a model by many other Aboriginal broadcast groups and its philosophy has been readily adopted by them.

CAAMA broadcasts up to 10 hours a day on the ABC's High-Frequency Inland Radio Service (shortwave) to areas within a 450-km radius. The association uses ABC transmitters in Alice Springs and Tennant Creek under a sharing arrangement. Programs are broadcast in six Aboriginal languages, and there are plans to introduce a seventh Aboriginal language (Freda Glynn, personal communication, November 24, 1988). The federal government, through ATSIC, directly funds the CAAMA radio station.

CAAMA broadcasts in some of the most widely spoken Australian Aboriginal languages: in three dialects of Arrernte, Warlpiri, and Pitjantjatjara. Freda Glynn, who is the director of Imparja, which is partly owned by CAAMA, stated that a recent "beat the grog" (alcohol)

program was very successful and that CAAMA has become part of the
Central Australian landscape:

> When we first broadcast, I've seen women cry when they heard [Aborigi-
> nal] language on the radio—just so excited and laughing and joking, you
> know. And I don't think people could manage now without CAAMA;
> without having a radio station broadcasting in their own language. (ABC,
> 1987)

One of CAAMA's many Aboriginal broadcasters echoes Glynn's obvious
pride:

> When you hear your own language and what's being spoken, you take a lot
> more notice. Since CAAMA, people are more aware of what politics is
> about because we can interpret what the people are saying exactly. And we
> can let the community know what people are saying. (ABC Radio, 1987)

In many ways, CAAMA's real success is with radio. Its involvement
with television is a different story. Phillip Batty (1986), CAAMA
projects manager, argues that the real motivation behind the launching
of the AUSSAT satellite was to favor existing commercial television
networks not to provide telecommunication services to remote Aboriginal Australians. According to Batty (1986), Aboriginal people were left
with two options when the Australian government moved to extend
television broadcasting to the nation's center: either to ignore the fact
that Aboriginal people had once more been left out of the debate or to
apply for a Remote Commercial Television License to ensure that
Aborigines would eventually get an adequate and comprehensive service. CAAMA chose the second option.

Winning the license was a major struggle in itself. Imparja Television
Pty. Ltd. is a private company owned by a group of Aboriginal organizations and individuals. Shareholders include CAAMA and the
Pitjantjatjara, Central, and Northern Aboriginal land councils. CAAMA
formed this company in 1984 to apply for the remote commercial
television license being offered and in August 1986, after two long
hearings, the Australian Broadcasting Tribunal awarded Imparja the
license. Imparja's bid was supported by the Australian Bicentennial
Authority ($2.5 million), the Aboriginal Development Commission
($1.8 million) and the South Australian government ($1 million). However, the Northern Territory government, a supporter of the unsuccessful

applicant for the license, bitterly opposed Imparja (Corker, 1986; Crisp, 1987). Later, after losing a Federal Court appeal against the tribunal's decision, the territorial government refused to give CAAMA the $2 million promised to the winning applicant. The refusal by the Northern Territory to subsidize Imparja threatened to prevent the company from having access to a satellite transponder that would enable it to broadcast to its planned Central Australian footprint (Crisp, 1987). Despite such attempts at sabotage, Australia's first Aboriginally owned television station began broadcasting by satellite on January 15, 1988, with the federal government providing funding at the last moment.

Largely because of commercial constraints, Imparja has been broadcasting a selection of mainstream English-language programs from Australia's three commercial networks. In fact, 98% of its output is standard commercial fare (CAAMA, 1989). The Aboriginal component on Central Australian television was limited to advertisements in Aboriginal languages and two Aboriginally generated programs: a current affairs show, *Urrpeye* (*Messenger*), and a magazine-format program, *Nganampa-Anwernekenhe* (*Ours*). The latter was broadcast with English subtitles in Arrente, Warlpiri, and Pitjantjatjara (Cochrane, 1988). However, production costs have forced Imparja to reduce even this small amount of Aboriginal programming. In 1990, Imparja reduced its local output to just half an hour a week of Aboriginal-language programs. *Urrpeye* is no longer produced (Freda Glynn, personal communication, December 6, 1990).

According to Glynn, the organization would like to aim for the maintenance of Aboriginal cultures rather than appealing to a non-Aboriginal audience, but this is not commercially viable. Subtitling to make programs acceptable to non-Aborigines used to take up to 60% of Imparja's time. Thus it has been eliminated. Another difficulty facing Imparja is the lack of sponsorship for locally produced programs. Glynn stated that it is ironic that most Aboriginal communities receiving Imparja television own or need four-wheel drive vehicles, yet even Toyota has so far declined to buy advertising time to support special Aboriginal programs. Glynn is philosophical about the dilemma. Aboriginal people are generally glad to receive television, but she admits the remote commercial service may never be financially viable—something Imparja knew when it applied for the license. One positive influence of Imparja is that its existence has encouraged the other two remote commercial television stations to make Aboriginal programs.

Queensland Satellite Television has set up a program-advisory group made up entirely of Aboriginal and Torres Strait Islander representatives. This followed criticism of the station's programming by the Australian Broadcasting Tribunal (1988).

Serving about 280,000 people, Imparja operates one of three Remote Commercial Television Service footprints across Australia. All three services are required to take account of the needs of Aboriginal and Torres Strait Islander audiences and all do so in different ways. None of the services is profitable in its present state nor are they likely to be in the foreseeable future. In the late 1980s they were losing between $12 and $13 million annually, despite subsidies from the state and federal governments (Department of Transport and Communications [DOTAC], 1990). A federal government review has suggested that the only financially viable options are to revert to one national broadcasting network or to have the three services become part of the program distribution of major networks (DOTAC, 1990). Either of these options would seem to further erode the chances of an increase in Aboriginal or Torres Strait Islander-generated material being broadcast and would further deemphasize the regional nature of the audiences.

The Broadcasting for Remote Aboriginal Communities Scheme

The Broadcasting for Remote Aboriginal Communities Scheme (BRACS) was announced in 1987 as a means of delivering satellite radio and television to 28,000 remote Aboriginal Australians (Venner, 1988). By 1990, more than 80 Aboriginal and Torres Strait Island communities had received a package of equipment that included a satellite dish, an FM radio aerial, two videocassette recorders and a video camera. This electronic equipment enables communities to receive one of three available ABC radio services (national, regional, and FM) and the one available ABC television service. Commercial television programs are also available via satellite, with communities making the decision about which service to accept. BRACS provides basic facilities for communities to produce and broadcast their own community radio and television programs, including those in their own languages, should they so desire. Control of programming is at the point of entry of the signal from the satellite, enabling communities to switch it off and insert relevant programs of their choice. The Department of

Aboriginal Affairs, which funded the program, claims culturally offensive material can be deleted by individual communities (DAA, 1988). The BRACS scheme is a direct result of the 1984 task force recommendations (Willmot, 1984), but has been criticized on a number of significant counts. Almost all communities claim there was little or no consultation before the BRACS equipment was installed. Some communities already had production equipment and would have preferred to choose additional equipment rather than receive duplications. Others stated that the standard BRACS package arrived without warning and that it has remained locked away because no one knows how to operate it. All communities received basically the same package. There was little or no room for negotiation. Another common complaint from communities is that there has been little subsequent funding for training and maintenance of the equipment (Corker, 1989). Communities were supposed to provide air-conditioned accommodation for the units but many were not aware of this until the equipment arrived. Some communities have been able to add extra equipment while others have not.

The federal government has yet to develop a clear policy on Aboriginal broadcasting and has only recently introduced a system of licensing to cover community television broadcasting. The uncoordinated introduction of the scheme has left a bitter taste in many mouths although some have taken to the system with relish. Communities in North Queensland are already using BRACS to videotape and broadcast local sporting events and to inform the community of important local news. A federally funded training program for community BRACS operators has had mixed success. An advanced broadcast training course is being developed through a new college of education in the Northern Territory, Batchelor College, and this has generally been welcomed.

Under the BRACS scheme, each community is encouraged to form a community media association to control and administer its own facilities (DAA, 1988). The scheme goes part of the way toward giving communities control over the type of television and radio they can experience. But it remains to be seen how much pressure will be exerted from within the communities to watch programs in Warlpiri, Pitjantjatjara, or Aboriginal English rather than satellite television with the lure of such popular programs as *Miami Vice* or the Australian soap opera *A Country Practice.*

Some researchers stress that BRACS is an experiment and, if successful, could become an important tool of cultural development: "Through BRACS, communities will have the opportunity to use media technology to maintain and develop their language and cultural identity instead of being the passive recipients of alien communicators" (Venner, 1988, p. 43). Nonetheless, it seems that ATSIC (or DAA) has given only token support to recommendations designed to ensure some Aboriginal control over television broadcasting to remote communities (Corker, 1989). The crucial notion of self-determination underlies the entire debate—a debate that ATSIC has not yet been able to address satisfactorily.

Public Broadcasting

Until the advent of BRACS, public radio was the fastest-growing sector of Aboriginal broadcasting in Australia with around 40 Aboriginal groups putting to air in 1990 between 180 to 200 hours of locally produced programs each week. In 1984, in contrast, 20 groups were producing about 60 hours of Aboriginal programming each week. Apart from CAAMA's operations in Alice Springs public radio is largely the domain of urban and regional Aboriginal voices.

From humble beginnings in 1974 (Law, 1986) to its current crop of 77 stations throughout Australia (Australian Broadcasting Tribunal [ABT], 1988-1989), public radio has been at the forefront of Aboriginal broadcasting. Access for Aborigines has been encouraged and most programs are broadcast in major urban areas, complementing existing broadcast facilities. Willmot (1984) contends that the Aboriginal presence on public radio represents a resource for the further development of Aboriginal broadcasting in general. Evidence also suggests that public radio is a major training ground for people moving into the mainstream (Marson, 1986), but few Aboriginal broadcasters see this as fulfilling a true community role. Most are dedicated to staying on—more often than not as volunteers—to provide a much-needed community service. Most Aboriginal broadcasting groups throughout Australia cannot pay their broadcasters and so are staffed by volunteers.

CAAMA's public radio station at Alice Springs is a success story, but there are many others, particularly in urban areas. Radio Redfern in Sydney broadcasts between 20 and 30 hours of Aboriginal programming each week, through public radio station Radio Skid Row. The Murri Hour Collective, through station 4ZZZ in Brisbane, airs about 17 hours of Aboriginal programs a week, produced, as in other major centers, by a local Aboriginal media association. A milestone for the Brisbane Murri Hour Collective and Radio Redfern in Sydney, was a land-line hookup for short periods during the 2-week preparation for the Bicentennial Sydney Protest march on January 26, 1988. The link made Aboriginal broadcast history in Australia, although it was ignored by the mainstream media.

ATSIC supports Aboriginal broadcasting through grants to the Public Broadcasting Foundation. In addition, the federal government provides direct funding to Aboriginal public broadcasters to enable them to buy basic equipment to make programs. However, the major funding for Aboriginal public broadcasting comes from the federal Department of Transport and Communications. ATSIC does not directly fund Aboriginal public broadcasting groups (DAA, 1988).

The federal government does occasionally subsidize groups on the understanding that an agreement exists with the ABC for the purchase of the programs. The funding limit of the Department of Aboriginal Affairs for 1988 was just over $1 million and went to Aboriginal media groups in Townsville, Thursday Island, Alice Springs (CAAMA), and Perth (DAA, 1988). CAAMA attracted almost half of the money available. Funds are also provided for semi-yearly meetings of an Aboriginal Broadcasting Consultative Group, made up of Aboriginal broadcasters from remote areas, representatives from ABC, SBS, the Public Broadcasting Foundation, and the federal Department of Employment, Education and Training. The group fulfills an advisory role (DAA, 1988). DAA also supports an Aboriginal standing committee within the Public Broadcasting Association of Australia—another body set up to administer the public broadcasting sector.

For some years, the National Aboriginal and Islander Broadcasting Association (NAIBA) existed to represent the needs of Aboriginal broadcasters for a lobbying voice. The organization has since ceased functioning, although there are attempts to revive the idea. Most Aboriginal and Torres Strait Islander groups working in radio must conform in some way to the constraints of their host broadcaster. This is one of the primary reasons why many groups intend to apply for their own license, enabling them to broadcast to their own communities—in their own way.

The mainstream media organizations described in this chapter have not experimented a great deal with alternatives to the standard commercial formats of broadcast media. However, some Aboriginal radio programs do experiment, adopting a format based on intimacy and informality. Often, half a dozen or more people will be in the studio at any one time, discussing various issues of concern, interspersed almost exclusively with contemporary Aboriginal music. The Murri Hour Collective operating out of the Brisbane studios of public radio 4ZZZ FM is a good example. The stated aims of the collective are to inform, educate, and entertain:

> We attempt to do this by regularly canvassing our community on the streets, in the parks, prisons and service organizations. People with information to broadcast are encouraged to attend in person if possible to maximise the number of different voices on air. (Murri Hour Collective, 1988)

There are other stylistic differences, including a slower pace of delivery and even long reflective periods of silence between spoken sentences, particularly on radio produced in remote Aboriginal communities. It is part of a pattern of development of new, culturally more appropriate ways of using broadcasting in Aboriginal Australia (Browne, 1990).

It seems that local, community-based radio and television stations are the keys that will unlock and perhaps ease open the door into the "silent land." The words of a Northern Territory Milingimbi Aboriginal counselor may well prove to be prophetic: "We are living in a new time. You people teach us and show us new things. We must know these things if we are to survive" (Liddle, 1980, p. 14).

Notes

1. Indigenous people in Australia use the following terms, loosely based on geographical boundaries, to identify themselves: Koorie (Tasmania, Victoria, and New South Wales), Murri (Queensland), Nyunga (southern Western Australia), and Nyungga (South Australia). They are generally preferred over the generic European term *Aborigine* (noun), or *Aboriginal* (adjective). Eve Fesl (1990) explains that the use of the term *Aboriginal* effectively sustains the notion of *terra nullius*—the legal concept that the Australian continent was a vast empty land when it was "discovered" by Europeans.

2. The Torres Strait Islands are located between New Guinea and the Cape York Peninsula of Queensland. They were annexed by Queensland in 1870. The islanders are a mixture of Polynesians, Melanesians, and Aborigines. Because Europeans were more interested in exploiting the islands' marine resources than in establishing permanent settlements, early contacts were less traumatic for the islanders than they were for Australian Aborigines. See Beckett (1987) for an account of the islands as an internal colony of Australia.

References

Australian Broadcasting Corporation. (1987, October 24). Aboriginal broadcasting, *Talking history* [audiotape]. ABC Radio.

Australian Broadcasting Corporation. (1988-1989). *Annual report.* Sydney: Author.

Australian Broadcasting Tribunal. (1988, October). *Inquiry into varying conditions on license of Queensland satellite television.* Canberra: Australian Government Publishing Service.

Australian Broadcasting Tribunal. (1988-1989). *Annual report.*

Batty, P. (1986). *The Aboriginal invention of television central Australia 1982-1986.* Canberra: Australian Institute of Aboriginal Studies.

Beckett, J. (1987). *Torres strait islanders: Customs and colonialism.* Cambridge: Cambride University Press.

Bell, D. (1983). *Daughters of the dreaming.* Melbourne: McPhee Gribble/George Allen & Unwin.

Bostock, L. (1990). *The greater perspective: Guidelines for the production of television and film about aborigines and Torres Strait Islanders.* Special Broadcasting Service, Sydney.

Browne, D. R. (1990). Aboriginal radio in Australia: From dreamtime to prime time? *Journal of Communication, 40*(1), 111-120.

Central Australian Aboriginal Media Association. (1989). *Review of the CAAMA group.* Alice Springs: Central Australian Aboriginal Media Association Productions.

Cochrane, P. (1988, April 16). Aboriginal network produces own current affairs show. *Sydney Morning Herald,* p. 2.

Cohen, P. (1982). The NUJ and race: The work of the union's race relations' working party. In P. Cohen & C. Gardner (Eds.), *It ain't half racist, mum* (pp. 90-95). London: Comedia Publishing Group.

Corker, J. (1986, June). An Aboriginal commercial television station. *Legal Service Bulletin, 11,* 115-120.

Corker, J. (1989). BRACS—Destined to fail? *Media Information Australia, 51,* 43-44.

Crisp, L. (1987, October 18). Black TV takes Dallas to the desert. *National Times on Sunday,* pp. 23-24.

Department of Aboriginal Affairs. (1984). *Aboriginal social indicators.* Canberra: Australian Government Publishing Service.

Department of Aboriginal Affairs. (1988). *Aboriginal broadcasting policy documents.* Canberra: Australian Government Publishing Service.

Department of Transport and Communications. (1990). *Review of remote area television services* (discussion paper). Canberra: Australian Government Publishing Service.

Evans, H. (1987). Prospects for the SBS. *Media Information Australia, 46,* 17-25.

Fesl, E. (1990). How the English language is used to put Koories down and deny us rights. *Social Alternatives, 9*(2), 35-37.

Grassby, A. (1981). Aborigines and the media. *Identity, 4*(3), 12-13.

Harris, S. (1980). *Culture and learning: Tradition and education in Northeast Arnhem Land.* Professional Services Branch, Northern Territory Department of Education, Darwin.

Hodge, R. (1990). Aboriginal truth and white media: Eric Michaels meets the spirit of Aboriginalism. *Continuum, 3*(2), 201-225.

Katz, E. (1977, Spring). Can authentic cultures survive new media? *Journal of Communication, 27,* 119-120.

Law, M. (1986). Public radio: Where is it headed and will it get there? *Media Information Australia, 41,* 31-35.

Liddle, R. (1980). [Untitled article.] *Identity, 4*(1), 13-14.

Mackay, H. C. (1985). The illusion of the global village. *Transactions of the Menzies Foundation, 9,* 141-144.

Marson, L. (1986, August). Public radio in national training bid. *Broadcast,* pp. 20-21, 29.

McCarthy, W. (1985). The value of the national broadcaster in new communications technology. *Transactions of the Menzies Foundation, 9,* 145-151.

Meadows, M. (1987). People power: Reporting or racism? *Australian Journalism Review, 9*(1-2), 102-112.

Meadows, M. (1989). Getting the right message across. *Australian Journalism Review, 10*(1-2), 140-153.

Michaels, E. (1983). Aboriginal "air rights." *Media Information Australia, 34,* 51-61.

Michaels, E. (1984). The social organization of an Aboriginal video workplace. *Australian Aboriginal Studies, 1,* 26-34.

Michaels, E. (1985). Constraints on knowledge in an economy of oral information. *Current Anthropology, 26*(4), 505-510.

Michaels, E. (1986). *Aboriginal invention of television Central Australia 1982-1986.* Australian Institute of Aboriginal Studies, Canberra.

Michaels, E. (1987). Hundreds shot at Aboriginal community: ABC makes documentary at Yuendumu. *Media Information Australia, 45,* 7-17.

Moore, R. (1976). *Aboriginal radio.* Paper presented by the Research Section, Department of Aboriginal Affairs, ATSIC Library, Canberra.

Murri Hour Collective. (1988). *Policy document.* Brisbane: Brisbane Indigenous Media Association..

Noble, G. (1980). Something stirring in the bush: Media and Aborigines. *Media Information Australia, 18,* 3-9.

Obijiofor, L. M. (1988). *ABC television and remote Aboriginal communities: An exploratory study.* Unpublished masters' thesis, Queensland Institute of Technology, Brisbane.

O'Hara, J. (1988, April). ABC funding: A revealing analysis. *Australian Society,* pp. 30-31.

Snow, M., & Noble, G. (1986). Urban Aboriginal self-images and the mass media. *Media Information Australia, 42,* 41-48.

Thompson, D. (1983). Claims of stardom. *Education News, 18*(5), 10-13.

Thompson, D. (1984). Action and no action—Aboriginal children's classification of films in an isolated community. *Aboriginal Child at School, 12,* 19-27.

Venner, M. (1988). Broadcasting for remote Aboriginal communities scheme. *Media Information Australia, 47,* 37-43.

Walsh, M. (1981). Language policy—Australia. In Robert B. Kaplan et al. (Eds.), *Annual review of applied linguistics* (pp. 21-32). Rowley, MA: Newbury House.

Wangkiyuparnanapurru, Puranyangu-Rangka, Kerrem, & Waringarri (1989). *Aboriginal radio in the Kimberley: A study of the broadcasting needs of Aboriginal people in the Kimberley district of Western Australia.* Sydney: Australia Broadcasting Corporation.

Watson, S., Jr. (1978). Blacks and the media. *Social Alternatives, 1*(3), 27-28.

Willmot, E. (1984). *Out of the silent land* (Report of the Task Force on Aboriginal and Islander Broadcasting and Communications). Canberra: Australian Government Publishing Service.

Wilson, C. C., & Gutierrez, F. (1985). *Minorities and the media: Diversity and the end of mass communication.* Beverly Hills, CA: Sage.

Worth, S., & Adair, J. (1972). *Through Navajo eyes: An exploration in film communication and anthropology.* Bloomington: Indiana University Press.

5

Inadvertent Assimilationism
in the Canadian Native Press

STEPHEN HAROLD RIGGINS

Introduction

One of the intended aims of ethnic minority journalism is to encourage audiences to retain their cultural values. Thus it is ironic that some of the best sociological studies of this type of journalism have concluded that it furthered the integration of minority audiences into the surrounding dominant society (e.g., Bogardus, 1933; Park, 1922; Zubrzycki, 1958). The assimilationist aspects of ethnic minority media are likely to be overlooked by minority journalists because it brings into question the legitimacy of their role. But research concentrating on assimilationist content—even though it may be somewhat biased—might be seen as a service to minority journalists who rarely have the leisure to reflect about the ideology of their own work. It might also be hypothesized that a substantial part of the assimilationist content, that which is accidental or inadvertent, could be avoided if journalists had a better understanding of ideology and had more control over the organizational structure of minority mass media.

To conceptualize media content as a measure of assimilation requires that a researcher have a detailed knowledge of both dominant and minority cultures. Because this is unrealistic with respect to a variety of topics, this research concentrates on one topic, the environmental philosophy of Canadian native newspapers. Native ideas about nature were widely perceived in the past as one of the features of their cultures that distinguished them most clearly from the early European settlers in North America. To anticipate the argument this chapter will make, it is assumed that traditional native attitudes toward nature were examples of "deep ecology." If modern native newspapers have a different environmental philosophy, this may indicate native assimilation.

Native communications societies have been very active in Canada during the last two decades (Price, 1972; Raudsepp, 1984; Riggins, 1983a, 1983b; Roth & Valaskakis, 1989; Rupert, 1982; Valaskakis & Wilson, 1985). A total of 19 native communications societies existed in Canada in the late 1980s, some concentrating on broadcast media; others, on print media. The increasing professionalism of the native media in the 1980s was recognized by the creation of journalism programs for natives at the university level and by annual native journalism awards.

This study is based on a sample of newspapers derived from the 1988 Canadian native journalism awards (National Aboriginal Communications Society [NACS], 1988). Using the criteria of professionalism and regional diversity, 5 of the 10 newspapers entered in the competition that year were chosen.[1] The sample is composed of the *Native Press* (published in the Northwest Territories), *Windspeaker* and *Kainai News* (published in Alberta), *Wawatay News* (published in Ontario), and *Micmac News* (published in Nova Scotia).[2] Unfortunately, the publishing schedule of the 5 newspapers varies.[3] Three appear monthly and two, weekly. But given the small number of newspapers available, it was not possible to avoid this. Natives from the province of Alberta were also overrepresented in the sample, because both weekly newspapers were published there. It should be noted that all articles on religion were included in the sample in order to be consistent with traditional native attitudes which imputed religious or spiritual meaning to nature. However, the newspapers contained so few religions articles that this had little effect on the study.

A sample of 150 articles was derived from the five newspapers. Those specifically discussed in this chapter are listed anonymously (by article title) in the references to protect the privacy of the authors. However, nearly all of these articles are signed and are the work of identifiable individuals. I would like to emphasize that this research should not be read as criticism of individual reporters. I have worked as a reporter for a native newspaper, the *Toronto Native Times,* and am personally aware of the difficulties of this type of work, especially when undertaken by nonnatives who have little personal contact with native communities. I could have chosen some of my own articles from the *Toronto Native Times* as examples of statements about nature that represent an inadvertently assimilationist and conservative position (e.g., Riggins, 1981).

The methodology used for this research is *discourse analysis* (Riggins, 1990; Van Dijk, 1988a, 1988b). Although discourse analysis is compatible with the older methodology of content analysis, the former encourages a researcher to pay closer attention to the stylistic and rhetorical elements of articles and to the presuppositions of statements. Discourse analysis relies less on mathematical summaries of articles, a procedure criticized for its superficiality and assumption that the meaning of statements is obvious. A radical questioning of the factuality of the media is encouraged by discourse analysis conceptualizing content as news "stories." With respect to the topic of ethnicity, some of the best examples of the methodology are provided by Van Dijk (1988b). The real strength of discourse analysis becomes apparent when a whole study dissects only one or two newspaper articles. However, as this study is based on an examination of a large sample, the discussion of individual articles will have to be less systematic and thorough than is the ideal for the methodology.

Deep Ecology Versus
Shallow Environmentalism: From Traditional Values
to Modern Political Options

The following two quotations are representative statements by natives about the philosophical/religious aspects of nature. The first quotation, taken from the First Salmon Ceremony of the Kwakiutl Indians of British Columbia, was recorded about 1900. The second statement was made by Crow Chief Plenty-Coup in the last quarter of the 19th century. He speaks about his relationship with his horse during war parties:

O, Swimmers, this is the dream given by you, to be the way of my late grandfathers when they first caught you at your playground in this river. Now you will be the same way, Swimmers. I do not club you twice, for I do not wish to club to death your souls so that you may go home to the place where you came from, Supernatural Ones, you, Givers-of-Heavy-Weight. I mean this, Swimmers, why should I not go to my house, Supernatural Ones, you, Swimmers. (cited in Stewart, 1977, p. 164)

To be alone with our war-horses at such a time teaches them to understand us, and us to understand them. My horse fights with me and fasts with me, because if he is to carry me in battle he must know my heart and I must know his or we shall never become brothers. I have been told that the white man, who is almost a god, and yet a great fool, does not believe that the horse has a spirit (soul). This cannot be true. I have many times seen my horse's soul in his eyes. And this day on that knoll I knew my horse understood. I saw his soul in his eyes. (cited by Lawrence, 1985, p. 17)

These speakers appear to believe that no significant distinction exists between humans and animals; humans are just one species of animal. They assume that animate forms of nonhuman life—even those as simple as fish—are able to understand human speech and motives. It is noteworthy that horses, fish, and humans have *souls,* although the exact meaning of that concept is not apparent in such brief quotations. The speakers recognize that the gift of life comes from nature itself, more precisely from what we eat. The human use of animals is conceptualized as reciprocal gift giving; both human and nonhuman participants are supposed to benefit through this exchange, although it may result in the death of an animal or plant and a full stomach for a human.

Environmental philosopher J. Baird Callicott (1989) concluded from his study of Ojibway mythology that the ideal relation natives established with nature involved courtesy, caution, mutual reciprocity, deference, and diplomacy, "forms of conduct which must be maintained to sustain the interspecies social structure. . . . From a sociobiological point of view, this is the sum and substance of an ethic—an American Indian land or environmental ethic" (p. 216). One of the most complete surveys of native environmentalism (Vecsey, 1980) also seems to share Callicott's evaluation of traditional knowledge.

In contrast, the environmental philospher Tom Regan (1982, pp. 206-239) stresses the pragmatic aspect of native ideas and practices, not morality or ethics. According to Regan, natives had to be keen observers of nature in order to survive. They understood the potential threat of overharvesting to their long-term interests as hunters and gatherers and for that practical reason rationally avoided altering the environment. This chapter is based on the assumption that Callicott is correct and that Regan is wrong although it must be admitted that the evidence arising from oral cultures is bound to be inconclusive. Regan may have been influenced too much by Calvin Martin's (1978) research on native participation in the fur trade which several scholars have found to be seriously flawed, logically inconsistent, and marred by rhetorical excesses (Callicott, 1989, pp. 177-201; Krech, 1981). Because the fur trade was controlled by whites, it may be a poor reflection of traditional native beliefs.

The fact that North America appeared to early European settlers to be a virgin wilderness despite thousands of years of human habitation is proof natives followed effective conservation practices. Natives did not hunt predatory animals to extinction. Nor did they alter the landscape to the extent that was possible even with simple technology because they intuitively understood one of the insights of modern ecology, the dynamic interaction of species and their environment. Admittedly, there are recorded exceptions to this generalization, isolated cases of overhunting and waste (see, e.g., Martin, 1978; Vecsey, 1980).[4] *Animism* is the term anthropologist Edward Tyler (1871) coined to refer to the belief that nature is animated by invisible conscious beings such as spirits. Animism was not unique to North American natives, but is a worldwide phenomenon. Societies in which animism is common share some features distinguishing them from modern industrialized societies: (1) They tend to be small societies whose populations know the local environments intimately, (2) they tend to be nonliterate societies, (3) respect for nature is usually accompanied by a fear of environmental failure, (4) the environment is understood as a system of interrelated species.

Contemporary attitudes toward environmentalism crisscross the political spectrum in the sense that both a capitalist and a socialist might be an environmental activist (Marchak, 1988). But some environmental ideologies are more radical than others; some people want to fine-tune the present economic system for environmental reasons whereas others envision a very different kind of economy. This distinction is also made among environmentalists: the *light greens* and the *dark greens* (Porritt & Winner, 1988), the *nature conservationists* and the *vanguard* (Milbrath, 1984), the *homocentrists* and the *ecocentrists* (Hay, 1988). Probably the best known terms are *shallow environmentalists* and *deep ecologists* (Regan, 1982). For that reason they will be used in this chapter, although they are not without bias.

Shallow environmentalism and deep ecology can be conceptualized as "media packages" or "interpretive packages" (Gamson & Modigliani, 1989). It should be possible to interpret the major themes in newspaper articles on environmental issues in the light of these two categories. They may not be equally evident in all newspaper articles. Some reporters may merely hint at a package, requiring that it be inferred by the reader on the basis of a few standard catch phrases or images; in other instances it may be highly explicit.[5] Shallow environmentalists believe that nature exists for the benefit of humanity; there is no reason to show any special respect or reverence for nature. It is an avowedly utilitarian ethic, but distinguished from the crude exploitation of nature in that restraint is advocated as a means of rationally extracting wealth from natural resources for as long as possible.

Evidence of shallow environmentalism in the media would include relatively little coverage of environmental issues, because they would not be perceived as urgent social problems. There would either be little criticism of developmental projects or rhetorical appeals about the practical necessity of balancing employment considerations and environmental protection. In reality, the short-term employment potential of projects would count more than long-term environmental protection. *Progress* and the more progressive *reform* are key words symbolizing the perspective. Modern scientific principles replace animism.

Deep ecology represents a more radical challenge to industrialization in both its capitalist and socialist forms. It is the belief that nature has value in its own right, irrespective of its value to people. Nature would not be judged solely in terms of its potential to provide for human prosperity or its potential to further human happiness. Humans would relate to nature with a reverential spirit. They would thus see the unnecessary suffering that we have inflicted on other species. Evidence of deep ecology in the media would include references to human ethical obligations to all forms of animate life. Ethics would take precedence over economics. Major environmental changes would be rejected even if they resulted in increased prosperity because one would suspect that the human benefits would be of short duration and would not counterbalance long-term disadvantages. The viability of environmentally relevant projects would be judged in terms of a very long perspective, several generations, because a hunting and gathering life-style may have existed for *80,000* generations whereas only about 8 generations have been born since the advent of industrialism (Catton, 1982). *Sustainable development* would be a key phrase symbolizing the perspective. Deep ecologists would be receptive to methods of direct action, such as protests and boycotts, to achieve their goals. They might be receptive to nonnative sources of ideological support, even though this raises the specter of assimilation. The receptiveness might take the form of favorable coverage of the international Green Movement, animal liberation, environmental theology, or positive references to some of the classic statements of deep ecology such as Aldo Leopold's *A Sand County Almanac* (1949/1987). Finally, more attention would be devoted to the members of native communities who are most in tune with traditional life.

It is unlikely that minority journalists will be able to give equal coverage to all segments of a community. The operation of ethnic media consequently implies some definition, explicit or implicit, of the boundaries of the ethnic group at which the media are targeted and the meaning of group membership. This has implications for the ideology of the content. It is consistent with shallow environmentalism for the targeted audience to be conceptualized in terms of ethnic background or geographical region, a concern for all people who have some minority ancestry, rather than in terms of specifically native values. A native engineer who is the director of an ambitious dam-building project would be as appropriate for a personal profile as the elder still engaged in subsistence hunting. But for deep ecologists what can be preserved from a hunting and gathering life-style, although perhaps reformulated and modernized to some extent, is a major consideration. Thus they would publicize natives who live a more traditional life-style. Some idealization of hunting and gathering societies would be expected, symbolized for example by the slogan of native activist Winona Laduke (n.d.): "From nature to synthetic and back again" (p. i).

When Animals Make the News

The most frequent topic in the sample used here is the management of renewable resources, generally timber, fish, and fur-bearing animals (Table 5.1). Many of these articles report on native efforts to counteract the lobbying activities of animal rights groups in Great Britain, which were campaigning for more humane technics of trapping. The tone and substance of the articles vary, but there is practically no sympathy for the position of the animal rights activists. Indeed, many reporters take an openly hostile position, documenting how the two sides conduct a deaf dialogue. The January issue of *Wawatay News* reported a conversation with a trapper from the Northwest Territories: "He does not care much for the animal rights movement and has a hard time understanding people who condemn an activity he views as the natural order of things. 'Living in a high-rise in Toronto, sitting in front of a computer is not my life,' he says, 'It's none of my business how other people live. I don't tell them how to live. So why should they tell me I can't hunt and trap?' " (Trout Lake, 1988). A few articles do report on the activities of animal rights groups in an impartial manner and with the degree of coverage reserved for major issues. Typical of this approach is an article

TABLE 5.1. Major Topics of Articles

Topic	Number of Articles
Management of Renewable Resources	36
Reports on Developmental Projects	22
Environmental Degradation	20
Environmental Activism	17
Occupationally Relevant Information	13
Religion	10
Success Stories	9
Miscellaneous	7
Fishing and Hunting as Leisure Activities	6
Farming	5
Improvements in the Environment	3
Nostalgia	2
Total Number of Articles	150

in the *Native Press* titled "Anti-Trapping Groups Have a Big Network." Although the headline might be read as highlighting the element of threat, the article itself serves the educational function of informing readers, in a nonjudgmental manner, about opinions they are unlikely to share, those of the World Society for the Protection of Animals and the Association for the Protection of Fur-Bearing Animals.

One of the rhetorically most elaborate articles about animal rights, reprinted in several papers, was titled "Bunny Huggers in Britain Are Getting Out of Hand." The following is the lead paragraph:

> Skonongohwe! The bunny-huggers in Britain are getting out of hand and I think it's time to do something about them. I call them "bunny-huggers" but they're not as innocent as the name suggests. They are narrow-minded, humorless fanatics who want to put 50,000 native trappers (and 50,000 non-native trappers) out of business. Putting natives out of the trapping business probably means putting them on welfare—permanently—but those loony tunes don't care what happens to trappers because they care more about animals than they do about people. They've already convinced the British Government to place warning labels on furs to tell potential buyers that the fur may have been caught in a leg-hold trap (1988, p. 4).

This article is similar to many others on animal rights in that the controversy is framed largely in economic terms. The reporter borrows the negative labels *bunny-hugger, looney tunes,* and *redneck* from the dominant culture. Hugging bunnies is an overreaction by nature lovers because wild rabbits do not seem to enjoy physical contact with humans. Nor are they threatened with extinction, because they are famous in folklore for their reproductive ability. Respect for rabbits hardly needs to reach this illogical extreme, however. No effort is made to discover common ground between native traditions and animal rights (Sperling, 1988). The fact that the movement threatens many nonnative economic interests, farmers, medical researchers, the cosmetic industry, and so forth is presumably irrelevant. Indeed, bunny-huggers are related to all of the other evils that natives have suffered since the European discovery of North America. The author is very pessimistic about the chances that natives will be able to defeat animal rights activists. "We might not be able to win the war against booze, bingo, dependence, brainwashing or racism, but we have to do something. After all, the bunny-huggers are out there and they don't plan to give up until we're all wearing plastic shoes and nylon sweaters and eating yogurt and bean sprouts" ("Bunny Huggers," 1988, p. 4).

The controversy over trapping technics might have provided native journalists an occasion to reflect on the ethics of commercial trapping and subsistence hunting, both of which are presently done by natives (Tanner, 1979). Are the ethics as different as animal rights activists believe? Little in these newspaper articles criticizes the commercialism of the fur industry. Some members of the anti-fur lobby have argued that the fur industry in Canada is basically a commercial business run by nonnatives and that the native portion of the profits is rather small. They claim that the industry uses natives as public spokespersons because activists who are opposed to killing animals are also sympathetic to the preservation of traditional life-styles ("Anti-Trapping," 1988; "Animal Rights Groups," 1988). This is a crucial bit of information for understanding reactions to the controversy, but the articles do not give readers sufficient information to judge this claim. (Anthropologist George Wenzel, 1991, provides an excellent summary of how animal rights activists have misperceived the way commercial hunting continues to reinforce traditional sharing and community cooperation.)

In 1988 the *Native Press* published a regular column written by an employee of the management board of a caribou herd. The article of

January 22 is especially interesting because of the way the author jokes at the expense of animals ("R-2000 Deer," 1988). He thought his column was too serious and wanted to be humorous in order to make scientific information more appealing to a larger readership. The depiction of caribou is reminiscent of the animals in Gary Larson's syndicated cartoon *The Far Side.* Caribou are described as "cute and funny." However, much of their humor is unintentional, a result of apparent stupidity. Caribou are so dumb that they "can not count." If a caribou were to follow two hunters, one hunter could hide and the animal would continue following the visible hunter, never realizing that it was being outwitted and could easily be shot. The curious behavior of caribou includes eating "wolf poop." Caribou are reluctant to jump over low fences made of driftwood and antlers, to cross a ribbon of metal or even tire tracks. The implication is that the cause is low intelligence as no effort is made to offer an explanation, either animistic or scientific.

> What other animal is apt to run toward you after being fired at by a high powered rifle? Or can be coaxed within camera range by lying on your back and kicking your feet in the air? On several occasions while trudging down a frozen lake, I have looked back to find a small band of woodland caribou happily following me. Every time I stopped they would stop and watch me with that goofy inquisitive look of an awestruck bunch of school kids. ("R-2000 Deer," 1988, p. 10)

Richard Nelson (1983) in his study of the environmental knowledge of the Koyukon Indians in Alaska, *Make Prayers to the Raven,* also writes that caribou can be "foolishly unafraid" and are fascinated by people who appear to have antlers (p. 171). However, Nelson recorded another side of the caribou that the writer of "R-2000 Deer" ignored. An informant told Nelson (1983) of shooting a young caribou. After the mother nuzzled the calf, it recovered instantly and ran away. The informant believed that the caribou "made medicine to her child" (21). The story is one of the many illustrations of the way the Koyukon blur the distinction between humans and animals in a manner that assumes both are highly intelligent. In the *Native Press* caribou are also related to a category of people, but the comparison is with one of the least sophisticated categories, "an awestruck bunch of school kids."

Developmental Projects and
Environmental Activism

Reports on developmental projects are the second most frequent topic in the sample. This includes not only projects such as tourist camps but also plans for uranium and gold mines. The *Native Press* published four articles about future plans for a uranium mine ("Council Undecided," 1988; "Don't Mine Uranium," 1988; "Full Review," 1988; "Uranium Mine," 1988). The project was supposed to consist of two open-pit mines providing up to 15,000 tons of uranium ore daily. The company also wanted to build an airport for jet aircraft, a marine terminal capable of handling cargo ships and oceangoing barges, and a winter road. Even though it was thought the project would have a substantial impact on the local community, only one of the four articles voiced strong opposition. This was a letter written by a representative of Nuclear Free North, a nonnative association.

The article, highlighted by its placement on the front page, begins with the topic of employment opportunities ("Uranium Mine," 1988). The mine was expected to employ 250 people. The first 12 paragraphs provide an overview of the company's plans. Then a Member of the Legislative Assembly is given 3 paragraphs of speaking space. He also talks first about jobs, not social or environmental change, but he does question the accuracy of the company's estimate of the number of jobs that would be created. The subsequent 5 paragraphs provide more detail concerning the company's plans and the article ends with 3 short paragraphs of criticisms from Nuclear Free North. Only at the very conclusion is there a discussion of nuclear weapons. The reporter does not mention well-publicized cases of natives resisting the opening of uranium mines on or near reserves (Goldstick, 1987). The other two articles about the uranium mine in the same issue of the newspaper are rather technical reports on the composition of an environmental review panel and on public participation in another panel that had been allotted the task of deciding if the mine would be given permission to open. Devoting space in these articles to the critics of nuclear energy and nuclear warfare would have counterbalanced the reassuring tone of the front page.

The May 13 issue of the *Native Press* contains two reports on a future gold mine ("Gold Mine Impacts," 1988; "New Gold Mine," 1988). The opening paragraph of the article on page one highlights the incompatibility between the mine and the local community: "One of the largest gold mines on the continent is moving in next to one of the smallest, traditional communities in Denendeh" (Western Canadian Artic). But the article's ominous beginning is not further elaborated. The expected theme of cultural conflict gives way in the following paragraphs to an optimistic discussion of jobs, occupational training, and business opportunities. One of the exceptions seems unintended. The vice-president of the development who talks in glowing terms about his company does not seem to realize the irony of his comment "it's a big, big project. We've got a tiger by the tail here" ("New Gold Mine," 1988). The other article, "Gold Mine Impacts Snare Lake," understated by its position on page two and its shorter length, appears to be the more logical development of the lead paragraph of the first article. According to this second article, the mine and the large number of land speculators making claims in the area do threaten trappers. However, no one in the community is interviewed other than the executive director of the Dogrib Tribal Council. He is quoted as saying that there is "not yet" opposition in the community and he appears to accept the project with ambiguous resignation. On one hand he is quoted as saying, "I can't see that it's had anything but a favorable impact," on the other hand he contradicts this by saying, "The people 'moved out there . . . to get away from community life. But community life is going to hit them right in the forehead.' " While this is an ideologically complex article, it also eventually slants the message in a reassuring direction.

The May 6 issue of *Windspeaker* contains an article about plans for a new $500 million pulp and paper mill titled "Community Response to Daishowa Varies." The caption under the illustration reads, ". . . expected to supply $22 million in salaries." Here the company plans are shifted to the concluding section of the article but are extensively described and are not questioned. Native reactions to the project, judging from the article, are not so "varied." They "have been anticipating a boost in the economy." Some communities are preparing projects of their own that link with Daishowa. Those who are most worried about the mill have either been "assured" or they make very bland statements about monitoring the environmental impact. *Windspeaker* may distance itself from the pulp mill more than *Native Press* did from the uranium and gold mines, but the differences in environmental politics seems superficial. On November 23 *Kainai News* reported on the plans for a $65 million irrigation project for the Blood Tribe in Alberta ("Blood Tribe Announces," 1988). The expectations for the project were that it would allow farming on 25,000 acres of otherwise infertile land. A band survey found that 90% of the population favored the project. There is an extensive literature on agricultural irrigation in the American West arguing that it may be a short-term, hazardous solution and that the more sound alternative is to adjust to a dry landscape (see, e.g., Bartlett, 1988). The potential hazards are ignored in the article. Exploration near Muskrat Dam in Ontario is discussed in the October issue of *Wawatay News* ("Confrontation Averted," 1988). Native activism is the theme of the article, noticeable in both the illustrations and text. The front-page illustration is a portrait of a chief apparently speaking in public. Little space is given to a spokesperson from Eldorado Mines. However, it appears that the real issue is one of ownership; capitalism and industrialism are not questioned. The chief is quoted as saying, "We are not opposed to development. We want benefits, both monetary and otherwise, but we have to be involved from the ground up" (cited in "Confrontation Averted," 1988, p. 1).

The third and fourth most frequent topics in the sample are environmental degradation and environmental activism. It is in these categories that *Wawatay News* expressed most passionately its concern with environmental problems in 1988. The February issue reported that PCBs had been discovered in the blood samples of the residents of two northern Ontario reserves ("High Chemical Count," 1988). Subsequent articles throughout the summer and fall kept the topic alive ("Chief Threatens," 1988; "Group Protests," 1988; "Group to Track Down," 1988; "New Society," 1988; "Search for Toxic," 1988). The May article "Group Protests in Toronto" is part of this series and shows that the residents of Big Trout Lake have a good understanding of what makes a successful media event. The article is about a group of residents of the Big Trout Lake Reserve who flew to Toronto to demonstrate in front of the Ontario provincial parliament. The protesters marched carrying signs made by the elementary-school children in Big Trout Lake. The accompanying photograph shows a chief speaking in public as he hands a child's piggy bank full of money to a Member of the Provincial Parliament (MPP). It is the native who is shown in an activist posture while the more passive MPP looks down at the bank in his hands and seems to frown. As if to shame the MPP, a protester displayed a child's protest sign in the background.

The initial verbal imagery helps to establish an identification between the reader and the native protesters who are not depicted as threatening but as a group that is acted upon: "Small groups of native Canadians huddled under somber umbrellas." The drama of the confrontation is heightened somewhat in the early paragraphs. Although the writer must have already known the conclusion of the day's events before writing the story, the article begins with the suspense of not knowing if the chief would, as he had threatened, dump a PCB contaminated capacitor on the grounds of the parliament. Speaking space in the article is given only to official political representatives, the Grand Chief of Nishnawbe-Aski Nation and the chief for the Big Trout Lake Reserve. One other native person is mentioned by name. This is a pregnant woman, one of the individuals who might be most affected by PCBs. No official statement by anyone of nonnative ancestry is quoted, but a joke told by the nonnative MPP is reported. Identification between the residents of Big Trout Lake and the reader is also built into the article by the writer mentioning that they could be distinguished from the other people present by their greater concern for personal appearance and their seriousness: "Many were women and children wearing their brightest scarves and newest shoes. All were quiet and respectful of the legislature. They shared none of the holiday laughter of the young Indians from Toronto" ("Group Protests," 1988, p. 2). The kicker that concludes the article is a memorable commentary on the photograph: "Four young children from Big Trout Lake have sent their life savings ($105) to the [provincial and federal] government, $52.50 to each level. They want the chemical cleaned up and are willing to put their money where their mouths are—they challenge the governments to do the same."

The frequency of articles on environmental activism in the sample is largely due to *Windspeaker* and *Wawatay News* whose journalists may have had more of these stories to report, but they also use an activist angle in these stories that seems to be less common in the other papers. Several of the articles in *Windspeaker* are about protests against the building of a dam on the Oldman River which would affect the Peigan Reserve. Some refer to the spiritual element in the controversy. On August 19 *Windspeaker* also reported that a committee had been formed by native women who were concerned with the environment ("Economics versus Environment," 1988). *Micmac News* in July wrote about the efforts of an individual native to protest the operations of a Swedish lumber company in Nova Scotia ("Fighting," 1988). On November 10 *Native Press* reported on the protests of the Haida Indians against logging in British Columbia ("Haida Standing Firm," 1988). The article is an eloquent expression of traditional ideas about nature that reiterates the religious component:

A Haida vision of the world teaches that we must respect the earth and take our place in the tribe of the animal. The division between the different animals, fish and birds is a very fine line. Loss of respect and improper behavior leads to suffering and finally chaos.

Today in this time of the subduer, it is still true that disrespectful sacrifice demanded of the earth will lead to this lack of balance and an untimely end.

But what isn't often appreciated is the inherent weakness of the subduers. Once removed of the false cloak of respectability they stand exposed in naked shame. ("Haida Standing Firm," 1988, p. 1)

Big Business, Exotic Dreams

The fifth most frequent topic in the articles was occupationally relevant information. To give a flavor of these articles, they have titles such as "New Traps Could Prove Helpful," "Trapline Tips," and "Spring Hunt Rules Announced." Despite the straightforward and impartial presentation of utilitarian information, one could not say that they make no political statement. The failure to question the present organization of commercial fishing and trapping surely indicates assimilation or economic conservatism. Although it might be argued that these articles help establish a secure economic base for the readership and thus strengthen cultural pluralism, the practical advice is given in a context in which major economic decisions are the privilege of others.

In general, these newspapers are as highly secularized or despiritualized as the mainstream metropolitan press of southern Canada. Religion seems to be perceived as too insignificant, controversial, or inappropriate to report. It is typical that a March article in *Micmac News,* reporting on the sophisticated understanding of traditional natives, attempts to gain prestige by relating this knowledge to science instead of religion, ethics or philosophy ("Indians Survived," 1988). The religion discussed in most articles is Christianity. In August *Micmac News* published an ambitious series of articles on 17th-century native Kateri Tekakwitha, who was declared "blessed" in 1980 by Pope John Paul II (*"Micmac* Tribute," 1988). A mission priest is quoted as saying that Tekakwitha "was a true daughter of her people. All the days of her life, she showed that an Indian can live as a Catholic. If she can follow Christ, then so can we. Kateri Tekakwitha never stopped being Indian, she always maintained her traditions" (*"Micmac* Tribute," 1988, p. 14). This statement loses much of its impact when no attempt is made in the series to explain exactly what were the native beliefs of Tekakwitha. Without that kind of detail, the statement seems to serve only a rhetorical function.

Only one article, on an earth healing ceremony, compares traditional native spirituality with modern nonnative religions, in the process idealizing the mosaic of cultural pluralism: "The non-native—native vision has been that of Chief John Snow and I [Dwayne Rourke, an organizer of the ceremony]. And we both realize the unity of our cultures and the possibilities for us to draw from both worlds and the best to converge. To weave that which is into a truly unique and modern tapestry of being, a combined expression of cultures" ("Earth Healing," 1988, p. 10).

The occupational success of natives is a frequent theme in native newspapers. The strength and endurance required to trap, hunt, and fish easily lend themselves to this kind of treatment (e.g., "Trapper Jack," 1988). The June issue of *Micmac News* includes a profile of a young fisherman who is one of the few people on his reserve who has a lobster license ("Fisherman," 1988). The article devotes attention to the conflict with both the weather and white fishermen. Readers learn that he defines fishing as "big business," an idea substantiated by many references to costs and prices and the prestige acquired by dealing in large sums of money. His profits appear to be in the range of present professional salaries. The article demonstrates strong support for native endeavors: " 'It's pretty dirty out there. . . . Once a fisherman ran right over our buoy on purpose. . . . [Non-Indian fishermen] never want to see an Indian get ahead in the game. It's like a battle out there' " ("Fisherman," 1988, p. 27). But the article is structured around an assimilationist theme, a native succeeding in a nonnative world. The article says little about his occupational practices that could be linked with traditional beliefs.

Also classified in the category of success story is an article in the January issue of *Micmac News* "Hunter Dreams of 'Exotic' Hunt . . . Big Horn Sheep and Elephants." The illustration shows the hunter surrounded by his impressive collection of big game and fish trophies, the stuffed heads of moose, bear, deer, and so on, preserved through taxidermy. Referring to a moose that the interviewee had killed, the journalist notes, "He hunted the animal in accordance with the guidelines of the Treaty of 1752, to practice his right to 'netukulimk'—the act of providing for the physical, spiritual and medicinal needs of himself, his family and community" ("Hunter Dreams," 1988, p. 30). This remark is somewhat gratuitous in the context of the overall article, because the spiritual and medicinal are completely ignored and instead the journalist records the interviewee's hunting stories. The interviewee takes pride in having speared and mounted a rare yellow eel, the only one that he had ever seen. " 'Maybe I could go to Africa and shoot down an elephant,' he added jokingly. 'Then my fellow hunters would eat their hearts out' " ("Hunter Dreams," 1988, p. 31). The article seems to show a nontraditional scale of values in which the trophy collection serves as an ostentatious conversation piece.

Miscellaneous Themes

The final categories of topics include articles that might be viewed as fillers, reprints of free information provided by organizations such as provincial wildlife agencies (e.g.,"First Season at Greenhouse a Success," 1988; "Trapping Books Published," 1988). Six articles are about fishing and hunting as leisure activities, five are about farming, three are about improvements in the environment, and two were classified as nostalgia. The category called "information relevant to fishing and hunting as leisure activities" consists largely of weather reports and the activities of organizations such as Ducks Unlimited. All of the articles on farming are about commercial agriculture and show no appreciation of the sophistication of traditional technics that have been rediscovered by agricultural specialists (e.g., Nabhan, 1989; Hurt, 1987). No one would suspect from these articles that North American natives bred as many as 155 varieties of domesticated plants (Vecsey, 1980). The few articles about improvements in the environment concern an increase in the number of buffalo and whooping cranes. The nostalgia articles are reminiscences of past hunting and trapping experiences. A typical title is "Trout Lake Elder Prefers Old Methods of Trapping" (1988). These articles lament or fondly recall the past, while making no effort to actualize the values that the past represented.

Conclusion: Who's Afraid of
Mother Earth?

To summarize the preceding sections, all five newspapers contain some articles that would appeal to deep ecologists, but the overall coverage given environmental issues in all five illustrates shallow environmentalism. Animism and the concept of an exchange relationship between humans and animals are largely absent; few articles depict nature as an active spiritual force that has to be negotiated. Instead, the environment seems to have been turned into a collection of exploitable commodities. The two most frequent topics in the sample, reports on renewable resources and developmental projects, are devoid of basic criticism of industrialism and capitalism. They merely advocate a reallocation of wealth so that natives receive a larger share. The yardstick for judging developmental projects generally seems to be employment opportunities. The animal rights movement is harshly criticized; reporters do not relate native spirituality to the concerns of the movement. Christian themes form the content of most religious articles and little is said about the spirituality of nature. The newspapers appear to define newsworthiness in terms of ancestry rather than values. For all of these reasons, the newspapers illustrate a conservative vision of the native press and a considerable degree of assimilation.

The contemporary native press could be a source for a radical critique of industrialism. The potential certainly exists in the traditions. But this portion of the ideological spectrum is largely missing today. Its absence may be a true reflection of public opinion, but there are reasons for believing that it might as well be a reflection of the organizational structure of the native press. Organizational structure is understood here as "the routine ways people coordinate their efforts in actualizing a symbolic product or service" (Peterson, 1982, p. 147). The key features of the structure include dependence on nonnative journalists, insufficient funding, and an affiliation with native organizations. Despite some dramatic improvements during the past few years, most notably the launching in 1992 of Television Northern Canada, the largest aboriginal television network in the world and one that will broadcast in 15 native languages (Platiel, 1992), work in native media remains a career with relatively meager financial rewards. This discourages long-term commitment to the native press and has resulted in a continual turnover of staff as well as the hiring of writers of nonnative ancestry. Despite the good intentions of nonnative staff and volunteers, they are obviously a source for some of the content that is viewed as assimilationist.

The philosophy of the press that these newspapers embody appears to be a combination of the libertarian model and the social responsibility model (Lorimer & McNulty, 1987). The commonsense notions of objectivity and neutrality, which are part of the libertarian model and the professional identity of mainstream journalists today (Schudson, 1978), have strongly influenced the papers in the sample. But these newspapers do aim to be more than independent watchdogs guarding the interests of natives; writers clearly want to create socially useful information, a defining characteristic of the social responsibility model. Both philosophies can be seen in one of the longest statements about the politics of the Canadian native press in 1988, which was published in the form of a public letter by the board of directors for the Wawatay Native Communications Society. The public letter was written in response to complaints from some readers that *Wawatay News* had been "uncooperative" in reporting on a hunger strike protesting inadequate health services for natives. The journalists at *Wawatay News* felt that they had in fact been cooperative with protesters but that some readers misunderstood the role of the newspaper within the community. The letter reads, in part:

> Wawatay is an agent for news and information to the Cree and Ojibway people of the Nishnawbe-Aski Nation. As an agent of news and information, Wawatay does not and will not be influenced in its role as a media organization by political forces.
>
> Wawatay's position is such that it will continue to maintain its role as a free press for the Indian people it is intended to serve. Wawatay will provide news and information that is fair, balanced, impartial and accurate. Wawatay will continue to provide not just news and information programs in the Cree and Ojibway languages. It will provide programming that will cover the traditional and culture elements of the people of the Nishnawbe-Aski Nation from editorials to features, to entertainment, covering all aspects of life of the Indian people. . . .
>
> Wawatay must maintain its editorial credibility at all times, in order for Wawatay to present facts in a fair, balanced, impartial and accurate manner. Wawatay journalists must abide by professional journalistic standards and ethics.
>
> It is not Wawatay's intention to provide or be seen to provide a service that is in any way negative to the people of the Nishnawbe-Aski Nation. To do so would only be going against the principles and ethics of the organization as taught by the elders of the Indian people. Rather Wawatay should be viewed in a manner that will strengthen and unify the people of the Nishnawbe-Aski Nation. (Wawatay Native Communications Society, 1988, p. 4)

The libertarian philosophy of the press is wholeheartedly endorsed in the letter. The commitment to provide supportive coverage of native activities can be seen as indicating some agreement with the notion of social responsibility, although freedom of the press is presented as a prerequisite. To many scholars (e.g., Epstein, 1973; Fishman, 1980; Gurevitch et al., 1982; Herman & Chomsky, 1988; Schudson, 1978; Tuchman, 1978; Van Dijk, 1988a, 1988b), a belief that the media convey balanced and impartial information is a delusion that is occupationally useful to journalists because it provides a public legitimation for their profession. Balance is rarely a realistic depiction of media content. Gamson and Modigliani (1989) state that influential media packages are sponsored by organizations that try to influence media coverage to their advantage through press releases and contacts with journalists. In the case of environmental issues in Canada, these organizations would include the Canadian Manufacturers' Association and Greenpeace. But within native communities there are very few environmental organizations. Thus a passive native press that waits for officials or community organizations to set the agenda for public debate on the environment or to create *news pegs* for stories will have little to say about the topic. The more activist role of the press, embodied in the social responsibility model, may for that reason be a better way of addressing this topic. How journalists can define themselves professionally as social activists while working for a newspaper that is strongly identified with objective coverage is discussed by Robert Miraldi (1989) in his study of the new muckraking. Journalists who vary the types of articles they write (news analysis and background news allow reporters more freedom to state opinions than does spot news), who co-operate with journalists employed by other organizations whose stories will then help to create news pegs and a momentum for reform, and who share information with high-placed informants may be both politically neutral and social activists.

Political influence on the native press is more pervasive ("Defend Freedom," 1988; "Report on Meetings." 1988) than the kind of incident, direct pressure from one segment of the readership, which prompted the letter from the Wawatay Native Communications Society at *Wawatay News.* The Canadian native press is profoundly affected by its potential readership being too small, too scattered, and too poor to be of much interest to advertisers. Consequently, all the newspapers depend on governmental subsidization, either directly through grants and paid advertisements or indirectly from funds channeled through native associations. Politicians are of crucial importance in the raising of funds. Irrespective of their ethnicity, politicians have a stake in maintaining the native press at an underfunded level, which restricts its critical potential. A flourishing native press is a threat to all politicians, because it has the potential of publicizing cases of corruption and mismanagement. Surely it is unrealistic to expect that many politicians will have the public spirit to subsidize their critics. They pay lip service to an independent native press, but a genuine appreciation of its cultural role, coupled with financial generosity, seems unlikely in the near future. The result is a press that is conservative and accommodating and that surreptitiously reinforces assimilationist drives.

Notes

1. At the 1988 annual Canadian native journalism awards, *Wawatay News* was chosen as the "best overall newspaper." Additional awards were won by *Windspeaker* and *Micmac News* (NACS, 1988). In 1987 the award for the "best overall newspaper" was given to the *Native Press*. Additional awards were won by *Kainai News, Micmac News, Windspeaker,* and *Kahtou* (NACS, 1987).

2. The newspapers that were chosen are the following: (a) *Native Press* is a tabloid of about 24 pages per issue, published every 2 weeks in Yellowknife, Northwest Territories, by the Native Communications Society of the Western Northwest Territories (1988 is volume 18). (b) *Windspeaker* is a tabloid of about 24 pages per issue, published weekly in Edmonton, Alberta, by the Aboriginal Multi-Media Society of Alberta (1988 covers portions of volumes 5 and 6). (c) *Kainai News* is a tabloid of about 16 pages per issue, published weekly in Standoff, Alberta, by the Communication Society of Indian News Media (1988 is volume 21). (d) *Wawatay News* is a newspaper published monthly in Sioux Lookout, Ontario, by the Wawatay Native Communications Society. At the beginning of 1988 *Wawatay News* was published in a broadsheet format but shifted to a tabloid format in November. As a broadsheet, the paper tended to be about 24 pages per issue and as a tabloid about 44 (1988 is volume 15). (e) *Micmac News* is a tabloid of about 40 pages, published monthly in Sydney, Nova Scotia, by the Native Communications Society of Nova Scotia (1988 is volume 19).

3. All of the articles that were examined for this study were published between January 1 and December 31, 1988. All are in English, the predominant language of the North American native press. *Wawatay News* is the only bilingual newspaper in the sample, but it provides an English translation of practically all the content. Initially, all articles were examined that included any reference to nature. But frequently this information was so superficial that many articles were excluded. For instance, the sample does not include any articles on rodeos. Although rodeos are of potential interest because they involve human-animal interaction, the articles dealt almost solely with rodeos as sporting events and provided little information about participants' attitudes toward animals. Articles on land claims and hunting and fishing regulations were excluded if they dealt with questions of ownership rather than use. Many articles had headlines about hunting, fishing, or a natural occurrence such as a storm, but were excluded when they were simply lists of recent community events. Letters to the editor that represented an individual's opinion rather than the policy of an organization were not included. Finally, all articles less than 200 words in length were excluded. To illustrate the difficulty of classifying the main topics of articles, *Windspeaker* published an article titled "Trapping Methods Easier, but

Wildlife Getting Scarcer" (September 16). The article has been classified as a success story because it is a personal profile of an older hunter. However, environmental degradation is a minor theme, as can be seen from the title, and it also provides some occupationally useful information. Articles that were reprinted were counted every time they appeared in print.

4. The literature that claims that the sharing of land and resources, as was done by natives, inevitably results in exploitation, the "tragedy of the commons," is presently seen as simplistic. Collective ownership occurs in a variety of patterns, some of which protect the sustained use of renewable resources (Berkes et al., 1989).

5. In case a reader mistakenly assume that most of the mainstream press is biased in favor of environmentalism, it might be noted that a survey by Milbrath (1984) found a considerable number of nonnative media gatekeepers to be unsympathetic toward all forms of environmentalism.

References

Animal rights groups leave exhibit alone. (1988, January). *Wawatay News.* p. 7.

Anti-trapping groups have a big network. (1988, October 14). *Native Press,* pp. 1, 14.

Bartlett, R. V. (1988). Adapt or get out: The Garrison diversion project and controversy. *Environmental Review, 12,* 57-74.

Berkes, F., Fenny, D., McCay, B. J., & Acheson, J. M. (1989). The benefits of the commons. *Nature, 340,* 91-93.

Blood Tribe announces $65 million irrigation project. (1988, November 23). *Kainai News,* p. 6

Bogardus, E. S. (1933). The Filipino press in the U.S. *Sociology/Social Research, 28,* 581-585.

Bunny huggers in Britain are getting out of hand. (1988, June 29). *Kainai News,* p. 4.

Callicott, J. B. (1989). *In defense of the land ethic: Essays in environmental philosophy.* Albany: State University of New York Press.

Catton, W. (1982). *Overshoot: The ecological basis of revolutionary change.* Urbana: University of Illinois Press.

Chief threatens to send chemicals to Toronto. (1988, May). *Wawatay News,* pp. 1, 6.

Community response to Daishowa varies. (1988, May 6). *Windspeaker,* p. 2.

Confrontation averted after drilling operation stops. (1988, October). *Wawatay News,* pp. 1-2.

Council undecided on uranium. (1988, June 10). *Native Press,* p. 21.

Defend freedom of the press. (1988, April) *Wawatay News,* p. 4. (Also published in the *Native Press,* March 31, p. 7.)

Don't mine uranium. (1988, April 15). *Native Press,* p., 28.

Earth healing ceremony draws 80 to Morley. (1988, June 8). *Kainai News,* p. 10.

Economics versus environment. (1988, August 19). *Windspeaker,* p. 4.

Environmentalist discourages trapping. (1988, April 8). *Windspeaker,* p. 2.

Epstein, E. J. (1973). *News from nowhere: Television and the news.* New York: Vintage.

Fighting a forestry giant. (1988, July) *Micmac News,* p. 19.

First season at greenhouse a success. (1988, August). *Wawatay News,* p. 6.

Fisherman nearly wiped out by storm. (1988, June). *Micmac News,* pp. 26-27.

Fishman, M. (1980). *Manufacturing the news.* Austin: University of Texas Press.

Full review coming for new uranium mine. (1988, November 10). *Native Press,* p. 12.

Gamson, W., & Modigliani, A. (1989). Media discourse and public opinion on nuclear power: A constructionist approach. *American Journal of Sociology, 95*(1), 1-37.

Gold mine impacts Snare Lake. (1988, May 13). *Native Press,* p. 2.

Goldstick, M. (1987). *Wollaston: People resisting genocide.* Montreal: Black Rose Books.

Group protests in Toronto. (1988, May). *Wawatay News,* p. 2.

Group to track down toxic chemicals. (1988, June). *Wawatay News,* p. 5.

Gurevitch, M., Bennett, T., Curran, J., & Wollacott, J. (1982). *Culture, society and the media.* London: Methuen.

Haida standing firm to protect the land. (1988, November 10). *Native Press,* p. 1.

Hay, P. R. (1988). The contemporary environmental movement as neo-romanticism. *Environmental Review, 12,* 39-59.

Herman, E. S., & Chomsky, N. (1988). *Manufacturing consent: The political economy of the mass media.* New York: Pantheon Books.

High chemical count found in residents of two northern reserves. (1988, February). *Wawatay News,* pp. 1, 3.

Hunter dreams of "exotic" hunt . . . big horn sheep and elephants. (1988, January). *Micmac News,* pp. 30-31.

Hurt, R. D. (1987). *Indian agriculture in America: Prehistory to the present.* Lawrence: University Press of Kansas.

Indians survived by knowing nature. (1988, March, 20). *Micmac News.*

Krech, S., III (Ed.). (1981). *Indians, animals, and the fur trade: A critique of Keepers of the game.* Athens: University of Georgia Press.

Laduke, W. (n.d.). Preface: Natural to synthetic and back. In W. Churchill (Ed.), *Marxism and native Americans* (pp. i-viii). Boston: South End Press.

Lawrence, E. A. (1985). *Hoofbeats and society: Studies of human-horse interactions.* Bloomington: Indiana University Press.

Leopold, A. (1987). *A Sand County almanac.* New York: Oxford University Press. (Original work published in 1949.)

Lorimer, R., & McNulty, J. (1987). *Mass communication in Canada.* Toronto: McClelland & Stewart.

Low levels of toxic chemical found in Sandy Lake School. (1988, October). *Wawatay News,* p. 1.

Marchak, M. P. (1988). *Ideological perspectives on Canada* (3rd. ed.). Toronto: McGraw-Hill Ryerson.

Martin, C. (1978). *Keepers of the game.* Berkeley: University of California Press.

Micmac tribute to St. Ann. (1988, August). *Micmac News,* 14-23.

Milbrath, L. W. (1984). *Environmentalists: Vanguard for a new society.* Albany: State University of New York Press.

Miraldi, R. (1989, August). Objectivity and the new muckraking: John L. Hess and the nursing home scandal. *Journalism Monographs* (No. 115). Association for Education in Journalism and Mass Communication. Columbia: University of South Carolina.

Nabhan, G. P. (1989). *Enduring seeds: Native American agriculture and wild plant conservation.* San Francisco: North Point Press.

National Aboriginal Communications Society. (1987, June 4). Native media organization presents national awards (press release). Ottawa: Author.

National Aboriginal Communications Society. (1988, July 8). Media awards cap festival (press release). Ottawa: Author.

Nelson, R. (1983). *Make prayers to the raven: A Koyukon view of the northern forest.* Chicago: University of Chicago Press.

New gold mine nation's largest. (1988, May 13). *Native Press,* pp. 1-2.

New traps could prove helpful. (1988, January 22). *Native Press,* p. 11.

New pulp mill "good news" for job seekers. (1988, December 23). *Windspeaker,* pp. 1-2.

New society takes active role in stopping pollution of Earth. (1988, August). *Wawatay News,* pp. 10, 19.

Park, R. E. (1922). *The immigrant press and its control.* New York: Harper & Brothers.

Peterson, R. (1982). Five constraints on the production of culture: Law, technology, market, organizational structure and occupational careers. *Journal of Popular Culture, 16,* 143-153.

Platiel, R. (1992, January 18). North channels own resources into prime time. *The Globe and Mail,* sec. A, p. 7.

Porritt, J., & Winner, D. (1988). *The coming of the greens.* London: Fontana/Collins.

Price, J. A. (1972). US and Canadian Indian periodicals. *Canadian Review of Sociology and Anthropology, 9,* 150-162.

R-2000 deer are curious creatures. (1988, January 22). *Native Press,* p. 10.

Raudsepp, E. (1984). The native press in Canada. *Journal of Native Education, 12,* 10-23.

Regan, T. (1982). *All that dwell therein: Animal rights and environmental ethics.* Berkeley: University of California Press.

Report on the meetings of the National Aboriginal Communications Society. (1988, July). *Micmac News,* pp. 23-31.

Riggins, S. H. (1981, March 7). Overhunting and inadequate management threaten moose. *Toronto Native Times,* p. 7.

Riggins, S. H. (Ed.). (1983a). Native North Americans and the media: Studies in minority journalism [Special Issue]. *Anthropologica, 25*(1).

Riggins, S. H. (1983b). The organizational structure of the *Toronto Native Times (1968-1981). Anthropologica, 25*(1), 37-52.

Riggins, S. H. (1990). News as texts and actions. *Semiotica, 78*(3/4), 359-374.

Roth, L., & Valaskakis, G. G. (1989). Aboriginal broadcasting in Canada: A case study in democratization. In M. Raboy & P. A. Bruck (Eds.), *Communication for and against democracy* (pp. 221-234). Montreal: Black Rose Books.

Rupert, R. (1982). Native communications in Canada (Report to the Interdepartmental Committee on Native Communications). Ottawa: Secretary of State, Native Citizens Directorate.

Schudson, M. (1978). *Discovering the news: A social history of American newspapers.* New York: Basic Books.

Search for toxic chemical begins. (1988, August). *Wawatay News,* p. 9.

Sperling, S. (1988). *Animal liberators: Research and morality.* Berkeley: University of California Press.

Spring hunt rules announced. (1988, May 3). *Wawatay News.*

Stewart, H. (1977). *Indian fishing: Early methods on the Northwest Coast.* Seattle: University of Washington Press.

Tanner, A. (1979). *Bringing home animals: Religious ideology and mode of production of the Mistassini Cree hunters.* New York: St. Martin's Press.

Trapline tips. (1988, December 5). *Wawatay News,* p. 1.

Trapper Jack tells tales about hunting. (1988, September 16). *Windspeaker,* p. 9.

Trapping books published. (1988, April). *Wawatay News,* p. 16.

Trapping methods easier, but wildlife getting scarcer. (1988, September 16). *Windspeaker.*

Trout Lake elder prefers old methods of trapping. (1988, January). *Wawatay News,* p. 7.

Tuchman, G. (1978). *Making news: A study in the construction of reality.* New York: Free Press.

Tyler, E. B. (1871). *Primitive culture.* London: J. Murray.

Uranium mine is planned near Thelon. (1988, March 4). *Native Press,* p. 1.

Valaskakis, G., & Wilson, T. (1985). *The Inuit Broadcasting Corporation: A survey of viewing behavior and audience preference among the Inuit of seven communities in the Baffin and Keewatin regions of the Northwest Territories.* Montreal: Concordia University.

Van Dijk, T. (1988a). *News as discourse.* Hillsdale, NJ: Lawrence Erlbaum.

Van Dijk, T. (1988b). *News analysis: Case studies of international and national news in the press.* Hillsdale, NJ: Lawrence Erlbaum.

Vecsey, C. (1980). American Indian environmental religions. In C. Vecsey & R. Venable (Eds.). *American Indian environments: Ecological issues in native American history* (pp. 1-37). Syracuse, NY: Syracuse University Press.

Wawatay Native Communications Society. (1988, March). Public statement on the media role of Wawatay Native Communications Society in northern Ontario. *Wawatay News,* p. 4.

Wenzel, G. (1991). *Animal rights, human rights: Ecology, economy and ideology in the Canadian Arctic.* Toronto: University of Toronto Press.

Zubrzycki, J. (1958). The role of the foreign language press in immigrant integration. *Population Studies, 12,* 73-82.

6

A Radio for the Mapuches of Chile: From Popular Education to Political Awareness

RAYMOND COLLE

The only private institution in Chile that uses radio for both educational and entertainment purposes is the Foundation for Rural Development Through School Radio (FREDER is the Spanish acronym for Fundación RadioEscuelas para el Desarrollo Rural). Created in 1967, FREDER has devoted its activities to the peasants in the south of the country and especially to the most disadvantaged who are part of a marginalized ethnic population, the Mapuche Indians. The term *Mapuche* refers to all of the indigenous populations south of Santiago. Today, the Huilliche groups in the 10th administrative district of Chile, where FREDER is located, still consider themselves to be Mapuches.

The social impact of FREDER comes from an interesting combination of three complementary forms of communication: radio broadcasting; written communication as a means of reinforcing broadcasts, especially the foundation's educational courses; and direct oral communication through educators and monitors who visit or reside in peasant communities. Because all of these forms of communication are related to the same goal, it is not possible to discuss radio broadcasting in isolation from the direct personal interaction sponsored by the foundation. Its radio station, called the "Voice of the Coast," presently broadcasts 17 hours per day and remains the main link between the foundation and the public.

A common way of establishing minority media is through an affiliation with a stable, well-financed organization. For North and South American natives this is likely to be a *friendship center,* a regional

EDITORS' NOTE: English Translation by Stephen Harold Riggins and Paul Bouissac.

native association, a labor union, or a church. Such organizational sponsors may be the actual source of money for the media or an agency redirecting funds from other sources. In either case, the sponsor may exert considerable influence on editorial policy and hiring. Because I was employed as a technical adviser for FREDER during its early years and remain sympathetic to its aims, this chapter should be read as an idealistic presentation of the goals of an organizational sponsor of ethnic media. There are an exceptional number of radio stations in South America that have taken social activist positions. Several are affiliated with the Catholic church and broadcast part-time in native languages. Indeed, O'Connor (1990a) writes: "the experiences of *radio popular* over the last three decades have put Latin America in the leading position for community radio. Nowhere else in the world are there so many examples of alternative uses of radio broadcasting" (p. 81). Even though I shall describe an organizational structure and religious/educational philosophy that many South American stations share, they nonetheless have very different histories. This chapter is a case study of only one station. Comparative case studies can be found in O'Connor (1990a, 1990b) and Tealdo (1989).

The Social Situation of the Mapuches

The 10th administrative district of Chile covers a total area of 68,247 km^2. The district includes four continental provinces (Valdivia, Osorno, Llanquihue, and Palena) and the first of the islands of the archipelago which extends to the Strait of Magellan (the province of Chiloé). The 10th district is divided geographically from west to east into three segments: the coastal chain of mountains along the Pacific Ocean, the altitude of which varies between 300 and 600 m; the central valley; and the Andes. In the province of Chiloé the mountains extend under the sea and create an area of islands, bays, straits, and fjords. Throughout the whole area the general climate is temperate and rainy. Natural resources include soils that are appropriate for cattle raising and silviculture on the foothills of the Andes. The central valley produces annual crops such as wheat, barley, sugar beets, and oats, as well as prime-quality cattle. Near the coast the soils are also good for cattle raising and silviculture, but for historical reasons they are used for subsistence agriculture in a way that exhausts the soil (Velasco et al., 1975).

In 1536 when the Spanish arrived in Chile they found a wide and fertile valley south of the Atacama Desert, running north and south between two mountain ranges, which was already inhabited. This area had been inhabited for at least 12,000 years, following migrations from North America:

A tribe of people lived between the Aconcagua River [slightly north of Santiago] and the Gulf of Reloncavi [where the southern archipelago begins] which was divided into several lineages. They called themselves "Mapuches" or "people of the earth." Spread over a rather large territory, they were characterized by differences due, for the most part, to their adaptation to different environmental conditions. These differences were observed primarily in their agricultural systems, the forms and dimension of their huts, their arms and their clothes. For this reason, three groups are distinguished: the Picunches, who lived between the Aconcagua and Itata rivers; the Araucans between the Itata and Tolten rivers; and the Huilliches south of the Tolten River. (Galdames & Silva, 1984, Vol. 1, p. 39)

The natives of the central valleys (Picunches) posed almost no resistance to the first Spaniards. However, Gomez de Alvarado, sent to survey the southern part of the country, encountered resistance at Reinoguelen near the Maule River (270 km south of Santiago). Alvardo returned to join Almagro and the two left the country they called Chile. In 1540 Pedro de Valdivia undertook the final conquest of the territory. This time he met strong resistance but succeeded nonetheless in establishing a settlement, founding Santiago in 1541, and conquering the rest of the country as far as the Maule River. Farther south, the country was explored by sea and several ports were established, but it was not until 1550 that it was possible to conquer the territory as far as the Bio-Bio River, after having made an alliance with the natives of the central zone.

This new frontier was more difficult to conquer. The Mapuche Indians were concentrated in a region, called Arauco by the Spanish, that extended from the Bio-Bio River to Cautin, which is 500 to 670 km south of Santiago. They were the most belligerent Araucans, and they fiercely opposed the invaders for a century. "From the battle of Reinoguelen in 1536 until the middle of the 17th century, about 30,000 Spaniards, more than 60,000 auxiliary Indian troops, and about 200,000 Mapuches died in Arauco. Chile was soon called the 'Indian Flanders,' and a Spanish governor declared that 'the war of Arauco cost more than the whole conquest of America' " (Encina & Castedo, 1985, p. 78).

The inhabitants of the region south of Arauco, who were of Huilliche ancestry, appeared to be less belligerent. This characteristic permitted the early foundation of cities such as Valdivia and Osorno. Osorno was founded in 1553 but was later destroyed by the Indians of the region who united with the Araucans. The Spanish and Araucans concluded a treaty in 1641 according to which the Bio-Bio River was made the frontier. This was not, however, the end of the fighting. More revolts took place later, but after 1700 the relations became increasing peaceful.

Until independence in 1818, there was practically no Spanish or Creole population, except in the forts and military garrisons, such as Valdivia, Villarica, and Osorno, which was destroyed and rebuilt several times. Mixed marriages occurred essentially in the peaceful region north of the Bio-Bio River. In the south, intermarriage was less frequent and tended to be of a different kind; Spanish women were abducted by the Araucans and taken as wives (Encina & Castedo, 1985). Until 1826, the cities south of the Bio-Bio River remained in the power of the Spanish; the surrounding territory was not occupied. It was only after this date that the Spanish presence ended and the definitive occupation of the liberated territories began.

The German crisis of 1848 produced the first German migration: in 1850, a total of 397 colonies of settlers were established, mainly at Valdivia. As the flow continued, it was necessary to find new land. Vicente Pérez Rosales was charged with opening a new section of the country. He went to the rapids that separated the continent and the island of Chiloé, disembarked on the continental side, and burned an enormous stretch of uninhabited and impenetrable forest (Encina & Castedo, 1985). Thus the settlement of the province of Llanquihue began with settlers moving from the south to the north. It was only after 1880 that the flow of Creoles coming by land from the north, with military support, reached the flow of migrants coming from the south and finally assured the occupation of all the Mapuche territories as well as the political unity of the country (Galdames & Silva, 1984). Thus the 10th administrative district is inhabited today by two ethnic groups: (a) people of almost pure native ancestry (the Mapuches-Huilliches), the descendants of the natives and the Spanish (Creoles), and the Metis (from the central region) and (b) people of German ancestry who have maintained a European culture. The latter form the majority in the cities and own several large rural properties, whereas the Mapuches form a majority in the small rural communities.

The Mapuches lived in small communities equivalent to extended families, a unit headed by a *lonko,* or elder, who was the head of the family lineage. Related lineages constituted a wider community that owned an established territory. Their chief (the *cacique*) was elected by the community. His role was limited to presiding over ceremonies and rendering justice. The Mapuches met occasionally in large assembles but only to declare war, in which case they elected a supreme chief (the *toqui*) whose authority lasted only until the end of the conflict. Their means of survival were mainly agricultural activities done entirely by the women. Men were involved in hunting or occasionally in warfare. Because their farming techniques rapidly exhausted the soil, they had to move frequently, and thus the population was dispersed over a rather large area. They believed in a single supreme god, Pillan, who controlled nature and in other secondary divinities who were forces of good and evil and in life after death, all concepts that are very close to Christianity (Galdames & Silva, 1984).

With the exception of some large agricultural properties in the central valley, the socioeconomic situation of the Mapuches in the 20th century has generally been desperate. In many cases the ownership of land has been transferred to the government as a result of the failure to pay taxes, and the indigenous population has kept only the right to farm the land. In other cases there were peace treaties with land concessions, but either the Mapuches do not have the official documents or the validity of these documents is questioned by the current government authorities. Because the territories were by tradition communally and not individually owned, property titles compatible with modern legal practices do not exist. As a result, the area that was legally owned and traditionally occupied has been constantly reduced. This is a phenomenon called *minifundio* ("reduced territory"). Today the size of the territory is less than the minimum necessary for subsistence farming, unless intensive techniques or cooperative systems are used. Because the law now demands property titles as a prerequisite for using the land, as well as for transporting and marketing the produce, agricultural work has become increasingly difficult for natives, if at all possible.

Twenty years ago most adults were illiterate; children attended only primary schools if they were located close to their homes, but they rarely attended beyond the second year. Poor nutrition, alcoholism, delinquency, prostitution, suicide, and drug addiction had become a natural part of the life of the Mapuches. Women were maintained in an inferior position, were less prepared for specialized work, and were personally repressed. This is the situation that FREDER found when it started its activities in a climate of passivity and despair, which was common among almost all the indigenous communities of the Andes from Colombia to the Tierra del Fuego.

The Foundation and Its Goals

FREDER is a nonprofit, private foundation that was incorporated in December 1966 and became operational in 1967. Created by Dutch Capuchin missionaries who arrived in Chile in the early 1960s, its goal is to "manage a radio school dedicated to the religious, cultural and social development of the peasant population" (FREDER, 1978). Although local development is a central preoccupation of FREDER, it does not restrict its activities purely to economic development, but instead advocates a broader religious framework within which individuals are seen as conscious actors ultimately responsible for their own development. The whole project is of a theological nature; individuals are expected to participate in a mood of solidarity as images of God desiring a better world for everyone.

The decision to create a radio station was made because of the neglect, illiteracy, lack of roads, infant mortality, and other problems of the population living on the coast of Osorno. The radio was called the Voice of the Coast to identify with the most needy peasants that inhabit the area. After a period of research and planning, its broadcasting and other services started on August 10, 1968. The people who were hired for this association, including some teachers specializing in adult education, actively participated in the preliminary phase. Having a power of 1 kW, the station covered approximately 150 km. Within this territory and under the direction of the association, radio schools were created in which teams of supervisors and students were directed from a distance by the teachers. The organization included a public relations department, a training center for the supervisors, and a printing press for the publication of pedagogical material.

From the outset the foundation fostered collaboration with other Christian denominations and with institutions representing or serving the needy population in the district. The financing of the foundation comes mainly from European and North American foundations for international cooperation and development. The general objectives of FREDER were defined as follows: (a) to contribute to the integral development of the rural population, (b) to contribute to the efficient use of the mass media in educating adult peasants, (c) to help coordinate all the various efforts directed toward rural development, (d) to help plan and implement pastoral programs. Such objectives imply the creation and promotion of programs that raise the level of literacy; advance the level of vocational training to enable peasants to understand and use agricultural resources better; develop craft activities and other forms of production; ameliorate the general quality of life in the areas of health, hygiene, nutrition, and lodging; reinforce and revitalize local organizations; work toward the improvement of leisure, the preservation of ethnic culture, and the general characteristics of the region; improve business conditions, credit, and technical assistance for the peasants; foster a critical consciousness among the population and an active participation in the life of the region and the country; and inspire developmental planning at all levels in a way that takes into consideration the cultural features, interests, needs and potential of the region.

FREDER is inspired by two main sources of ideas: first and foremost, by the doctrines of the Catholic church and on a technical level by the complementary philosophy and pedagogical methods developed by Brazilian Paulo Freire in the 1960s.[1] Thus FREDER is committed to a system of values that emphasizes the human individual as being understood as an active and responsible subject, created in the image of God, and therefore, worthy of the respect of the Creator. As stated by the 34th assembly of bishops in Pueblo, Mexico: "the ultimate aim of this doctrine of the church is always the promotion and integral liberation of the human person in its earthly and transcendental dimension" (Conferencia general del episcopado latinoamericano, 1979). Liberation must start here and now and must strive for the construction of a better world, first on earth and then in the final kingdom.

This construction is viewed as progressing through the development of three sets of values: a stable family, peace, and justice. These values must emerge and be expressed in each society, taking into account the existing sociocultural context, to nurture humane qualities. *Culture* is not understood here as simply an accumulation of knowledge of technical achievements; its central core is the system of values that arise out of communal life and are projected into the social structures. This is why it may be necessary to change unjust structures so that they become better able to express true respect for all human beings through respect for human rights. Essentially, the presence of these values is measured by the degree of social participation of all people in the decisions that affect society at its various levels. All people have the right to create their own destiny. Various degrees and rhythms of participation may exist, but everyone should participate in one way or another. This is a right that cannot be denied any group and that includes the right to education, free opinion, the election of politicians, and the creation and repeal of laws.

Education is for FREDER the main means by which humanity extends its rights and actively participates in the integral development of society. Education is an activity that arises out of the very nature of humanity. On this point the concepts of the Catholic church concur with the philosophy that is the basis of Freire's methodology. In Freire's (1969) own words (which are paraphrased in Conferencia, 1979): "no one educates anyone and no one educates himself alone: humans educate each other through the mediation of the world" (p. 14). In other words, all possibilities of manipulating students are rejected; the problems of knowledge find their solution in a social relationship that avoids abstract discussions that do not correspond to the perception students have of their world. The result of this concept is an active method in which the educator is a guide, not someone who has an answer for every question. This approach is based on the assumption that students know much more than they realize and that it is possible to help students to formulate, express, organize, and develop what they already know.

A community can find a solution to problems that no individual in isolation is able to solve. FREDER believes that the self-development of communities can only be a result of local autonomy because this facilitates the development of a critical consciousness and the appreciation of personal abilities and knowledge. Autonomy frees the creative capacity for administering community resources, making it possible to discover appropriate solutions for the problems that are encountered. Thus human beings should seek development through a participatory framework connected with the interests and aspirations of the community to which they belong. This will enable them to insert themselves in a process of communication that facilitates the sharing of the results of educational activities.

Organization and Structure of FREDER

FREDER has now become a well-known institution in the 10th district, mainly because of its radio. But when it started its activities, it could not even count on the radio for publicity because very few peasants had receivers. Its early success depended almost entirely on its promotion department. It was far more difficult 20 years ago to make the initial contact with people and to organize a first meeting. Moreover, less emphasis was put on the process of local organization. The stages of making contacts and negotiating cooperation were, however, practically the same in the 1960s as they are in the 1990s. The promoter or coordinator of a small subregional area makes contact with the members of the community and invites them to a meeting through written invitations that are sent to everybody and through verbal invitations. The radio also publicizes the scheduled project in its information programs. During the first meeting, the purpose of which is to motivate the participants, the promoter explains the aims of FREDER and what it offers, underlining the subject matters that it can teach and the needs of the community that it could help to solve through technical assistance. If the community shows interest in one of these aspects, a verbal agreement is reached between the community and the representatives of FREDER.

Once an agreement has been made the community must elect a representative who had the title *monitor* in the early years and is now called the *coordinador local*. This person directs future activities in permanent contact with his or her neighbors and with the coordinator of FREDER. The local coordinator is then invited to a 2- or 3-day seminar at the training center of FREDER, which is located in the countryside a few kilometers from the city of Osorno. Through the mutual exchange of information, these seminars provide an opportunity for establishing a precise profile of each community that is represented. The goals and activities of FREDER are again explained to the participants and the various programs available are reviewed and related to the needs that have been identified. The coordinator also learns the basic methods for community work.

Once the local coordinator has returned home, he or she invites community members to at least four meetings to establish firmly the basis for a community center. The local coordinator must explain the various roles that the members play before the community center forms its own executive committee and devises a working plan. This plan is limited at first to the identification of some of the urgent measures such as the construction of roads, the teaching of techniques for pruning fruit trees, and the building of enclosures for cattle. (During the first years, literacy courses were started immediately, without including this preliminary stage.) Once specific activities have been selected, they are publicized through the radio, which also broadcasts programs relevant to these tasks. FREDER sends brochures and manuals and initiates a cycle of regular visits by its coordinators and educators. The local coordinator is invited to participate regularly in new seminars both in general education and in practical training. Other members of the local community center also have the chance to participate in these seminars.

To achieve its goals, FREDER employs about 30 people, comprising the following administrative units: management, promotion and training, the Voice of the Coast radio station, administrative secretary, accounting, legal and social assistance, and documentation. The department of promotion and training is mainly composed of middle-level professional technicians assisted by a minimal number of employees with university training. Curricula and pedagogical methods are usually formulated in cooperation with other institutions, which makes FRE-DER dependent on external support. At first it was often necessary to rely on institutions in Santiago, but later it became possible to reduce this dependence and to rely more on regional cooperation without lowering the quality of the programs.

Historic Development of FREDER: 1966-1972

The history of FREDER can be divided into three main stages in which the educational priorities and procedures were significantly modified. The earliest period (1966-1972) is marked by the influence of the first radio schools in Latin America: the model of Radio Sutatenza created in Colombia in 1948 by Father Salcedo. However, in our case the methodology of Paulo Freire was followed as far as pedagogy was concerned. FREDER considered that the peasants needed a basic formal education, and for this reason, it created a curriculum that included much of the state primary education program for adults. Thus the programs of FREDER were officially integrated into the Chilean system of education and benefited from the participation of specialized teachers paid by the state.

The most important achievement of this stage was the training of monitors and the promotion of "schools," which were essentially reception centers: Groups of peasants wishing to learn elected a monitor and were given a radio receiver so that they could listen to the classes. A total of 3,000 receivers were distributed. In the beginning only restricted receivers were given, which could not be turned to any frequencies other than those of FREDER. The monitor was trained to serve as a guide—the eyes and hands of the absent teacher—even though his or her level of literacy was hardly superior to the other members of the group. The radio told the guide what to do, for instance, distribute the textbooks, write on the blackboard, and collect the exercises. The monitor also provided a means of feedback, thanks to periodic meetings organized by the training center of FREDER and the field visits made by the teachers. Parallel to this, every day the Voice of the Coast broadcast 6 hours of radio school, 2 hours of programs devoted to the development of local organizations, and 8 hours of programs concerned with family issues, religion, youth, music, and local and international news.

Due to the isolation of the area the personal message service of the station became a great success and was transformed into an important means of publicity for the radio. It amounted to a sort of oral telegraph not unlike the BBC's broadcasts for the resistance movement in Europe during World War II. It allowed personal information or information relevant to small groups to circulate from the city to the countryside, a phenomenon of great importance for those who had no other means of rapid communication. These messages were transmitted three to four times a day at set times and attracted the station's largest audiences.

About 1972 it became obvious that the monitors' role of puppet, which did not allow for any initiative on their part, was inadequate and that it would be better for them to receive a higher level of training so that they could more effectively contribute to the educational process. FREDER also found that the curriculum it offered was not as attractive as it could have been and reoriented it more to the real needs of the target population. Another reason for restructuring the program was that it became clear that the teachers assigned to the radio schools by the Ministry of Education were taking advantage of their position to voice their political inclinations and attempted to use the broadcasts to advocate socialism or Marxism. In so doing they betrayed the Christian and apolitical objectives of FREDER and jeopardized its survival.

"Radio Vision": 1973-1981

During the period from 1973 to 1981, the focus became occupational training. The content of the programs dealt with agricultural production, health care, craft development, and so on. At the same time that FREDER's elementary courses were broadcast on the radio, they were supplemented by printed material and series of slides presented by monitors in the community centers. Hence, the name *radio vision*. The main objectives were then related to the economic development of the family. This was particularly difficult because of the economic and agricultural policies of the military government that came to power in 1973. Government programs in support of the poorer segment of the peasant population were reduced or canceled, credit became more expensive, and powerful companies monopolized the market for agricultural produce at the expense of small producers who were left defenseless.

To have a better chance of success in meeting these challenges, FREDER sought the technical assistance of universities and specialized international institutions. It secured the collaboration of UNESCO, the Austral University of Valdivia, the University of Chile (Santiago), the Center for Research and Development of Education (CIDE), and the *Centro de Perfeccionamiento del Magisterio*. The new project that was implemented involved a multidisciplinary study of the rural conditions of the province of Osorno and the creation of an appropriate curriculum as well as the training of FREDER's personnel in educational research and communication.

A regional study enabled FREDER to assess better the shortcomings of the state educational system in terms of the local population. With the help of specialists from Austral University, FREDER produced a new curriculum that was experimentally applied to all 8 years of primary education in two area schools. These experiments involved the participation of agricultural scientists, ecologists, and specialists in forestry, in addition to educators. The young students were expected to receive, as a supplement to the general education appropriate to this level, a professional training equivalent to the title of forester or wood technician or in other specialties useful for rural development. This initiative received the support of regional authorities from the Ministry of Education and was recognized by the state, but was not directly managed by FREDER.

Training courses for adults through radio vision were also developed. Each course lasted one week and was repeated several times, because there were not enough sets of slides to be simultaneously available to all the communities concerned. The broadcast lectures that accompanied these training courses were directed by two monitors in each listening center and lasted half an hour. When the radio lecture ended, the monitors spent a full hour in discussion with the group, answering questions and reinforcing technical training. Every day, 7 hours were devoted to practical work under the supervision of the monitors. This is why these courses were considered intensive and were so brief. The most frequent themes were the pruning of trees, grafting, vegetable growing and rabbit raising. Courses for women followed a similar method, but without radio broadcasts and lasted only a few hours a day. They dealt with weaving and the making of clothes.

To address family problems FREDER secured the support of the Research and Development Center in Education in Santiago and created a program called "fathers and sons" the aim of which was to facilitate reflection about children and family relationships. It attempted to develop the educational capacity of the family for both the children and adults of rural and urban communities. In addition to a special radio broadcast, educators created and distributed printed brochures specifically aimed at the population of the region. Here, too, the method was interactive and participatory and included discussions after the group had listened to the radio program. This program was received with enthusiasm and was repeated for several years.

Another program dealt with health problems and was directed principally to volunteers who were to serve as diffusion agents in their respective communities. It consisted of four stages: (a) the self-instruction of the volunteers through the study of 30 printed lessons that had been prepared by FREDER, (b) ninety 45-minute radio programs broadcast at various times as a complement to the self-instruction, (c) regional meetings for the evaluation and reinforcement of the self-instruction, and (d) community meetings directed by the coordinators and supported by posters.

FREDER also created a training program for prospective union members, because courses given by other organizations were directed exclusively toward the training of leaders. It was thus necessary to create new booklets for the rank-and-file union members because the leaders did not have any literature of this sort and were not pedagogically prepared to instruct their members. Representatives of several unions collaborated in writing the material. Here, too, the pedagogical methods of Freire were applied. The material developed the members' motivation through a critical analysis of the social conditions of their communities.

Finally, in its capacity as a Catholic foundation FREDER sponsored a special program of catechism. It was organized in cooperation with the diocese office of catechism and supplemented the religious instruction in the rural schools of the region through radio theater and printed booklets.

Preserving the Mapuche Culture and
Community: Activities Since 1982

In 1981 the idea of scheduling events aimed at preserving the Mapuche language (*tse su 'ngun*) and culture was suggested up by the Mapuches themselves. They were by then seriously threatened with extinction; their language was gradually disappearing. At the end of 1982 they formed a working group called *Monku Kusobkien*, and FREDER supported and incorporated it in its regular activities. Thus the promotion of the Mapuche cultural centers started. The means used for this purpose were visiting rural communities, promoting traditional organizations and institutions (*lonkos* and *caciques*) as well as stimulating folk activities, particularly among the young. They expressed their goal in this manner: "to rediscover the language of the Mapuche people, to maintain their cultural and ecological identity as a nation different from Chilean society with deep historic roots, and to modernize the language in view of the present technological era" (*Monku Newsletter,* p. 1). Such a project includes the intention of enriching the vocabulary with newly coined words so that the language can maintain its currency in today's world. It also includes a research project designed to collect linguistic forms in the field that are still in use. The first course in *tse su 'ngun* took place in 1984 and had 300 registrants.

To assist these activities the Voice of the Coast launched a program called *Our Roots,* which was prepared exclusively by native collaborators. This program very quickly attracted a large audience. The aim of the program was described in this manner:

> Our objective is to broadcast the different aspects of the life of the Mapuche people (culture, language, history, music and organization) in order to break the ostracism from Chilean society which they have submitted to for a century and to regain the right of existence as an ethnic group.
> Claiming to be superior, Chilean society has a tendency to eradicate ethnic minorities from its territory by imposing the reproduction and the diffusion of its own model of civilization through the mass media and the schools. At the same time it disqualifies the culture of other ethnic groups and denies them any possibility of communicating their ideas. One of the objectives of the Mapuche program is to oppose this project of ethnocide. (Cagnulef, 1987)

The cultural activities of the Mapuches were also strengthened by a program for the development of folklore, which had been created at the same time as the foundation and which consisted of organizing every December a regional folklore festival attracting about 10,000 participants. Even in its earliest years FREDER took into account the traditional organization of the indigenous communities that were still in existence, but only in recent years has the foundation decided to give absolute priority to activities destined to revive them.

As a result of 20 years of encouraging community organization, many communities that were no longer electing traditional authorities revived this custom. In 1983 two great institutions came into existence: a *junta de caciques* and a regional council formed by all the communities' chiefs. That year the communities' chiefs celebrated a parliament of peace. A total of 14 *caciques* gathered to represent 137 communities in order to oppose expulsions and expropriations. They wrote a petition, which was presented by a delegation in 1984 to the central government. But as of January 1989 no response had been made. The only option left was to protest during the public sales of community lands and the result was that some potential buyers were scared away by their fear of a trial at a later date. They could also denounce injustices through the opposition parties. FREDER did create a legal department that has been able to prevent numerous expulsions and to legalize many ownership titles. It has also had many opportunities to request habeas corpus in defense of human rights. In 1983 a group of specialists completed an historic study of the landownership problems of the Mapuches. This study was directed by lawyer Eduardo Castillo, who presented the findings to the Human Rights Commission of Santiago, FREDER and the *junta de caciques*. It was decided to reformulate the report and to publish it in the future, if funds are available.

In all the territory covered by its radio station, FREDER has started to organize a network of *comunicadores populares*. These volunteers regularly attend training seminars in which they are taught how to organize community meetings and how to produce alternative forms of communication. According to the possibilities within their community this may simply be a mimeographed paper with a small circulation or it could be what is called *wall journalism*. In the latter case an advertising panel is placed at a spot, such as a community center or a church, that many people pass. Information considered important by the local community is placed on the panel: press clips, texts written by typewriter, or even very legible manuscripts chosen or prepared by the *comunicador popular*. These people are also taught how to write press releases for the mass media and to analyze critically the news that they receive from them. They also create and record sociodramas, which are sometimes broadcast by the Voice of the Coast or sent to other communities on cassettes. In 1987 the objective was to train 120 *comunicadores populares*; however, the goal was not attained. FREDER admits that it was useless to form *comunicadores populares* in an isolated manner. The idea has not been abandoned and has been continually discussed in meetings. There is, nonetheless, a crisis in the network of communication, and FREDER is now rethinking its strategy. The Association of Volunteer Peasant Educators was formally constituted in 1980 and this is also in a state of crisis. The association was supposed to include the previous monitors and the current local coordinators or other leaders trained by FREDER or by private agrarian organizations. The association directly participated in the planning of the foundation's activities. This ensured that feedback was more complete and more efficient as it reached the very level at which decisions were made. Many of these volunteers have now either left their community or this type of activity.

The deterioration of urban conditions prompted FREDER to launch activities involving socioeconomic assistance for the urban population: a social assistance office provides direct consultation regarding health, law, social security, and family problems. Matters of general interest are also addressed through the radio. FREDER has helped create an association for unemployed persons and supports some essential services: soup kitchens, medical and dental consultations, and courses for women in making clothes. Moreover, the social assistance office participated in the creation of a local committee for the defense of human rights, an association of epileptics, an association for parents of children with cleft palates, and several centers for youth recreation. It must not be forgotten that many of the organizations that are today independent were originally created under the aegis of FREDER.

One indication of positive changes occurring in recent years is the founding of a native political party in Chile. Although such activism was not the explicit purpose of FREDER, there is little doubt that it contributed to the social awareness that is a prerequisite for founding a political party. Following the legislation on political parties that took effect in 1987 and the results of the plebiscite of October 1988—in which General Pinochet lost the possibility of continuing his regime—the three native peoples existing in Chile (Aymaas in the north, Mapuches in the south, and Rapa-nui on Easter Island) concluded for the first time a common agreement to form a political party called the Party for the

Earth and Identity (*Partido por la Tierra y la Identidad*). The decision was taken by the leadership of 28 organizations, who met on January 2, 1989, in Santiago, and the constitution of the new party was announced to the press by the Mapuche leaders on February 5 of that year. The legalization of the party was to be the culmination of the desire of the ethnic Chilean minorities to attain a type of social development compatible with their cultures. Aspiring to be represented in the future parliament, they hoped to have their existence and languages officially recognized and to obtain a bilingual and bicultural education for their children.

The declaration of principles that the new party was legally required to publish contained ideas capable of enriching the local political spectrum: "Our historical compromise is with mother nature, the relation humanity-earth-heaven that has always been our inspiration and the support of the native world view." The reason why the members of the party felt responsible for the mission of protecting the harmony and equilibrium of the natural environment, which is threatened by technological progress, is that "there is a cosmic order that affects all life. The party proposes a vision of economic development in which humanity, society and technology are at the service of the natural order." This is a call to the defense of the environment based on a millenarian philosophy. As Carrasco (1989) indicated in an editorial in the newspaper: "What is notable is that the native world raises this metaphysical banner precisely at the moment of serious poverty and when the most reasonable choice would seem to be for them to concentrate on immediate demands. This is a tremendous lesson for the long-range politics of today!" (p. 7).

The Political Persecution of FREDER

The history of FREDER is complex, loaded with emotion and marked by a succession of positive and negative events. In the words of its executive director, "FREDER has lived, survived, and overcome the storms of two democratic governments and one dictatorship (the presidencies of Frei, Allende, and Pinochet)" (FREDER, 1978). Indeed, the foundation has experienced a long series of dramatic events which few organizations share: occupation, violent attacks, arson, arrests, and constant threats. However, it has never given up its responsibilities to the rural and urban poor.

There is a clear distinction between the people who support its work and those who criticize and fight it. The former are the people who come by the hundreds to visit the studios of the station, listen to its broadcasts, and finance its activities or the reconstruction of bombed buildings, participate in the folklore festivals, and form community groups. The latter are those who hurt the foundation by spreading false rumors among the press, take it to court under unsubstantiated pretexts, destroy its premises and antennas, shoot at the personnel or have them arrested, impose fines or administrative penalties, make threats and spy on its activities.

The hesitation and suspicion of some local and regional administrators have delayed FREDER's activities and created a hostile mood among civil servants and bureaucrats. The main accusation is always political and is accompanied by pressure and threats that aim to frighten the population and to paralyze them so that they do not take advantage of the opportunities offered by the foundation for educational and social advancement. Administrative authorities (mayors and educational bureaucrats) have made public their intention of putting obstacles in the way of these projects because they are annoyed by the agitation that is caused by the revival of traditional native customs and the protests against legislation that deprives the native population of their rights.

It goes without saying that this situation is primarily typical of the years when the military regime suspected anybody taking care of the underprivileged of being Marxists. During its first 5 years the existence of FREDER was not put in jeopardy and security services never investigated it. But after 1973 there is a long list of physical violence and attacks in the press.

1977: Arson against the antenna and broadcasting equipment (cost: $25,000 US).

1983: Bombing of the antenna, bombing of the director's residence, slogans painted on the facade of the foundation's premises, a formal agreement between the regional mayors for the surveillance of its activities, arbitrary arrest of the foundation's lawyer.

1984: A campaign to frighten native leaders who resisted expropriations and forced sales of property. The newspaper *Diario Austral* falsely accused the foundation of distributing proterrorist propaganda.

1986: The provincial governor came in person to visit the station's premises to protest against its encouragement of unrest. The *Diario Austral* published a letter from a reader accusing the radio of "exciting the people as in Nicaragua or Cuba where violence is everywhere." The *Diario*

Austral published an article reporting that a *cacique* accused FREDER of causing disturbances in his community and thus undermining his authority. The headline for the article read "Struggle for the Title of Cacique Caused by Activists." In its editorial the same newspaper insisted that FREDER was responsible for creating "an underground movement in the country with the purpose of bringing back the situation to what it was more than thirteen years ago." The *Diario Austral* published an article with the headline "Authorities Reassert That There Are Agitators in the Rural Zone" and reported that the prefect of police was speaking of FREDER.

1987: An announcer for the radio was wounded by gunshot during an attack against the studio. The provincial governor came in person to visit the place of the attack but in a later declaration played down the incident.

Confronted by these attacks, the response of the peasants has always been solidarity to the extent that, for example, when the antenna was destroyed, it was rebuilt within 15 days thanks to popular support and despite the current level of poverty. The answer of the foundation has always remained the same: to persist.

Conclusion

It is difficult to measure statistically the results of FREDER's activities because the foundation does not have the personnel and resources for establishing such records. Annual reports do exist that clearly show that a large number of activities have taken place, but without any attempt to assess their cost-effectiveness. These reports generally offer few figures. Planning is formulated on the basis of experiencing how the population reacts and what they still need; it is not the result of formal research, because that tends to be perceived as a waste of time. Only on two occasions have outside investigators produced an objective evaluation. The first study was titled "The Research Project on the Use of Radio in Educational Programs for Disadvantaged Adults" and was completed in 1972 and 1973 by two private Chilean foundations providing technical support to institutions such as FREDER: the *Secretariado de Comunicacion Social* (SEDECOS) and the *Centro Latino Americano de Education de Adultos* (CLEA) (see *Secretariado de Comunicacion Social*, 1976). The second study, titled "Analysis of Systems of Radio Education" was completed in 1980-1981 by a team from the *Associacion Latinoamericana de Educacion Radiofonica* (1981). Naturally, an assessment of FREDER's achievements must take into consideration the abilities and, above all, the dedication of the institution's personnel as well as the fact that financial resources, without which FREDER could not survive, come from other countries. For these foreign foundations, the annual reports published by FREDER listing only its activities without any assessment of their cost-effectiveness are generally sufficient.

The results of the above inquiries show that in 1973, five years after the creation of the Voice of the Coast, 80% of the coastal population and more than 60% of those in the central valley knew and regularly listened to this station. In the coastal zone, where the native population is more important, the percentage of women among the audience was greater than the percentage of men. However, at that time only 4% of the native population formally attended the radio schools. The news generally attracts the most interest, but the technical programs, helpful for the working activities of the population, have been in great demand. In other words, the listeners quickly became aware of their need for information and training aimed at coping with short-term agricultural problems.

As far as the schools are concerned, 3,500 people had become literate by 1973 and 200 peasants had received their primary degree. Moreover, 250 others were trained as monitors and progressively became the communication leaders within their communities. The sense of participation, which was a high priority for FREDER, gradually became more appreciated by the peasants and was enhanced by the numerous visits made in the field by the promoters and teachers, thus facilitating the creation of community centers and other forms of association that had not existed earlier. This process revitalized the traditional institutions that were no longer perceived as important.

Until 1973 FREDER worked in collaboration with many organizations, both private (institutes of rural education, peasant confederations, etc.) and public (the Ministry of Education, Institute of Agricultural Development, Office for Agriculture and Cattle Raising, National Health Service, Corporation for Agrarian Reform, etc.). This collaboration resulted in dramatic progress as far as the socioeconomic conditions of the region were concerned. SEDECOS-CLEA's study of the various radio schools in Latin America showed that FREDER had achieved the best results in the shortest time precisely because of the collaboration, which was unique to Chile (*Secretariado de Comunicacion Social*, 1976). Unfortunately, after 1974 the suspicion and distrust on the part of local authorities were responsible for the decline and disappearance of joint efforts. As a result, FREDER continued its activities practically alone. It had to seek other partners and received understanding help from the University of Chile (which was a state institution but operating in Santiago), the Austral University (in the neighboring city of Valdivia), the regional UNESCO office, and the Education Research and Development Center (a private organization located in Santiago). These institutions were of vital importance for FREDER, because they provided the specialized technical assistance that it needed to develop its training program in recent years.

In 1975 there were 78 peasant communities involved with the activities of FREDER. According to annual reports, from 1975 to 1979 more than 20,000 people benefited from these activities: more than 6,700 participated in the training programs, and more than 5,800 in the program fathers and sons. A total of 360 participated in the women's program, and 565 in the program for community organization. During the same period 2,300 people were educated at the training center of the foundation.

Two decades of active presence in a neglected region have enabled FREDER to offer a vital educational service with the optimum creative participation of those concerned. This has furthered real progress among the native communities, which now benefit more from their natural resources, better preserve and reassert their own culture, and better communicate among themselves and with the rest of the nation, both directly and through the mass media. Education is now for the peasants of this region—both native and nonnative—something that they understand, appreciate, and desire. This is not the lesser of the results obtained by FREDER and recognized by the indigenous communities. When it was possible to teach religion to children through the radio, FREDER found that it created better motivation and mutual understanding, more sense of responsibility, more spontaneity and joy, and a closer rapport with the sacraments.

Today, FREDER regularly interacts with approximately 240,000 people, half of whom benefit directly from the community organizations, educational programs, and social services. After 20 years FREDER is neither complacent nor exhausted. It maintains its vigor and hope while acknowledging that the complete transformation of the social conditions of the underprivileged and the full development of the rural and urban communities of the 10th district of Chile is a long way ahead.

Note

1. Brazilian educator Paolo Freire developed a method for teaching literacy based on the identification of a small number of words relevant to concrete situations familiar to students. The method is meant to provoke a dialogue and to motivate illiterate students by anchoring the teaching process in their real world. For instance, in Chile the method is based on significant contradictions such as *boss/worker, leader/followers,* and so on. Photographs are made of typical situations illustrating these themes and are presented in the form of slides or posters to the students. Following Bertrand Russell's concept of *minimal vocabulary,* the whole method gravitates around locally relevant key words, which are the starting point of phonetic investigations that call on the creativity of the students. The basic idea is to acquire literacy, not as something imposed from above but as something that emerges from the students' own mental activity.

References

Associacion Latinoamericana de Educacion Radiofonica. (1981). *Análisis de sistemas educativos radiofónicos: FREDER.* Unpublished manuscript.

Cagnulef, E. (1987). *Proyecto "Mapuche Werken"* Unpublished manuscript.

Carrasco, E. (1989, February 24). [Editorial]. *La Epoca,* p. 7.

Conferencia general del episcopado latinoamericano. (1979). *Documento de Pueblo.* Santiago: San Pablo.

Encina, F., & Castedo, L. (1985). *Resumen de le historia de Chile.* Santiago: Zig-zag.

FREDER. (1968-1988). *Informes de actividades.* Osorno, Chile: Author.

FREDER. (1978). *Boletin conmemorativo X^o aniversario.* Osorno, Chile: Author.

Freire, P. (1969). *Sobre la acción cultural.* Santiago: ICIRA.

Galdames, F., & Silva, O. (1984). *Conocimientos específicos de historia y geografia de Chile.* Santiago: Tercera de la Hora.

O'Connor, A. (1990a). Between culture and organization: The radio studios of Cotopaxi, Ecuador. *Gazette, 46,* 81-91.

O'Connor, A. (1990b). The miners' radio stations in Bolivia: A culture of resistance. *Journal of Communication, 40*(1), 102-110.

Secretariado de Comunicacion Social. (1976). *Efectos sociales de la educacion radiofonica en sectores populares de América Latina.* Santiago: Author.

Tealdo, A. R. (Ed.). (1989). *Radio y democracia en América Latin.* Lima, Peru: IPAL.

Velasco, N., et al. (1975). *Geochile, primera enciclopedia de la regionalización.* Santiago: Lord Cochrane.

7

Flaws in the Melting Pot: Hawaiian Media

JOHN HENNINGHAM

In Hawaii every ethnic group is a minority, and in the past all have had their own forms of mass media. For much of the 19th century and into the early 20th century, Hawaii boasted a remarkable plurality of vigorous ethnic-language media. But the 20th century has seen a withering of most minority media in the state, as the dominant culture has strengthened in power and influence.

The first newspapers in Hawaii were produced in the Hawaiian language, and newspapers in that language in the late 19th century became widespread and potent political instruments. Today, however, Hawaiian journalism is barely visible. This is despite the signs, as the 20th century draws to its close, of a reawakening of minority ethnic consciousness, including a realization of the value of ethnic media as a support for minority culture. This chapter will concentrate on the media produced by or for Hawaii's indigenous people, providing both an historical sketch and an overview of the contemporary situation.

Historical Background

Hawaii was colonized by stealth. For more than a century after Captain James Cook happened on the islands in 1778, their Polynesian population enjoyed an internationally recognized sovereignty over their own land: In fact it is significant that Cook and his successors failed to lay claim to the islands for the British crown, as they had done elsewhere in the Pacific. Hawaii was, however, too valuable and too vulnerable to be left an independent kingdom for long. In particular, American business and military interests found Hawaii to be a plum ripe for the plucking—and connived to have it annexed by the United States by 1898.

The plantation interests of white settlers also eventually resulted in the establishment of a multiethnic population, with the employment of cheap imported labor from Asia—in particular China, Japan, and the Philippines—as well as from Portugal and Puerto Rico. The major ethnic groupings in contemporary Hawaiian society are Caucasian (23.4%), Japanese (23%), Hawaiian or part-Hawaiian (20%), Filipino (11.3%), Chinese (4.8%), African-American (2.3%), and Korean (1.3%).

The first media development in Hawaii was at the hands of the well-meaning if culturally insensitive Congregational missionaries from New England who became the islands' first permanent white settlers. Newspapers produced in the mission schools beginning in 1834 were designed more for education than journalism, but one of their spinoffs was the training of a whole generation of mission-educated young men in the printing technology.

In the 1860s the first independent Hawaiian-language newspapers appeared. The first, *Ka Hoku o ka Pakipika* (*The Star of the Pacific*), expressed the concerns of educated Hawaiians about the submergence of their culture by the increasing flood of foreigners. Editors, including David Kalakaua, later to become king of Hawaii, sounded the first warnings of the threat to the Hawaiian language posed by the spread of English (Mookini, 1974). Dozens of titles, mostly ephemeral, were to appear in the next three decades. They tended to be highly political, representing the views of different factions in the struggles to maintain Hawaiian control over their nation.

Especially in the last quarter of the 19th century, as absorption by the United States loomed more and more as a threat, the Hawaiian-language newspapers were marked by a strong political role. Also reflected in the Hawaiian press were the factional issues that plagued royal court circles. The key figures in the strongly pro-Hawaiian journalism of this era were generally sympathetic Caucasians or missionary-trained part-Hawaiians.

An early foreboding about annexation was expressed by *Ke Au Okua* (a government-sponsored paper that merged with *Kuokoa* in 1873), which declared, "suspicions have entered our minds that the benefits would not be for the mass of the people but for a few" (Kuykendall, 1953, p. 226). Much stronger feelings were expressed in *Nuhou* (*News,* established in 1873), a political vehicle of controversial ex-Mormon missionary-turned-politician Walter Murray Gibson. *Nuhou* "became the public voice of the Hawaiians":

> Through his newspaper Gibson generated distrust of foreigners generally and Americans specifically, casting himself as the protector of the native Hawaiians. He denounced the haole [foreigner] as the enemy of Hawai'i and Hawaiians. (Mookini, 1976)

The newspaper had eight pages, two of which were in English, and carried the slogan "Hawai'i for Hawaiians." Among the causes vigorously fought by Gibson were the reciprocity treaty and the scheme to cede Pearl Harbor to the United States. *Nuhou* folded after a year, but Gibson had aroused sufficient support among the Hawaiian people to be elected to the legislature. He consolidated his influence in 1880 by starting another newspaper, *Ka Elele Poakolu,* as well as buying the English-language *Pacific Commercial Advertiser,* and he was appointed prime minister by King David Kalakaua.

Other significant writers to use Hawaiian-language newspapers on behalf of the Hawaiian cause were Daniel Lyons, John Bush, and Robert Wilcox. Together, Gibson and Lyons started *Ka Nupepa Elela* in 1885, which was a weekly that ran for 7 years. Bush and Wilcox emerged as influential figures following the overthrow of Gibson by haole business interests led by Lorrin Thurston. In *Ka Oiaio (The Truth)* and *Ka Leo o ka Lahui (The Voice of the Nation;* 1889-1896), Bush and Wilcox campaigned against haole domination and won seats for themselves in the legislature. Initially strong supporters of the kingdom's last monarch, Queen Liliuokalani, they eventually fell out of favor with the queen, who was ultimately overthrown by a coalition of American business interests. Although critical of the queen's administration, Wilcox and Bush saw the impending American annexation of Hawaii as the threat that they had been warning Hawaiians about for years. They were active in counterrevolutionary activity and were jailed by the new republican government. Bush was jailed for editorializing in *Ka Loa.*

The early years of the 20th century—when the Home Rule party was formed by former royalist leaders—saw the continuation of the Hawaiian-language press as a political force. Initially successful (with Wilcox representing the party as Hawaii's first territorial delegate to the U.S. Congress), the party produced two newspapers, *Kuokoa Home Rule* and *Ka Na'i Aupuni,* edited by Joseph Mokuohai Poepoe. With the demise of these papers, Poepoe accepted the editorship of *Aloha Aina* (1895-1920). Meanwhile, the Republican party regrouped to take over the local political scene, with the support of Hawaiian leaders including newspaper editors.

Republican dominance (which lasted until after World War II) meant the end of the Home Rule party and, ultimately, of the Hawaiian-language press. Only three newspapers survived to the 1920s, but the last of these (*Ka Hoku o Hawai'i*) closed in 1948. The Great Depression, followed by World War II, contributed to economic and cultural hardships that spelled the death knell of the Hawaiian press.

Johnson's (1976) translations of Hawaiian newspapers bear testimony to a growing sense of despair; the only glimmers of hope were seen in spiritual amalgamation with the United States and obeisance to the American flag. It was a sad end to an era that lasted only a little more than 80 years and that had, according to Mookini's (1974) research, spawned at least 102 Hawaiian-language titles.

Contemporary Developments

Hawaiian-language newspapers lost their purpose when the number of people speaking Hawaiian dropped to a negligible level. The decline has been particularly marked among young people: There are now only about 2,000 native speakers of Hawaiian in the islands, most of whom are aged 60 or more. It is estimated that only about 30 children under the age of 5 speak Hawaiian—almost all of these live on the tiny isolated island of Ni'ihau (Heckathorn, 1987).

Although the early waves of missionaries made a substantial contribution to the development of Hawaiian literacy through their translation and printing of religious and educational books, the establishment of an English-speaking ruling class by the mid-19th century diminished the status of the Hawaiian language and was ultimately responsible for its demise.

Hawaiians have had good reasons to look wistfully at other Polynesian island groups, many of which have been able to retain their independence as well as their language as a consequence of being located farther from North America than Hawaii is. Hawaiian linguist Larry Kimura, from the University of Hawaii, spoke of his own experience of culture shock when he encountered fluently bilingual children in the Cook Islands:

For people from Hawai'i, it was almost embarrassing to hear these little kids speak excellent British English. And they still had their own language. We Hawaiians were told we had to give up our language so that we would learn English better. We gave it up, and what did we get in return? Pidgin. (cited in Heckathorn, 1987, p. 111)

But more important than the decline in language—and obviously a root cause of it—was the gradual suppression of the Hawaiian people as a viable political and cultural force in their own land. Like many indigenous peoples, Hawaiians suffered the impact of disease and the stresses associated with colonization—including their reduction to a status similar to that of serfs. According to Young (1980):

Hawaiians began to disappear from the face of the earth. With the loss of identity, loss of prestige, and cultural confusion, the Hawaiians had no will to live and began to die at an alarming rate. Estimates are that approximately three hundred thousand Hawaiians were present in Hawaii in 1778. The number of Hawaiians was reduced to sixty thousand by 1930. Disease alone cannot account for the rapid decline. The emotional impact of the data can be felt in the Hawaiian saying *Na kanaka 'oku'u wale aku no i kau 'uhane,* "The people dismissed freely their souls and died." The Hawaiians had lost all the cultural elements that gave interest and meaning to their lives.

Yet the 1970s and 1980s witnessed a remarkable cultural renaissance among the Hawaiian people. Influenced by the civil rights movement of the 1960s and by parallel resurgences of political and cultural consciousness on the part of indigenous peoples throughout the postcolonial world, Hawaiians began to speak with pride of their achievements (Holt, 1974; Kanahele, 1982, 1986). A potent symbol of this rebirth was the construction of the canoe *Hokule'a* and its historic voyage to Tahiti in 1976, followed by numerous voyages around the Pacific. This activity emphasized the extraordinary achievements of the Polynesian adventurers of the past who peopled the Pacific islands and performed amazing feats of long-distance navigation hundreds of years before Europeans began their voyages of discovery.

Organizations such as *Alu Like* ("Working Together," which describes itself as a "private, non-profit community based advocate for Hawaiian economic and social self-sufficiency") and the Office of Hawaiian Affairs ("a constitutionally established state agency which coordinates services and programs for the Hawaiian people"), emerged to represent Hawaiian interests through social welfare, cultural activities, and to a lesser degree, the development of a political voice.

The extent to which Hawaiians as a people had been influenced by these developments was shown in the 1988 culmination of the Year of the Hawaiian, when some 50,000 people of Hawaiian ancestry gathered in the Aloha Stadium, Honolulu, for a day of celebration, known as *Ho'olohaki*. Hawaiians' success in shaking off their role as underdogs in society was illustrated by the election in 1986 of John Waihee, Hawaii's first governor of Hawaiian ancestry. Radical voices have also emerged, calling for much stronger assertion of native Hawaiian rights and for moves to limit American influence (e.g., Kent, 1983; Trask, 1984-1985, 1987).

Current Hawaiian Newspapers

The role of Hawaiians in the media continues to be minimal, and newspapers catering for Hawaiians are limited in their perspectives. Only two newspapers directed at Hawaiians are now published: *The Native Hawaiian,* by Alu Like, and *Ka Wai Ola O OHA* (*The Living Water of OHA*), by the Office of Hawaiian Affairs (OHA). Each newspaper betrays its institutional origins and dependence on state funding; neither paper goes beyond a somewhat bland editorial content, devoid of meaningful criticism or political positions. Both newspapers are in English.

Ka Wai Ola O OHA is mailed out monthly to about 35,000 households registered as electors of OHA trustees, and an additional 10,000 copies are distributed in bulk to schools, institutions, and other outlets. According to editor Ken Haina, the "main role is to keep the Hawaiian people as informed as possible about all benefits they may accrue through different kinds of federal and state legislation [as well as to] keep them appraised of what is happening in their own Hawaiian community" (personal communication, May 4, 1988).

Haina took particular pride in OHA and his newspaper's success in promoting Ho'olohaki: "Ho'olohaki at the stadium made many of them realize how proud they should be of being Hawaiian. . . . A display not seen for 120 years." He was critical of mainstream media coverage of Hawaiians: "It could be much better; I feel there's not enough. Only when we do something wrong they give us a lot of play. . . . Our newspaper's about the only voice" (personal communication, May 4, 1988).

But in addition to its supportive and welfare role, *Ka Wai Ola O OHA* is essentially a public relations organ, rather akin to a company's house magazine. It gives no coverage to controversial issues raging at the board level of OHA, such as the extent to which native Hawaiians should seek enactment of a right to sue for recovery of compensation for appropriated lands. Nor does it give any attention to more radical groupings within the Hawaiian population, some of which are highly critical and disdainful of OHA itself as an organization that has "sold out" Hawaiians' basic rights in return for becoming part of the establishment. On radical groups, Haina commented, "We stay away from that. I don't feel it's this newspaper's role to be involved in that kind of thing" (personal communication, May 4, 1988). Haina also saw no particular role for his newspaper in promoting the Hawaiian language, the development of which some see as fundamental to effective revitalization of Hawaiian culture. He said he would use Hawaiian-language articles if they were contributed.

Alu Like's *The Native Hawaiian* is similarly a house journal in style rather than an independent voice. Editor Gard Kealoha describes it as simply a "publication of this organization. . . . Our publication reflects the work that we do in this community" (personal communication, May 5, 1988). Published irregularly, with a print run of about 20,000, *The Native Hawaiian* features personality profiles, extolling the work and achievements of prominent Hawaiian people, as well as articles on Hawaiian history, culture, economic trends, and vocational guidance.

Kealoha also sees no great value in publishing articles written in the Hawaiian-language: "Nobody reads the language. There's been a resurgence [but] I don't know how successful that will be. In order for something to have a lasting effect there must be a felt need for it" (personal communication, May 5, 1988).

Kealoha referred to the success of festivals in Hawaii, such as the celebrations for May Day (known locally as Lei Day): "There's the making of leis, crafts, [the Lei Day concert]—a unique situation where you're really buying into that value of shared appreciation of the songs. The Brothers Cazimero show [including songs written in Hawaiian] has an audience of thousands: They don't understand the language, but bring to it a shared sense of *aloha*—a shared spirit of respecting each other. Isn't that a way of preserving a culture?"

Unlike Haina, Kealoha believes that mainstream media do a reasonable job in reporting on the Hawaiian people: "You see articles all the time about ethnic events. . . . Minorities have made a great deal of progress." But Kealoha thinks that the range of Hawaiian achievement at the individual level was often ignored:

> People concentrate on the poor downtrodden Hawaiian part of the stereotype. But the descendants of people who tilled the soil are now in the legislature and so on. It's a realization of the American dream. There are millionaire Hawaiians, a great deal of middle-class Hawaiians. It tells you something when you have that kind of variety.
>
> If you put the Hawaiian experience into the context of the struggle of all kinds of groups, the important thing is that the values which are universal are strengthened and reinforced. Diversity is something that makes our country stronger. . . . I think that Hawaiians are well on their way. If we had rampant racism here would we have a Hawaiian governor? (personal communication, May 5, 1988)

Musical Renaissance

Even though the Hawaiian language is rarely written or read, it is increasingly finding expression through Hawaiian music. Musical performance has been one of the most significant elements of Hawaiians' cultural renaissance of the last two decades. There has been a rediscovery of the expressive and narrative *hula* and accompanying chant as a cultural performance as well as the creation of means of communicating poetic themes, especially concerning nature, in contemporary musical form (Kanahele, 1979). Hawaiian contributions to music, such as the steel guitar, ukulele, and slack key guitar, have enthused a new generation of devotees, whereas ancient hula percussion instruments and the poetry of traditional chant have been learned anew. Groups such as Eddie Kamae and the Sons of Hawai'i, the Makaha Sons of Ni'ihau, and Kapena have popularized the singing of Hawaiian lyrics, a process well established by the legendary Gabby Pahinui, whose songs receive daily air-play a decade after his death.

Hawaiian music has fluctuated in popularity, but has had a continuing presence on radio since the 1920s. It enjoyed a peak of popularity in the 1930s, particularly in its *hapa haole*, or westernized form (Tatar, 1979). Yet much popularizing of Hawaiian music was in tourist terms—the music, together with a glib and sexualized version of the hula, designed only to entertain or titillate visiting outsiders. Lyrics such "a little brown gal, in a little grass skirt, in a little grass shack in Hawaii" reflect these predispositions.

Although exponents of the tourist versions of Hawaiian music continue to make a fortune in the night spots of Waikiki, the modern revival in Hawaiian music tends to eschew mainland tourists: It is directed very much at locals and is often performed at somewhat seedy nightclubs or rundown bars out of the sight of tourists. Its performers barely scratch a living from their music and typically hold day jobs in skilled or unskilled labor, such as in factories or the construction industry.

Radio

The only radio station in Honolulu committed to an Hawaiian format is KCCN, which has been broadcasting since 1966. Unlike most U.S. radio stations with an ethnic identity, KCCN is one of the front-runners in the local ratings battle. Although it began as a somewhat folksy local station (broadcasting at one stage from a tree in the International Marketplace!), KCCN has benefited from and contributed to the upsurge in popularity in Hawaiian music. The station has established a strong place in the commercial market. This has guaranteed the survival of its Hawaiian format, but its need to be profitable because of its mainland ownership has resulted in an essentially commercial and bland orientation (see Buck, 1983).

KCCN manager Michael Kelly is anxious to avoid the ethnic label: "If national agencies ask, 'Are you an ethnic station,' we say, 'No we're not an ethnic station.' We don't broadcast in Hawaiian, but in English. We're not like, say KISA [a Filipino station]" (personal communication, May 5, 1988). According to Kelly, market research by the station has shown that it has a wide non-Hawaiian audience, which he sees as necessary to attract national advertising. The Hawaiian-music format is interpreted broadly, to include music of all kinds performed by local artists.The Hawaiian connection is, however, strongly evidenced by the station's support for local events involving Hawaiian people—such as the Year of the Hawaiian and the Hokule'a as well as Kamehameha Day and other festivals. Most of the station's announcers and news readers are part-Hawaiian.

The station's news bulletins, however, provide no meaningful alternative to the approach used by other commercial radio stations: The emphasis is on national or state politics as well as crime and accidents. Journalistic work is done by announcers, who choose stories from wire service copy. There are no on-the-road reporters or any news commentators. Occasional voice reports supplied by the Office of Hawaiian Affairs, promoting OHA activities, are inserted into the news, but there is no concept of a uniquely Hawaiian journalism.

There are some other informational programs on KCCN, including a guide to the pronunciation of Hawaiian words, but a cultural discussion program (the *'Ohana Program*) supplied by Alu Like is tucked away in a Sunday night time slot. There are also direct broadcasts of Hawaiian church services on Sunday mornings.

Currently the Office of Hawaiian Affairs is trying to buy a radio license, with the aim of providing more informational and discussion programs of direct interest to native Hawaiians (K. Kanahele, personal communication, May 19, 1988).

Television

There are more than 30 on-air and cable channels available to the population of Honolulu. Despite such a wealth of media gateways, there is relatively little on television to represent the Hawaiian people. Selected aspects of traditional Hawaiian culture are aired regularly on local television: Their audiences are minimal, however, because they are shown mainly on public television and on community access cable.

Hawaii Public Television produces a weekly half-hour program, *Spectrum Hawaii,* which concentrates on arts and culture in the islands. Much of this program concerns native Hawaiian cultural activities, although other ethnic groups also receive substantial coverage. The public affairs program *Dialogue* has a question-and-answer format and acts as a forum for the discussion of local issues. Although the show concentrates mostly on politics, wider community issues are also canvassed, including from time to time issues of specific interest to Hawaiian people (for example, in 1987 to 1988 "Voices of the Hawaiian Nation" and "Racism in Hawaii").

Cable television is required by Hawaii State law to provide at least one public access channel as well as production facilities for interested individuals and groups. Major supplier Oceanic features several dozen ethnic- and community-based programs: These include shows prepared by Alu Like as well as by the Kamehameha schools (a pair of trust-funded schools for children of Hawaiian descent).

One information-and-discussion program on cable, *First Friday, The Unauthorized News,* is unique in its confrontation of controversial issues. In the opinion of one media critic, "It's one of the few sources of hard-core dissent available to residents of Honolulu" (White, 1989). The program is produced by a small group of volunteers (prominent among whom is radical Hawaiian studies professor Haunani-Kay Trask from the University of Hawaii) and gives considerable attention to Hawaiian issues. Yet its estimated 1,200 to 2,000 audience for a monthly half-hour episode indicates the lack of reach of alternative programming in Hawaii. Programming on the local affiliates of the major U.S. networks is almost indistinguishable from that on the U.S. mainland.

Flaws in the Melting Pot

It is clear that Hawaii lacks any sort of meaningful, independent news media aimed specifically at its Hawaiian and part-Hawaiian population. In a situation in which the indigenous minority is integrated into the total society at all levels such a gap may not matter much. Such cannot be claimed for Hawaii.

A common assertion about Hawaii is that it is a melting pot society— with various races and cultures in the process of blending to form a new mix. Novelist James Michener (1959) popularized such a view with his depiction of the "golden men"—offspring of the Caucasian, Asian, and Polynesian races. Indeed there is evidence that the degree of interracial marriage in Hawaii is leading to such a blend (Lind, 1980), although McDermott (1980) suggests there is more likely to develop a demarcation between Caucasians on the one hand and a mixture of Asian and island races on the other.

But in terms of hiring, the melting pot image seems to mean little to the established news media (Henningham, in press). Analysis of staff lists of the two major newspapers in Hawaii—the *Honolulu Advertiser* and the *Honolulu Star-Bulletin*—shows that in 1988, only 2% of the newspapers' journalists were of Hawaiian ancestry: This compares with 20% of the state's population who are Hawaiian or part-Hawaiian. By contrast, Caucasians comprise 70% of the two newspapers' journalists, but Caucasians represent slightly less than 25% of the total population. Similar results were found in a study conducted by the University of Hawaii's journalism department in 1985, although representation of Hawaiians in broadcast media was somewhat higher than in print (Minority Affairs Task Force, 1985).

The imbalance indicates that although Hawaiians are beginning to make an impact in some areas of society—such as law, politics, commerce, and medicine—the mass media is not an area in which an indigenous presence is felt. The situations in Australia (Henningham, 1986) and the U.S. mainland are remarkably similar (Wilson & Gutiérrez, 1985).

Alu Like's Kealoha is optimistic about trends toward full Hawaiian participation in society, but the organizational structure of the mass media indicates weakness in this case. Kealoha maintained that mass media did not lack Hawaiian representation: "Some of the most outstanding people in the mainstream media have been Hawaiian" (personal communication, May 5, 1988). But when pressed, he could name only the late Pierre Bowman, a well-known Hawaiian writer and commentator. Haina, from the Office of Hawaiian Affairs, could offer little practical solution to the absence of Hawaiians from the mainstream media: "Hawaiians are as smart; they need the drive, they need motivation" (personal communication, May 4, 1988).

It is unfortunate that the editors of Hawaiian newspapers see little need for reforming media employment practices. The situation is somewhat complicated in Hawaii, because there are many ethnic groups competing for fair representation. Caucasian domination of the media is clear-cut, but members of various Asian groups are all in need of greater representation.

One group pushing for reform is the Asian American Journalists' Association. The group does not, however, limit its claims to those of journalists of Asian ethnicity. Secretary of the association's Hawaii chapter Sandra Oshiro states that one aim of the chapter is to "promote the hiring of Pacific Islanders. . . . I think it's a tragedy. I do not know of any Hawaiian who is a reporter or an editor. It's really important that we encourage their participation in journalism" (remarks made during general discussion at a meeting of the Hawaii Chapter, Asian American Journalists' Association, Honolulu, April 30, 1988).

It is clear that a meaningful attempt by mainstream news media in Hawaii to recruit and train journalists and other media personnel of Hawaiian ancestry would be one way of giving native Hawaiians a clear voice in the Hawaii of the next century.

References

Buck, E. B. (1983). KCCN: Hawaiian radio. *Pacific Islands Communication Journal, 12*(2), 165-168.

Chapin, H. G. (1984). Newspapers of Hawaii 1834 to 1903: From "He Liona" to the Pacific Cable. *The Hawaiian Journal of History, 18,* 47-86.

Heckathorn, J. (1987, April). Can Hawaiian survive? (*Ua hiki anei ke ola ka 'olelo Hawaii?*). *Honolulu,* pp. 107-113.

Henningham, J. P. (1986). Ethnic minorities in Australian media. In UNESCO (Ed.), *Mass media and the minorities* (pp. 39-81). Bangkok: UNESCO.

Henningham, J. P. (in press). Multicultural journalism: A profile of Hawaii's newspeople. *Journalism Quarterly.*

Holt, J. D. (1974). *On being Hawaiian.* Honolulu: Topgallant.

Johnson, R. K. (1976). *Kukini 'aha'ilono (carry on the news): Over a century of native Hawaiian life and thought from the Hawaiian language newspapers of 1834 to 1948.* Honolulu: Topgallant.

Kanahele, G. (Ed.). (1979). *Hawaiian music and musicians: An illustrated history.* Honolulu: University of Hawaii Press.

Kanahele, G. (1982). *Hawaiian renaissance.* Honolulu: Project Waiaha.

Kanahele, G. (1986). *Ku kanaka, stand tall: A search for Hawaiian values.* Honolulu: University of Hawaii Press/Waiaha Foundation.

Kent, N. J. (1983) *Hawaii: Islands under the influence.* New York: Monthly Review Press.

Kuykendall, R. (1953). *The Hawaiian kingdom* (Vol. 2). Honolulu: University Press of Hawaii.

Lind, A. W. (1980). *Hawai'i's people* (4th ed.). Honolulu: University Press of Hawaii.

McDermott, J. F. (1980). Toward an interethnic society. In J. F. McDermott, W. -S. Tseng, & T. W. Maretzki (Eds.), *People and cultures of Hawai'i* (pp. 225-232). Honolulu: John A. Burns School of Medicine & University of Hawaii Press.

Michener, J. (1959). *Hawaii.* New York: Random House.

Minority Affairs Task Force. (1985). *1985 Survey of Hawaii's Newsrooms.* Unpublished manuscript, University of Hawaii, Department of Journalism, Honolulu.

Mookini, E. (1974). *The Hawaiian newspapers.* Honolulu: Topgallant.

Mookini, E. (1976). *Hawaiian newspapers. Encyclopedia of Hawaii.* Unpublished manuscript [microfilm]. University of Hawaii, Honolulu.

Tatar, E. (1979). Radio and Hawaiian music. In G. Kanahele (Ed.), *Hawaiian music and musicians: An illustrated history* (pp. 320-325). Honolulu: University of Hawaii Press.

Trask, H. (1984-1985). Hawaiians, American colonization, and the quest for independence. *Social Process in Hawaii, 31,* 101-137.

Trask, H. (1987). The birth of the modern Hawaiian movement: Kalama valley, O'ahu. *The Hawaiian Journal of History, 21,* 126-153.

White, J. W. (1989, April). One of the things they are. *Honolulu,* pp. 30-31.

Wilson, C. C., & Gutiérrez, F. (1985). *Minorities and the media: Diversity and the end of mass communication.* Beverly Hills, CA: Sage.

Young, B. (1980). The Hawaiians. In J. F. McDermott, W-S. Tseng, & T. W. Maretzki (Eds.), *People and cultures of Hawaii* (pp. 5-24). Honolulu: John A. Burns School of Medicine & University of Hawaii Press.

PART II

The Quest for Media Space by Immigrants and Indigenous, Integrated Minorities

8

Local Radio and Regional Languages in Southwestern France

JEAN-JACQUES CHEVAL

This chapter is a study of the creation and evolution of radio stations that broadcast in regional languages in the French province of Aquitaine. France is by tradition a nation that is highly centralized politically and culturally. However, it is also the home of diverse regional cultures the areas of which do not necessarily coincide with political borders. Southwestern France is a mosaic of marginal minorities through which national and provincial boundaries run irrespective of traditional and linguistic boundaries.

The Aquitaine region of southwestern France covers an area of 41,309 km^2 and includes five departments: Dordogne (or Périgord), Gironde, Landes, Lot-Garonne, and Pyrénées-Atlantiques. Sparsely populated, Aquitaine had only 2,665,000 inhabitants at the time of the census in 1982. The density of the population varies throughout the area but is fairly low. Gironde represents 24% of the total area of Aquitaine but has 42% of its population, primarily because the city of Bordeaux and its suburbs have a population of approximately 700,000 inhabitants. Two other centers of more than 100,000 people are located in the department of Pyrénées-Atlantiques: the city of Pau and an urban area located on the Basque coast that comprises the townships of Bayonne, Anglet, and Biarritz. Also found in Aquitaine is a set of small- and medium-size regions that are highly individualized by their history and geographical characteristics. These regions still maintain a marked personality (Braudel, 1986).

The population of Aquitaine is slightly older than the French average and the proportion of rural population (38%) remains higher than in the

---

EDITORS' NOTE: English Translation by Stephen Harold Riggins and Paul Bouissac.

rest of France (27%). In 1982 agriculture was the main occupation of 14% of the active population. About 33% of the population works in industry, primarily chemicals, aircraft and military weapons, and wine. But the greatest amount of employment is provided by the service industries, especially the booming tourist industry.

The southern part of this region is delineated by the Pyrénées, a range of mountains that marks the Spanish border. The other borders of Aquitaine are less distinct and have varied considerably throughout the course of history. The modern borders of Aquitaine as an administrative region were determined in 1955 and do not cover either a unique historic entity or a single cultural area. In brief, there are two cultural areas of unequal size: the Gascon-Occitan area, which occupies the major part of Aquitaine, and the Basque country. Although the latter includes three microprovinces (Labourd, Basse-Navarre, and Soule), it occupies only a part of the department of Pyrénées-Atlantiques. It should be kept in mind, though, that the Basque country is larger than this because there are four sister provinces in Spain, which is the location of the greater part of *Euskadi* (a term used to denote the entire Basque country). There are 237,000 Basques living in France compared with 2,861,000, in Spain. Even if indisputable historic ties, both cultural and linguistic, exist between the two parts of Euskadi, the French-Spanish border and the political and administrative gap that has prevailed for centuries has had consequences for their respective evolutions. French Euskadi, which has primarily a rural population markedly older than the average for Aquitaine, presents a striking contrast to the young and industrialized Spanish Euskadi.

Culturally, it would make sense to separate the city of Bordeaux from the Gascon-Occitan area where it is located. Bordeaux has almost completely lost touch with its hinterlands, because its economic activities have long involved wine export to Northern Europe and America as well as colonial trade with the Caribbean islands. Although it has attracted a large part of the rural exodus, the city of Bordeaux today has little in common culturally with its surrounding area except for its role as a centralizing political and administrative power, a role that is often resented by the rest of the Aquitaine population.

Aquitaine is part of the larger cultural area of Occitania, which covers the whole south of France and where the use of the *Langue d'Oc* distinguished its inhabitants from those who used French, or the *Langue d'Oïl*. Aquitaine coincides with what can be called the humid Atlantic Occitania as opposed to the dry Mediterranean Occitania of the east

(Escarpit, 1981). Langue d'Oc includes three families of dialects: middle Occitan (Provençal and Languedocien), north Occitan, and Gascon. Even though all three dialects are used in Aquitaine, Gascon is by far the most widely spoken. In fact, many people prefer the terms Gascon and Gascogne instead of Occitan and Occitania. However, all of Gascogne is not entirely within the borders of modern Aquitaine. According to the region, other terms are used to designate the vernacular language that is spoken locally. In Béarn, for instance, which shares the department of Pyrénées-Atlantiques with the Basque countries, people refer to the Béarnais language, or simply Béarnais. All over Aquitaine, people may refer to their own local dialect as a *patois*, without any derogatory connotations.

It is impossible to say how many people today speak Occitan daily in Aquitaine—or could if they wanted—or have a passive understanding of it. No sociolinguistic census has ever been conducted in the region. In fact, several conflicting figures circulate. For the totality of Occitania the figures vary between 1 and 20 million (Petrella, 1978). Phillippe Gardy (1987) writes that "no global statistical inquiry exists regarding the linguistic habits of France" (p. 28). There are only some limited studies from which estimates are drawn. Gardy believes that we are witnessing a constant decline in the use of this heritage language: "those who possess a definite linguistic competence in this language have fewer and fewer opportunities to use it functionally in their society. It is restricted to the exclusive domain of nostalgia at a time when the daily activities which could insure its survival are disappearing" (p. 28). However, he adds, "confronted with the disappearance of some usages, other forms of spoken Occitan appear as a contrived reaction against this advanced process of linguistic assimilation. . . . Occitan reappears by muddling through in institutions of formal speech which explicitly make an effort to bypass it" (Gardy, 1987, p. 28). Gardy specifically included local radio stations among these institutions.

The Basque country, probably because it is much smaller than Occitania, yields more consistent figures for the use of Euskara (the Basque language). These figures are also based on estimates from limited inquiries. In 1970 the number of people who could express themselves in Basque was supposed to be in the vicinity of 78,000. Today the estimated figure is only 60,000. The number of people who understand this language is higher; it varies from 24% on the coastal area (the urbanized area around Bayonne) to 60% and 72% in the hinterlands (Letamendia, 1987). According to a Gallup pole commissioned by the *Comunidad Autonoma del País Vasco,* the proportion of Basque speakers could be higher in France than in Spain (Rubio Tió, 1986).

Regionalist movements are present in Aquitaine as elsewhere in France. Borrowing the definition provided by Christian Coulon (1982, 1983), I will include among these movements all the various forms of defending the provinces that promote, through ideas and social action, an identity that weakens or opposes the process of national integration originating in Paris.

The Occitan regional movement is generally dated as beginning in 1854 when Frédéric Mistral founded the *Félibrige,* a Provencal literary movement that eventually spread to the whole *Langue d'Oc* area. Primarily a cultural association, the movement did not lead to a political revolt and might be characterized as traditional and conservative regionalism. The movement celebrates the soil, the ancestors, and the good old times and their customs in opposition to the modern world, which is urban, working class, and democratic. Politically compromised through its collaboration with the Pétain Regime during World War II, it has declined ever since, although it has not completely disappeared. At the time of the Liberation, the creation of the *Institut d'Etude Occitane* (IEO) revived regional cultural activities, but it then represented a different political orientation. More to the left, the IEO sponsored, among other activities, Occitan kindergartens called *calandretas.* The IEO is organized in departmental sections and is present in Aquitaine, but it does not have more than a few hundred members. Regional protest groups of a purely political nature—for example, the Occitan Nationalist party (created in 1959)—have attracted only a small number of activists. Another movement that was formed around the candidacy of Robert Lafont during the presidential election of 1974 was more serious. This movement, called *Volém Viure al País* ("We Want to Live at Home"), popularized the theme of protest and made demands that were not only cultural and linguistic but also economic, social, and political. This movement is autonomous, socialist, and *autogestionnaire,* and it holds a federalist concept of the French state. Some of its slogans, such as *Vivre et travailler au pays* ("Live and work at home"), have been borrowed by other organizations and spread beyond a narrow circle of militants. At the same time, a fad for regional music and songs broadened the general interest in Occitan culture so that it was no longer restricted to the purely literary domain. In spite of this, the candidates sponsored by *Volém Viure al País* in various elections did not even receive 3% of the local vote (Coulon, 1982).

In the Basque country, regional political claims are not well developed either, but they are more noticeable. The movements that are inspired by it, some of which go as far as promoting separatism, are a small minority and have no elected representatives. This is another point of contrast with the Spanish Basque country where the various nationalist parties have a majority and some participate in the management of the *Comunidad Autonoma del Païs Vasco*, because the Spanish constitution grants its provinces a strong degree of autonomy. Since 1982 this constitutional status has allowed the Basque government to have its own radio and television channel, Euskal Irrati Telebista, broadcasting entirely in Basque. However, the clandestine organization *Euskadi Ta Azkatasuna* (ETA) also exists, which engages in armed struggle against the Spanish state to obtain total independence for Euskadi. In the French Basque country, nationalist political radicalism does not enjoy the same degree of historical legitimacy that resulted from the fight against Franco's dictatorship in Spain. For a long time France was used as a shelter for Basque militants sought by the Spanish police. It is true that some Basques in the north became involved in terrorism following the model of ETA, but this has been a short-lived venture. The tense climate that prevails in the south, however, is not without repercussions in the north. The recent collaboration between French and Spanish police against those who are defined, depending on one's point of view, as political refugees or terrorists has triggered protests and demonstrations. There are also several associations and movements for the defense and promotion of Basque culture, language, and sports. For instance, Basque kindergartens, called *ikastolak* are the equivalent of the *calandretas*.

For both Basque and Occitan activists the defense of minority languages, the basis to a large extent of regional identities, is their central demand. The French state has endeavored since the 19th century to repress minority languages within its territory because of its ideology of centralization. Education was a powerful instrument for this policy, which was also helped by the rural exodus, the movement of populations, and the general conditions of modern life. This applies not only to the minority languages mentioned earlier but also to other languages in France such as Breton and Corse. Recent administrative measures that provide time for regional languages in national educational programs remain timid and do not amount, according to regionalist militants, to the historic measures of restoration, which they demand in compensation for what some call a real *ethnocide*. As for the media, they have ignored regional languages for a long time. At the end of the 1970s they were granted very little attention by public or private radio. In Aquitaine the regional television station FR3 devoted only 1 hour each month to Basque and completely ignored Gascon. The regional public radio stations were only marginally more receptive to minority languages, devoting 6 hours per month to Basque and 24 minutes to Gascon, and even this for only a portion of the potential listeners, the Béarnais-speaking people (Barelli, Boudy, & Darenco, 1980; Drouin, Cazenave, & Tudesq, 1982). The creator of Radio Adour Navarre, Alexandre de la Cerda, used to tell a story of how a pelote player refused to speak in front of a microphone because "the microphone is not a Basque instrument" (Akam, Begard, Diaz, & Ducasse, 1983, p. 81). This anecdote emphasizes the distance that may separate the modern means of communication from some form of expression of regional culture.

Local Radio in France and Aquitaine:
The Origin and History of *Radios Libres*

Until 1981 radio broadcasting in France was a state monopoly. Its control was relaxed for only a few large private companies, called *radios périphériques,* the antennas of which were located outside the national territory. However, in the case of Aquitaine they did not cover the whole region and the reception was technically poor in some areas. France's radio network was dominated by long-wave broadcasting, which enabled a powerful antenna to cover a vast territory. In the mid-1970s the state monopoly, instead of being perceived as a public service, was seen by many people as either a restriction of the freedom of expression or an ideological apparatus of the state (to use a popular phrase from the time) the task of which was to perpetuate the ideas and control of the dominant class. It is in this context that around 1975 the *radios libres,* "free radios," were born. They were clandestine and illegal and consequently forbidden and prosecuted.

Radio libres originated most often in political, ecological, cultural, or trade union movements in opposition to the current conservative majority in the government. From today's vantage point, they appear to be the last repercussion of the social upheavals of May 1968 and bear witness to the decline and transformation of this movement. Indeed, the free radios resulted in part from an acknowledgment of failure in that some militants, admitting that they could not totally change society, turned their attention to real but limited experimentation. The militants focused on a narrower range of actions than in 1968 through which they hoped they could implement an alternative political philosophy (Mattelart & Mattelart, 1986). A concern for action at the local level became the object of new attention. It was a time of *révolutions minuscules*, when microconcerns replaced macrotheories and in so doing reinforced regionalism.

What all the diverse free radio stations had in common was their local character and the fact that they broadcast in a discontinuous manner. The goal was to give a voice to those who until then had been kept in silence. Radio Périgueux 103 in Dordogne stated in 1981 that the reason the station was established was to enable ordinary people to express themselves without the intermediary of technicians, specialists, and intellectuals who already had that privilege (Tudesq, 1987). The micromedia, that is the radios libres, would achieve what the mass media could not do or did not want to do because of lack of space, time, or political will. The time had come at last to do away with the notion of a mass audience indiscriminately showered with messages from gigantic media organizations. According to sociologist Robert Escarpit (1981): "We know that a collective identity cannot exist without many interconnections at the small-group level both geographically and socially. It is precisely in these terms that the problem of the local or free radios in France must be assessed because they escape the control of both the state monopoly and the economic oligopolies" (pp. 126-127).

Before 1981 Aquitaine did not play a major role in the emergence of free radios. However, it is possible to list some experiments in the 1970s that clearly show an interest in regional cultures. Although several stations could be cited, I will mention only one example. On July 9, 1978, a radio station started broadcasting from the Spanish Basque territory programs that were destined for the French region of the Basque country. This was the first version of Radio Adour Navarre created by Alexandre de la Cerda. The programs were conceived in France and telephoned to Spain from where they were broadcast using the antenna of the Spanish station Radio Popular de Loyola, located near the city of San Sebastian. Radio Popular de Loyola was a member of a network of stations called *Cadena de Ondas Populares de España* (COPE), which was affiliated with the Spanish Catholic church and directed by Jesuit priest Father Arregui, and offered 2 hours a day to Radio Adour Navarre. Thus trilingual programs were produced in Basque, Gascon, and French. The station was organized as a corporation and gathered advertising income to pay employees (Tudesq, 1987).

Almost immediately after his election as president of the French Republic in 1981 and the arrival of a left-wing majority at the National Assembly, François Mitterrand authorized the granting of licenses for radio broadcasting to local organizations. This was in conformity with his electoral program. The new legislation, which was quickly passed, gave the radios libres legal existence and a new name. They became *radios locales privés* (RLP). The law required that the local radios conform to the status of an association. They had to be an activity sponsored by an association or they had to form a nonprofit association themselves, defined by the 1901 law. Considered to be *nouveaux espaces de liberté* ("new areas of freedom"), the RLPs were shielded from the forces of the market economy; financing through advertising was excluded. Furthermore, the creation of stations that would depend entirely on local administrative bodies was excluded as was the creation of networks and mergers. In addition, the RLPs had to maintain a local character; they could broadcast only on the FM frequency and their range could not exceed 30 km. At least 80% of the programming was to be conceived and produced by the station itself. To compensate for this restrictive legislation, the licensed stations were to benefit from an annual grant distributed by the state. Only a high administrative body independent of political parties, the *Haute Autorité de la Communication Audiovisuelle,* could grant licenses to broadcast.

This legal framework favored the birth of 1,001 projects in all quarters of France, and this time Aquitaine was far from lagging behind, particularly because of the department of Gironde and its capital, Bordeaux. Gironde is among the French departments that witnessed the creation of the largest number of private local radios. I have been able to locate 85 radio projects that existed in the department between 1981 and 1986; 44 of them were legally authorized. In Aquitaine a total of 109 different frequencies had been allocated by the end of 1985. This represents 7% of the 1,486 frequencies that were allocated in France at the time when the *Haute Autorité* was still being flooded with applications (Cheval, 1986). At the end of 1987, after many transformations, 108 frequencies were still broadcasting in Aquitaine.

Private Local Radios: 1981-1984

Between 1981 and 1984 almost all private local radio stations had few financial resources. Their small budgets were on average 200,000 francs (Fr) per year, an amount that did not allow them to pay their employees. They depended on volunteers and in addition received membership fees and donations from sympathizers. Their investments in office and studio space and in equipment were approximately 100,000 to 150,000 Fr in most cases. Generally, they used high-fidelity domestic equipment as the basis of their technical infrastructure, and their musical programs were supplemented by the personal record collections of the broadcasters. The first payments of the state subsidies were made in 1983; however, after that year they tended to be irregular. Contrary to the law, some municipal stations were created, but local administrative bodies remained cautious about organizations that were beyond their control.

Private local radios attracted an important number of participants. I have estimated that perhaps 1,500 persons were involved with RLPs in 1984 in Gironde. This would represent 0.13% of the total population of the department. After 1984 the participation in the RLPs declined in Gironde: 1,000 people in 1985 and approximately 700, in 1986 (Cheval, 1986). For the Aquitaine region as a whole no credible figure is available. Station members came mainly from the middle and upper classes and from the better-educated segments of the population. This is particularly obvious if one looks at the position of director at the RLPs. Thus the hope expressed by Radio Périgueux 103 that working-class people would become active in broadcasting does not appear to have met with success.

In the beginning, enthusiasm prevailed, a new mood appeared, projects abounded, groups and communities expressed themselves and made themselves known, and talented individuals sometimes emerged. This was a period of effervescence that included both the best and the worst. During this phase conversation formed a large part of the programming. Indeed, the great majority of the radios were essentially conceived as means of expressing ideas. The right to broadcast was a conquest that was too recent for anybody to think of using it for a purpose other than communicating ideas and knowledge or for sharing a passion or a hobby. There was no strict organization of the time allotted to each program, and most often no harmony existed between them. Each broadcaster was responsible for his or her time slot. Programming schedules looked like patchwork quilts without any unity. The quality of the programs suffered, as could be expected from the lack of resources available, the lack of professional education, and the amateur nature of the members.

There was an obvious gap between the intentions that had been proclaimed and the actual content of the programs. This is particularly true of the stations broadcasting in regional languages. In 1982 the members of Radio Côte d'Argent in Bordeaux stated in one of their introductory pamphlets that one aspect of local culture would be their priority: "Our purpose is to defend minority languages (Occitan and Basque) which have a very special place in our region" (Radio Côte d'Argent, 1982, p. 8). However, this project proved to be nothing but a pious wish and was soon abandoned by the station. Other stations formulated similar projects that were either not implemented at all or existed for only a brief period.

A small-scale study of the statutes of 32 RLPs in Gironde revealed that included in the frequently used vocabulary were the words *local, region,* and *culture,* which would obviously lead one to think that there was a strong commitment to regional cultures and issues (Cheval, 1986). In the same spirit numerous stations were planning to broadcast for the communities of immigrant workers in Aquitaine: North Africans, Spaniards, Portuguese, and so on. However, this does not mean that such programs were common. There is evidence that sometimes the main reason for these minority-oriented projects was to obtain a license to broadcast. The first pioneers of RLPs, who were left-wing militants or actively involved in social-cultural movements, were actually concerned with the expression of minorities, but this was not always the case for those who followed them. By repeating this type of project, they hoped to convince the authorities who were supposed to be inclined to favor such ideas. Finally, do not forget that the stations encountered many obstacles in implementing their projects; one of the most important was the difficulty of finding people interested in expressing themselves on the radio who were also competent in minority languages.

Not withstanding these reservations, it was probably during the first phase that the programs in regional languages or about regional cultures were the most numerous. Newly created stations sincerely believed that they could play a major part in the defense and reclaimation of regional cultures. They rightly thought that the media had been powerful instruments in the decline of minority languages and that they might be able to reverse the process.

The stations that were inspired by such a commitment formed regional federations. In Brittany, the *Fédération Bretonne des Radios Locales et de Pays* considered radio waves to be a natural resource that were limited and whose appropriation could only be collective. It also defined what was supposed to be the guiding principles of a local radio: to promote the development of the cultural identity and expression of a country or area, to be an instrument of participation for the population in the development of local life, to increase the flow of information between the population and its institutions, and finally, to facilitate learning techniques and methods of communication. These principles were approved by the *Fédération Nationale des Radios et Télévisions Occitanes*, which was created on July 26, 1981. It added to them the necessity of bilingualism and refused to let the Occitan language be marginalized in the worst time slots (*horaires-ghettos*) (Prot, 1985). The Occitan federation also demanded the right to create a specifically Occitan nonprofit network of programs or a radio channel. Several RLPs in Aquitaine adhered to or were influenced by this organization, which now seems to have disappeared.

In Gironde six stations are known to have broadcast in Gascon but none did so on a regular basis. A seventh station was the only one that claimed that broadcasting in Gascon was one of its main priorities. This is Radio Landes de Gascogne, which continues to produce programs in collaboration with the *calandretas* in its broadcasting area. I found only one Basque program in Gironde; it was, and still is, broadcast every Monday night by La Clé des Ondes, a station with the slogan *La radio qui se mouille pour qu'il fasse beau* ("The radio that does not hesitate to get its hands dirty for the sake of better days"). In conclusion, an examination of the situation in Gironde shows that the religious or foreign communities have a small but not inconsequential place in the private local radios; however, this is hardly the case for the indigenous cultural and linguistic communities.

The situation in the other departments of Aquitaine is markedly different. In the department of Pyrénées-Atlantiques, where Gascon and Basque are both found, the intentions and realizations are more significant and numerous.

The Evolution of Private
Local Radio: 1984-1988

In time, practically all the RLPs aimed at becoming permanent. They realized that the public had become weary of the amateurism and the mistakes of the early days and that each station required a sufficient audience and a minimum of organization and regularity in its programming. The stations that were carrying an alternative cultural project became discouraged and decided to turn toward entertainment styles that were more accessible to a large audience. Although they were becoming aware of the necessity of an audience, they changed the question *Who speaks to whom* into *Who listens to what.* People had naively thought in the beginning that to be popular it was enough to call oneself a popular station. It was assumed that introducing psychological, sociological, or cultural content in the programs would awaken and change the listeners. But surveys revealed that the private radios that were the most popular were not the most innovative, but the most musical. The militant and individualistic listener of the pioneer years was succeeded by a collective audience that formed a commercial target that advertisers started to court (Tudesq, 1987).

The political will to enforce the legislation concerning radio stations, particularly in terms of financing, did not exist in France. Furthermore, the stations had great difficulty in surviving if they respected the law, because the government grants that had been promised were slow in materializing. The associations in Aquitaine were not strong enough to meet the needs of several dozen stations, probably because an excessive number of authorizations had been granted. Clandestine advertising and hidden sources of financing started to develop. Remember that right at the outset many of the promoters of local radios sought to find employment and income in this activity by transforming the stations into small commercial companies. This was undoubtedly a legitimate endeavor at a time of economic crisis and unemployment. Because local radios benefited from the help of the state, they drew heavily from special employment funds. They used programs such as *Contrat Jeune Volontaire, Travaux d'Utilité Collective*, and others, which provided a small wage for young unemployed people who wanted to start getting involved in productive life. Through these programs the stations could attract employees who did not cost them anything. But there was a serious drawback in this system; this personnel was not always highly motivated, had not been properly trained, and had little hope of finding permanent employment at the stations.

Instead of enforcing a repressive policy, the French government chose to adjust the legislation, taking into account what was actually happening. In the summer of 1984 financing through advertising was allowed. Private local radio no longer needed to be nonprofit, and the annual grant was maintained only for those that renounced advertising. In spite of all these changes, the myth of free radio stations still remains intact in France.

The rush for income from advertising unavoidably entailed a quest for larger audiences and cost-efficient programs. Commercial financing led to concentration, to the negation of the local character of the stations. On the technical level, the stations tried to cover the greatest area possible and did not respect the power limitations on the antennas that had been assigned to them. To lower the cost and to take advantage of programs considered to be higher quality (or simply because they were forced to change because of lack of success), many stations chose to join national networks. More and more of the programs of these stations, which were essentially musical, consisted of broadcasting French and English productions. These programs were not produced in Aquitaine but by the heads of the Parisian or other networks and were shipped to the various stations by mail in the form of records, recorded tapes, and program suggestions or by a satellite link. Local radio stations thus became mere transmitters whose personnel had no other function than to gather messages for local advertising. The trend was toward stations that were conceived on the model of music and news in which, as in a *pâté d'alouette et de cheval,* a horse of commercial music was mixed with a lark of information, the latter rarely being local. As early as 1984 there were radio networks in Aquitaine, although they were to remain illegal until 1986. Following the change of government that occurred in France in 1986, these networks were legalized.

These networks could not afford to address themselves to only a part of the potential audience by broadcasting to regional minorities in their own language. When I visited the Bordeaux station of the most famous French network Nouvelle Radio Jeune (NRJ) in 1986, its director told me that a person in charge of introducing a program had been chosen because of his special training that taught him how to lose his regional accent. According to Claude Collin (1986), who observed a similar situation in the Grenoble area, "only a few of the stations defined as local presently produce or have ever produced programs concerning regional history, memory and culture" (p. 38). Later he said, "At this point of the inquiry one may wonder if one is not completely mistaken, if one is not inquiring about something which does not exist, if one has not projected one's desires and fantasies upon a reality which could not care less?" (p. 38).

It could be said that French local radio stations changed as soon as they were born. Even if it is not the case for all of them, the current reality is remote from the dreams and expectations raised by the 1981 authorization of free and independent radio stations. Today, the few associative stations with a commitment to social communication rather than money making are not in the limelight. Their number has decreased, and their marginalization is probably still progressing. In contrast, the concentration of national networks that share the same models and recipes for success and that offer a standardized product keep growing. But this negative conclusion must be qualified. Collin's disappointment may apply to the region of Grenoble as well as to other French regions and probably to the greater Bordeaux area and even to the department of Gironde. But it does not apply to Aquitaine as a whole. Private local radio stations have indeed been able to fulfill a beneficial role for the local culture and are still doing so. I will provide some examples to illustrate this assessment, but first I'll focus on the public local radios that compete most directly with the private stations.

Public Local Radio

The history of public local radio is simpler than that of private stations. French broadcasting remained very centralized for a long time, as noted earlier; however, a few small-scale regional stations were allowed to exist. In 1974 they were placed under the umbrella of the regional television channel FR3, whose main preoccupation was not the radio. As could be expected, the activity and development of the regional radio stations declined. In 1982 the public radio company, Radio France, assumed the management of the regional stations from FR3. Radio France had its own decentralization projects. As early as 1975 it was conducting market studies and in 1979 created three local FM stations. One was urban, another was regional, and the third, departmental. The experiment was continued because of its success. Eventually, permanent departmental stations were created in Aquitaine. Radio France Périgord started to broadcast in 1982, Radio France Landes and Radio France Bordeaux-Gironde followed in 1983, and finally Radio France Pays Basque and Radio France Pau Béarn, which shared the same facilities, appeared in 1985.

The financial and technical means that were at the disposal of the public local stations were incomparably superior to those of the RLPs. This was the case for all the public local radios. To create a public departmental radio station there had to be an agreement between Radio France and the elected departmental assemblies endowed with the proper authority. The latter paid the basic cost for the installation of the station, which was in the vicinity of 3 million Fr and Radio France provided the money for the management and the operation from the public funds coming from the audiovisual tax that every owner of a television set must pay. The annual budgets of the public local stations vary from 7 to 11 million Fr, the greater part of it going to salaries. Radio France Périgord, Radio France Landes, and Radio France Bordeaux Gironde had 35, 34, and 40 employees, respectively, in 1984, including 7 journalists at each station. In 1988, 42 people were working at the double station for the Pyrénées-Atlantiques. The abundant and competent personnel of the public local radios ensured a high degree of professionalism at all levels. If one keeps in mind that these radios also have first-class equipment, it seems obvious that they possess all the means for efficient work. However, their situation is not without constraints. Belonging to the network of Radio France entails the obligation of reporting to the national director. They are obliged to broadcast the news bulletins of the national network (France Inter). All major decisions are made in Paris, which includes among other things, the right to choose the personnel. The budgets of the stations of Radio France vary according to national budgetary decisions, and as a result, a global reduction in their budgets has led to a decrease in their own programs and an increase in the broadcasting of programs produced in Paris.

Perhaps it would be more appropriate to speak of a *deconcentration policy* of Radio France rather than true decentralization. The term *deconcentration* was preferred by Jean-Noël Jeanneney, the former president of Radio France, who saw an advantage in this policy. According to Jeanneney (1986), only the existence of a national company could guarantee that the stations would have the means of broadcasting nonpartisan information independent from both governmental power and local pressure groups.

The Achievements of Public Local Radio

Having surveyed the history of local radio stations in France, let us now turn to some examples to assess the past and present practices of the Aquitaine stations concerning the defense and promotion of regional languages and cultures. Because it is not possible to examine all the projects, I have selected some examples I consider to be the most significant.

When Radio France Périgord and Radio France Landes were created, the Occitan community leaders circulated petitions that demanded 5 hours of daily broadcasting in Occitan. In Landes 1,000 signatures were gathered, but without results. In 1984 Radio France Périgord did not broadcast any full-fledged programs in Occitan; however, in addition to Occitan records it was possible to hear some element of this language during programs scheduled every morning from 5:45 to 7:10 and on Wednesday evenings. This was very little indeed. But it should be noted that a phrase had been borrowed from the regionalist militants of the previous decade: One Saturday evening a program was titled *Vivre au Pays*. The program was about individuals who had been born in Périgord or had moved there and had found a way of making a living in the country.

No specifically Gascon program had been planned in the beginning for Radio France Landes either; only a musical homage was paid to Gascon sensitivity. A program in French, titled *We Speak and Sing Gascon,* was presented by a speaker who did not know anything about the Gascon language. The changes that followed were probably due to protests, which showed that there was a real need for more Gascon content. One of the highlights of the station became a 2.5-hour program that was broadcast every Sunday evening entirely in Gascon; that represented 2.5% of the weekly program in 1985-1986. This was then presented as "one of the major programs of Radio France Landes in the last two years." However, it is worth noting that it was scheduled at a time that coincided with heavy television viewing with which it had to compete. On the other hand, every day the station opened and concluded symbolically with the Landais hymn sung in Gascon and the morning presentation and the news included short sequences in Gascon. But rather than being the result of a deliberate decision, it seems that they were personal initiatives of the Gascon-speaking employees who managed to sneak some elements of their language into the program that they directed, without, it must be recognized, being prevented from doing so by the management. These efforts are warmly supported by the local Occitan publications, which also encourage listeners to participate in programs in Gascon and to communicate in the language in their contacts with Radio France Landes in order to win de facto, little by little, the 5 hours of daily broadcasting that they demanded. The community leaders also claim that the programming should include four news bulletins in Gascon. This request was turned down by Radio France under the pretext that the station employed only one journalist able to present these bulletins and that it would be impossible to present them during his days off and during vacations (Malecot, 1984).

Radio Pau Béarn and Radio Pays Basque form, as we mentioned earlier, a single station with two programs that address two populations that are close to, yet different from each other: the Basques and the Béarnais. For the most part the programming is the same except for in the morning between 6:00 and 8:30. During these hours 30% of the presentation is done in Basque on Radio France Pays Basque, according to Pierre-Jean Ferrer, the program director. One record out of four must be Basque or Béarnais. The titles of the news are given in Basque. From 1:00 to 2:00 p.m. Monday to Friday a program and news bulletin in Basque are produced by Radio France Pay Basque. This program is not a part of the regular broadcasts in FM but is broadcast in middle waves, something that is inconvenient for the listeners who have to tune their radio to a special wavelength that is not currently used in France. The Béarnais are not provided with a similar service, but they have their own hour-long weekly cultural program.

It is difficult to assess with precision the percentage of Béarnais and Basque that is broadcast by these stations. A quick survey by Pierre-Jean Ferrer suggested that approximately 10% is in Béarnais and 20% in Basque, but this includes both musical and spoken sequences. These percentages are significant but still far from the daily 5 hours in regional languages that are usually requested by the local cultural movements. Yves Laplume (1987), the director of the two stations, stated that "this type of program is obviously essential. Maintaining a linguistic presence in the regions, irrespective of the number of listeners, is one of the functions of the public service" (p. 7). However, to justify the relative weakness of the programs in Basque he claimed in an interview that the small number of listeners attracted to such programs was a justification, adding that in any case it is always possible to promote a culture in another language. According to Laplume, his station contributes to this promotion through many French programs devoted to Basque culture (in the case of Radio France Pays Basque) and Béarnais culture (in the case of Radio France Pau Bearn). One example of interest in the Basque language on the part of Radio France Pays Basque: Every week all the personnel are asked to participate in a 1-hour session of sensitization to Basque with the station's two broadcasters and two journalists who are native speakers of the language.

Basque Private Local Radio

In 1981 Radio Adour Navarre, which until then had broadcast from Spain, moved its studio to France. From that point the history of the station can be considered to be very representative of the evolution of many private local radios. The aim of this station was initially to put the medium of radio in the service of Basque and Gascon. Although it was a private station, it aspired to become a public service station assisting all the cultural and linguistic communities. The people who created the station also wanted it to be a news station, broadcasting 10 or so daily news bulletins in Basque in 1982. That year the station had 35 volunteer and 8 salaried employees, including 3 journalists. Radio Adour Navarre devoted 25% of its broadcasting time to the Basque language. In the evening, between 8:00 and 9:00, it broadcast an educational program sponsored by the *Gau Eskolak* ("night school"), the purpose of which was to teach and promote the use of Euskera among adults. Radio Adour Navarre also devoted 14% of its broadcasting time to Gascon. The rest was in French with the exception of 1 hour weekly that was produced in Portuguese for a community of Portuguese residents on the Basque coast, which might have 5,000 people. By practicing multilingualism, Radio Adour Navarre demonstrated its generosity but at the same time ran the risk of alienating each community instead of accumulating audiences. Moreover, it offered time every day to trade unionists (Akam et al., 1983).

To continue its action, Radio Adour Navarre was planning a budget of 700,000 Fr in 1983 with 80% of it coming from advertising. Therefore, its employees regretted the initial exclusion of advertising, but complied with this decision because of the public subsidies that were promised and that should have been sufficient for the needs of the station. As I pointed out, the government subsidies were not granted as they were supposed to be and Radio Adour Navarre also had no choice but to break the law until 1984. The absence of surveys during the first years of its operation makes it impossible to measure the success or failure of the station among listeners. But certainly its income, which was below expectations, can be considered a sign of limited success.

In 1985 when advertising became legal, Radio Adour Navarre decided to make a deal, because of its shaky financial situation, with a local advertising agency the director of which, M. Eguymendia, bought a controlling interest in the station (Oregi, 1987). Eguymendia was impressed by the team in charge of the radio and by its potential for expansion. His goal was to transform the station into a real professional company and it was soon employing up to 17 people. The substance of the programs remained basically the same. For 1.5 years the radio experienced a new life, but a short one. Financial difficulties led to new changes. The station made a contract with Radio-Télé Luxembourg, a major foreign station that directed its broadcasts to the northern half of France. This contract with Radio Adour Navarre allowed Radio Tele Luxembourg to be relayed in FM in the southwest of France, but by the same token the Basque station lost its independence and identity and soon became the mere relayer of commercial programs that were far removed from its initial concerns and commitments. Radio Adour Navarre kept only 5 hours daily for its own programs and retained only four employees to produce the local programs that made it possible for Radio Adour Navarre to continue receiving a portion of the local advertising. All the other employees were dismissed. Alexandre de la Cerda, the founder of Radio Adour Navarre, eventually left the station. With his departure, the last program in Basque and Gascon disappeared, and according to Eguymendia, all these programs were canceled in 1988. The reason given for their cancellation was that they attracted too few listeners. Eguymendia chose a type of mass-audience program that would harmonize with the Radio-Télé Luxembourg programs broadcast during the day.

A totally different history was experienced by *Gure Irratia* ("Our Radio") in Bayonne and two other stations that were created in its wake: *Irulégiko Herri* ("Radio Irouléguy"), which is located in a Basque valley of Basse-Navarre, and in Mauléon the station *Xiberoko Botza* ("The Voice of Soule"). Each station was thus located in one of the three small historic provinces of the French Basque country. Their uniqueness comes from the fact that they all use the Basque language almost exclusively.

The association *Entzen-Ikus* ("To See and to Hear") was formed at the Basque Museum of Bayonne. This association lobbied for the introduction of the Basque language in the media and had its own radio project. In the summer of 1981 the station Gure Irratia started to broadcast. It was the first important Basque station, because the one under the control of the Comunidad Autonoma del País Vasco in Spain was not active yet. The goal of the promoters of Gure Irratia was the creation of a joint radio service in which the public and private sectors would be represented, the former by Radio France and some local administrative bodies and the latter by community associations that were supposed to allow the listeners to influence the policy of the station. Meetings were arranged with the direction of Radio France but to no effect. The national radio company had its own project and did not want to enter into the kind of agreement proposed by the Basque association. Eventually, Gure Irratia implemented its project in the form of a typical private local station. It was a *radio associative,* formed in compliance with the French regulations that forbade advertising. A total of 30% of the seats on its board of directors were reserved for representatives of the other 12 associations that supported it. Gure Irratia was joined in 1982 by two more Basque stations. Working in the same spirit and for the same cause, these stations chose to join their efforts rather than compete with each other, but they kept their own structures, personnel, and programs.

The association supporting Gure Irratia had a membership of 160 in 1988; 20 people were working regularly at the station, most of them as volunteers. Only 4 were salaried, 2 as full-time employees earning 4,500 Fr per month and the other 2 worked part-time. Gure Irratia also took advantage of governmental programs subsidizing employment. Its budget was around 450,000 Fr annually, which came from government grants, campaign drives made by institutions and diverse groups, membership fees, and various events organized by the radio. Two other sources of income were important. The first provided by the public radio of the Spanish Basque country, Euskadi Irratia, totaled about 50,000 Fr annually. This was given to the station in exchange for being its correspondent in the French Basque Country and providing daily information and reports about the area. Second, Gure Irratia established an orderly way of financing: listener subscription, which was quite unusual for a French radio station. Listeners had their bank account automatically debited every month for 30, 50, or 100 Fr in favor of the station. This enabled the station to raise from 120,000 to 130,000 Fr per year because of 200 to 300 regular subscribers. This form of support was obvious evidence of the listeners' strong commitment to the station. The other two Basque-speaking stations used the same system. But for Irulegiko Herri Irratia, which covers a demographically much smaller area (27,000 people compared with 191,000), only 50 people subscribed this way. The budget of this station, a little less than 300,000 Fr, was substantially lower than the one for Gure Irratia. Attracting 40 volunteers, it employed three part-time workers who earned 2,600 Fr per month.

The programs of these three stations are in Basque for 90% or 95% of their broadcasting time, but in all other respects they try to be regular mainstream stations addressing the whole of the Basque-speaking population without distinction of age or cultural level. They offer the complete gamut of a mainstream station: news, education, and entertainment. Traditional Basque music is, of course, commonly broadcast but so is modern Basque songs and rock as well as music from other countries. If they do not grant much time to the French and international commercial music that floods the waves of competing stations, they do not hesitate to use types of programs, such as hit parades, that are strongly criticized by the activist stations. Irulegiko Herri Irratia organizes one in which the listeners vote by telephone for the performers and the songs that are presented. One of the announcers, quite pleased with her success, claims that she usually receives about 30 calls per half an hour.

Concerning the use of the Basque language, the only exceptions that are tolerated are instances in which those who want to express themselves cannot speak Basque. For example, this is the case for the ecology movement *Les Amis de la Terre*, which has a program on Irulegiko Herri Irratia. Another case occurs during news bulletins when a non-Basque-speaking person is interviewed about an important event. Indeed, if only politicians who spoke fluent Basque had the opportunity of speaking on the station it would lessen the objectivity of the news, because they are often champions of the regionalist cause.

The attitude of these stations toward Basque autonomy or nationalism is not neutral. Larçabal, a journalist at Gure Irratia, stated that the stations that originated in these movements had to grant them utmost attention (personal communication). This was considered by him as a kind of moral obligation. They do not treat such political activities in the same way as Radio France. Confronted with the arrest and expulsion of Spanish Basque activists by French police, Laplume, the director of Radio France Pays Basque, recognized that the public radio had at first treated this as a major event, but that by the time of the 128th expulsion Radio France Pays Basque was granting these events much less attention, although they were mentioned. The attitude is quite different at Gure Irratia where, according to Larçabal, the radio continues to highlight the expulsions despite their ordinary character. In his own words, "We don't take positions but we call attention to what is happening" (personal communication, February 1988). Needless to say, this is, of course, a way of taking a position.

It has been difficult to assess the degree of involvement of these stations in the nationalist movements by examining their programs or by interviews. However, it is obvious that the very existence of the stations, the fact that they use the Basque language almost exclusively, signifies a political position that goes beyond the simple cultural framework of a traditional centralist country such as France (Idieder, 1982). Undoubtedly, these stations shelter activists for Basque nationalism but those whom I interviewed were very cautious about this. It is possible that their silence and their refusal to proclaim positions betray a diversity of opinion and that only a politically neutral position provides a conciliatory ground for everybody involved in these stations.

The cooperation between the three stations involves common programs. Every Sunday morning they broadcast a Catholic Mass in Basque, which is recorded by each station in turn in a parish in the area it covers. The Basque country in France is a region where Catholic religious practices remain strong, hence the importance of this cooperation. Every afternoon during the week, Xiberoko Botza and Irulegiko Herri Irratia take turns producing a musical program that is broadcast on the two stations, while Gure Irratia prefers to relay the Euskadi Irratia program in France. But the production that the promoters of these stations are the most attached to is a multiplex that interconnects them each morning at 7:45 for a news bulletin made in common during which each one of the stations brings to the others the latest news of its province. For example, the following is a list of subjects treated by Irulegiko Herri Irratia between Monday, January 25 and Saturday, January 30, 1988:

Monday. A report on the first stage of the women's championship for pelote at Saint-Jean-Pied-de-Port and a report on a conference attended by the wine growers of Irouléguy.

Tuesday. The announcement of an increase in the broadcasting of television programs in Basque during an interview with an executive of FR3 who was making a film in the area covered by Irulegiko Herri Irratia.

Wednesday. A report on the furniture fair in Paris from the perspective of two local companies.

Thursday. A report on the general assembly of a local cheese cooperative.

Friday. An economic discussion of the decreasing sale price of lambs and an interview with a cattle trader who gave explanations for the drop in price.

Saturday. The presentation of the pelote league of the Basque countries and the presentation of a cassette of modern religious songs in Basque designed to renew that type of music along with an interview with the local women who were the composers and interpreters of the music.

This list shows that it is possible to produce local news without limiting oneself to a narrow provincialism (e.g., Wednesday's program) and at the same time dealing with a variety of topics. The stations also report events that are not local.

Béarnais Private Local Radio

A survey made in 1987 by the journal *Per Noste, Païs Gascons* indicated that there were 16 stations broadcasting in Gascon in the Aquitaine region (Bidot-Germa, 1987). If other Occitan languages spoken in this region are included, the total number of local radios reaches the figure of 23, including the 3 public service stations that devote some time, sporadically and irregularly, to Occitan. This is certainly a respectable figure, but it nevertheless remains congruent with the phenomenon of marginalization of regional broadcasts that was described earlier.

Occitan is used the most often in programs sometimes called *ghetto programs* or *alibi programs,* which instead of encouraging the daily use of the language encloses it within a kind of radio museum. Without totally agreeing with these views, it is nevertheless noticeable that a large part of the programs specifically devoted to minority languages are broadcast in the evening at times when the audience is bound to be small. Symbolically, it is significant that many such programs are called *veillées* or similar names. The word *veillée* refers to the rural world of the past when, in the absence of television and all other mass media, families and communities gathered after dusk at one another's farms to talk, sing, and listen to storytellers or musicians in a congenial atmosphere. The stations that use this term more or less consciously play on the nostalgic myth. They suggest that local radios could abolish time and the negative aspects of modernity by recreating this dimension of local collective life. Note also that the programs in regional languages frequently deal with history, customs, traditions, and memories of older people—all topics that also point to the past. There are short sequences in the Occitan language that are now and then introduced in the general programs produced in French. They have similar forms and content all over Aquitaine, including the public local radios. Such programs consist of riddles, proverbs, etymologies, and the meanings of Occitan family names or place names.

In Aquitaine, Béarn seems to be a region that has kept a genuine cultural life and a functional use of the traditional local languages (Kristol & Wüest, 1985). This is probably the reason why 10 out of the 16 stations listed in *Per Noste, Païs Gascons* are Béarnais stations. Since 1981, two private local stations, both claiming to champion regional culture, are competing in Pau, the capital city of Béarn. However, their situation and history are very different.

Radio Vivant was the first free radio to broadcast in the Pau area immediately after the 1981 elections. An association called *Vivre au Pays* had been created to support a local monthly magazine, *Le Pays,* which had been launched in 1976. The magazine was short lived, but the association was soon joined by others such as *Per Noste,* the Bearnais chapter of IEO and by Gascon groups of singers and musicians, such as *los de Nadau.* It is this association that was the origin of the station. At the beginning, it was a shoe-string operation with rudimentary equipment and a meager budget of 17,000 Fr. The station did not even have a telephone but nevertheless refused, on principle, to use advertising as a financial resource. As soon as it was created, Radio Vivant adhered to the *Fédération Nationale des Radios Télévisions Occitanes*

The promoters of Radio Vivant stated that "the Occitan language is a part of our culture and regains its leading role by becoming a language of mass communication. Radio is the means to reclaim this language and to prevent its extinction" (Lenguin, 1983, p. 21). This manifesto included a denunciation of *Parisianism,* a phenomenon that was described as "conveying a domineering model which in a light-hearted manner imposes on us a sterilized accent to which the country is invited to listen day after day on television and on radio" (Lenguin, 1983, p. 22). The cultural commitment was accompanied by political activities along the lines of the movement *Volèm Viure al Païs.*

The station functioned according to a system of self-management, refusing professionalism and any sort of hierarchy. For some of its broadcasters, Radio Vivant was only one facet of their activities, because they were also involved in *L'Hostau Biarnès,* a cultural center, and in a *calandreta,* which had been opened in 1980. Due to lack of money or because interorganizational and managerial problems were never settled, the station was never fully developed. Like many other RLPs it was richer in projects than in talent and means to implement them. When it disappeared in 1982, Radio Vivant was broadcasting only a few hours each week.

In 1981 another radio was created in Pau, La Voix du Béarn, primarily the work of a man endowed with a strong personality: Catholic priest Father Marrimpouey. In the summer of 1981, two associations were founded, one of which was to manage La Voix du Bearn (also called in Bearnais Votz de Noste, "Our Voice"). The purpose of the other association was to organize listener support for the station. The financial means of this station were 10 times those of Radio Vivant (Lenguin, 1983).

In 1982, the station was broadcasting 105 hours per week and devoted about 18% of its time to the use of the Béarnais language in the form of stories (for instance, the old *Pépé Arthur,* who recounted his own memories or the stories of Roger Lapassade, an Occitan writer more interested in contemporary realities), courses in the Béarnais language (15 minutes a day), and above all, a *veillée béarnaise* each evening. The time given Béarnais did not satisfy everybody. Even some members of the station thought it was insufficient and wanted to achieve real bilingualism. There was also opposition to Father Marrimpouey's personality and to his style of management, which was considered too personal and too paternalistic. In 1983 about 50 people left La Voix du Béarn and created Radio Païs. These departures impoverished the Bearnais dimension of the station but did not prevent it from continuing its activities. In 1988 the radio had only 5 or 6 Béarnais-speaking collaborators out of about 30.

At the present time the radio seems to gravitate essentially around one program, which was possibly its reason for being, the program by Father Marrimpouey: 7 days a week for the last 7 years he has spoken by telephone with his listeners between 10:30 p.m. and midnight. The program includes games and counseling, but all this is done in French. According to the radio's directors, its initial aims have remained unchanged but it is obvious that the percentage of time devoted to Béarnais has declined. In fact, there are only three weekly programs left, broadcast between 9:00 p.m. and 10:30 p.m. One deals with regional history, one is a talk show, and the third is concerned with local crafts and small businesses. It is also possible to hear Béarnais occasionally at other times of the day, but only sporadically, for instance, when a folklore record is played. A journalist from Pau defined La Voix du Béarn as a family station with a rather old audience (Grollier, 1987). Its news bulletins, purely local, occupy a small place in its program, but it is produced by a network of correspondents established by the radio who report every day about the events in their area.

Radio País, a station born from the team that left the Voix du Béarn, remained linked with the Occitan movement. Its statutes define its goals as "the promotion of Langue d'Oc in Béarn and Gascogne by audiovisual means, the broadcasting of programs specifically destined for the regional community, as well as neighboring communities. Its production will have a regional character in the domains of news, culture and leisure" (Lacaze, 1984-1988). Following the accidental destruction of its equipment, Radio País joined forces with Radio Vivant and the latter changed its name to that of the former. The new radio had about 100 collaborators, half of them speaking Occitan. In 1984 Radio País reached its objective of producing a bilingual program, 40% of it being Gascon, 40% in French, and the remaining 20% in Basque, Catalan, Portuguese, and Arabic (Lacaze, 1984-1988). The situation was practically unchanged in 1988. The proportion of Occitan to French varies, depending on the program and the announcers; it can reach 80% in the morning. In this case bilingualism would mean that people express themselves either in Occitan or in French in the same program or in the same conversation without translations. Each one uses the languages with which he or she is most comfortable.

La Voix du Béarn and Radio País are both good examples for understanding the diversity of attitudes and conceptions that the regional stations hold concerning the broadcasting of local languages. The opposition between La Voix du Béarn and Radio País focuses on the use of the Occitan label. La Voix du Béarn claims to be Béarnais more than anything else and has no use for the term *Occitan*. To its directors, *Occitan* is a politically loaded word that relates those who use it to the partisans of the Occitan autonomy or independence movement. They prefer to speak about Béarn and its language or *patois*. On the other hand, the members of Radio País point out that the position of La Voix du Béarn is no less political than their own. Indeed, they claim that by negating or refusing to take into consideration the Occitan cultural and linguistic unity, the promoters of La Voix du Béarn serve French centralist politicians for whom *Langue d'Oc* is nothing but a patchwork of local *patois* that impedes communication. They reproach La Voix du Béarn for refusing to speak about the future in Béarnais and for confining Béarnais to the role of folklore. Radio País does not confine Occitan to any particular type of program but uses it to deal with any topic whether it be traditional culture or the chemical industry of Lacq, which is located near Pau. Radio País aims at being a news station, broadcasting news bulletins three times a day. Depending on the journalist in charge they may be in Bearnais.

Confronted with this situation, it is tempting to interpret the conflict between these two radios in the light of the old division within the Occitan cultural movement. The division is between the advocates of independence or autonomy and those who want to keep cultural roots alive without weakening national unity. But in the absence of more thorough research this can only be a hypothesis for the time being. Also note that the two stations do have some common features. Both draw resources from advertising, something that does not solve all of their financial difficulties. An average budget of 180,000 Fr for La Voix du Béarn and double that amount for Radio Païs does not enable them to pay a single salary. Consequently, both function exclusively with volunteers and with employees paid by the state through the *travaux d'utilité* collective program.

Conclusion

The few examples that have been given in this chapter certainly do not exhaustively describe the diversity of approaches to broadcasting in local languages. The examples are simply case studies enabling one to form an idea of the present policies in Aquitaine. As has been shown, each radio is to some extent unique. But the attitude of the local stations can be the point of departure for establishing a tentative typology.

The first category in the typology would be those stations that do not grant any time to the regional languages. This is the case for about 80% of all the regional stations still existing in Aquitaine. Their number is increasing as the associative stations that are more prone to give time to regional cultures disappear or are transformed. This phenomenon illustrates the relative failure of the private local stations in France. The extent of this failure can be measured in terms of their initial ambitions that set one of their main goals as being community media in the service of the internal and external communication of particular social groups. I have already commented on the style and content of the music stations that are all too often deprived of originality but that attract large audiences. One may wonder whether it is really useful for the government to continue to license a large number of these stations that are obviously redundant with respect to each other. This is the opinion of

David Grosclaude, a journalist at Radio Païs, who asked ironically that those who have nothing to say be given the means of keeping silent.

The second category would include a great variety of stations. Those that broadcast some programs in regional languages or include some elements of these languages in their programs. The stations in this category do not form the majority of the regional radios, but their number is nonetheless important. This category comprises public local radios as well as stations such as La Voix du Béarn and the short-lived Radio Adour Navarre.

The third category would include the stations critical of the policy of isolating the regional languages from the rest of the programs and that thus promote bilingualism. Radio Païs is a good example.

The fourth category would include the stations whose language of broadcasting is exclusively the minority languages such as the three Basque stations. They are to my knowledge the only stations in Aquitaine that fall into this category. Both of the last two categories are found in Aquitaine only in the department of Pyrénées-Atlantiques.

The mass audience has chosen among these four types, and it is obviously the first category that the Aquitaines favor to a large extent. The notable exception is the public local stations in Dordogne and Landes that have secured audiences of a respectable size. Surveys show that the three other categories do not score well among the population at large. They are often credited with less than 1% of the total audience. Community local radios are quick to negate the validity of these surveys. For instance, the members of Gure Irratia questioned the general value of the surveys as far as they were concerned, arguing that they were partially valid but only for the coastal and urban part of the Basque country. Those whom I interviewed suggested different figures, such as 60% to 70% for the two other stations located in the mountains in rural environments. It is difficult to decide whether this is a faulty assessment of reality, bad faith, or the result of overestimating the sympathy that these stations are given but that do not necessarily translate into actual audiences. In the case of the Basque stations, the answer may be that the surveys were done there, as elsewhere, mainly in urban areas where the percentage of Basque-speaking people is low (10%). The rural areas, where the percentage is high, were outside the regions surveyed. But it is difficult to constantly deny the scientific validity of successive surveys when their results are consistent. Once the low impact of the minority-language stations is admitted, it is possible to question the absolute value represented by the number of listeners. A station that addresses a minority and captures the attention of a sizable part of its members may score poorly when compared with the total population of its broadcasting area. Nevertheless, it has obviously achieved its goal.

The future survival of most stations in the private sector is problematic. They address a restricted audience during at least a part of their operations, while seeking an income from advertising. It is obviously difficult to reconcile a credible commercial strategy and an audience that is inevitably small. Radio Adour Navarre experienced this contradiction. The results of La Voix du Béarn and Radio Païs are not encouraging either. Even if these two stations succeed in raising the minimum funds necessary for the continuation of their operation through advertising, neither will probably be able to raise the funds for paying salaries to their workers. The Basque stations discussed earlier are different because they survive principally through governmental subsidies and donations from their sympathizers, but even here their employees receive low salaries.

Two conditions seem to be a requirement for the survival of stations that broadcast programs for regional cultural minorities. First, it is necessary that their mode of financing and operation be solidly rooted in their environment. They must be trusted by active and motivated listeners the number of which is relatively unimportant. The existence of a real identity and cultural life is obviously the other condition as is the presence of a regional political claim that is more or less explicit. These are the prerequisites without which it is not possible to mobilize the listeners and promoters of these stations in a militant manner for a long period of time. The indefinite continuation of their activities is based to a large extent on this militant attitude. But in any case, help from the government or local administration remains necessary. Understandably, governments show some reluctance in subsidizing independent media that are sometimes openly hostile to them. This is, however, a moral obligation in a democratic society that wants to promote the self-expression of all its citizens. But at the time this chapter was written, government grants for RLPs—guaranteed by law—had not been paid in France for 2 years.

One might regret that local stations in the public sector sometimes yield to the temptation of trying to compete with private commercial stations for mass audiences even though their purpose is different. In spite of real achievements, the proportion of time they grant regional languages in Aquitaine remains small. It may be understandable that Radio France is reluctant to alienate the majority of its audience, which is French speaking, by devoting a sizable part of its programs to the smaller number of listeners who wish to hear broadcasts in regional languages. But, after all, this is its role. A possible solution might be to generalize the system adopted by Radio France Pays Basque and give all local stations in the Radio France network two FM frequencies or different wavelengths. Thus they could use one for minority audiences and the other for majority audiences. This solution is sometimes used in Spain, where cultural minorities are also numerous. Joint radio stations have the possibility of focusing on a variety of audiences without doubling the cost, because the infrastructure and part of the personnel can be shared.

What has been said about Breton by the journalist Fanch Broudig, employed at the regional television station of FR3 Bretagne, is equally applicable to all minority languages in France: "Breton has no legal existence in France. No legislation defines either the rights of those who speak Breton or the obligations of the state toward them [with the exception of the Diexonne Law which authorizes the optional teaching of Breton]" (quoted in Chapalain, 1988). Private and public local radio stations can be important factors in the functional survival of minority languages, but their long-term existence requires fundamental political decisions about the necessity of their survival and the appropriate means to ensure it. Until that happens one would have to be rather pessimistic about the long-term survival of nearly all the minority-language radio stations in France.

References

Akam, N., Begard, D., Diaz, A. -M., & Ducasse, R. (1983). *Les partenaires potentiels de la communication en région: Le local comme marché ou comme ressource*. Talence: Maison des Sciences de l'Homme/Lasic.

Barelli, Y., Boudy, J. -F., & Darenco, J. -F. (1980). *L'espérance Occitane*. Paris: Editions Ententes (Collection: Minorités).

Bidot-Germa, D. (1987). Cric et crac . . . lengua nosta e radios. *Per Noste, Païs Gascon, 123*, 17-18.

Braudel, F. (1986). *L'identité de la France: Espace et histoire*. Paris: Editions Arthaud-Flammarion.

Chapalain, J. -J. (1988). Fanch Broudig, le journalisme en langue Bretonne. *Ar Men, 13*, 52-56.

Cheval, J. -J. (1986). *Les radios locales privées en Aquitaine*. Unpublished doctoral dissertation, Université de Bordeaux III, Talence.

Collin, C. (1986). Radios locales et culture régionale: La grande désillusion. *Medias Pouvoirs, 3*, 34-48.

Coulon, C. (1982). Les régionalismes en Gascogne. In R. Escarpit (Ed.), *La Gascogne: Pays, nation, région?* (pp. 32-56). Paris. Editions Entente.

Coulon, C. (1983). Les régionalismes en Gascogne. *Les dossiers d'a noste qu'en: Les Gascons, 1,* 25-31.

Drouin, J.-C., Cazenave, E., & Tudesq, A.-J. (1982) L'information en Gascogne. In R. Escarpit (Ed.), *La Gascogne: Pays, nation, région?* Paris: Editions Entente.

Escarpit, R. (1981). *Théorie de l'information et pratique politique.* Paris: Editions Le Seuil.

Gardy, P. (1987). L'Occitan en 1987: Situation, statut, perspective. *La Lettre du Centre d'Information et de Recherche pour l'Enseignement et l'Emploi des Langues* (CIR-EEL), 2/3, 28-34.

Grollier, B. (1987, April 24). Radios locales Paloises: Le dernier carré des radios associatives. *La République des Pyrénées,* p. 20.

Idieder, J. (1982). *Les radios libres au Pays Basque Nord, un outil d'affirmation au de révélation de l'identité basque* (Mémoire de Maîtrise). Unpublished manuscript, Université de Bordeaux III, Institut des Sciences de l'Information et de la Communication, Talence.

Jeanneney, J. -N. (1986). *Echec à panurge: l'Audiovisuel public au service de la différence.* Paris: Edition du Seuil.

Krisol, A.-M., & Wüest, J.-T. (Eds.). (1985). *DRIN de TOT: Travaux de sociolinguistique et de dialectologie Béarnaises.* Berne: Edition Peter Langsa.

Lacaze, P. (1984-1988). *Rapports d'enquêtes sur les radios Paloises et d'Orthez.* Unpublished manuscript. Talence: Centre d'Études de Presse, Maison des Sciences de l'Home.

Laplume, Y. (1987). Interview. *La bonne fréquence, Bearn-Pays Basque, 2,* 7.

Lenguin, R. (1983). *La voix du Béarn et radio vivant, deux radios occitanes* (Mémoire Séminaire Vie Locale). Unpublished manuscript, Université de Bordeaux I, Institut d'Etudes Politiques, Talence.

Letamendia, P. (1987). *Nationalisme au pays Basque.* Talence: Presse Universitaire de Bordeaux/Maison des Pays Ibériques.

Malecot, J. (1984). *Les radios locales publiques en Aquitaine* (Mémoire de Diplôme d'Etudes Approfondies). Université de Bordeaux III, Institut des Sciences de l'Information et de la Communication, Talence.

Mattelart, A., & Mattelart, M. (1986). *Penser les médias.* Paris: Editions la Découverte.

Oregi, S. (1987). *L'Information radio-télévision dans le Pays Basque* (Mémoire de Diplôma Supérieur de Recherche). Unpublished manuscript, Université de Bordeaux III, Institut des Sciences de l'Information et de la Communication, Talence.

Petrella, R. (1978). *La renaissance des cultures régionales en Europe.* Paris: Editions Entente (Collection: Minorités).

Prot, R. (1985). *Des radios pour se parler: Les radios locales en France.* Paris: La Documentation Française.

Radio Côte d'Argent (1982). Unpublished document.

Rubio Tió, J. (1986). Quelques particularités d'Euskal Telebista: Une chaîne de télévision autonome. In *Les moyens d'information en Espagne* (pp. 249-277). Talence: Presse Universitaire de Bordeaux/Maison des Pays Ibériques.

Tudesq, A. -J. (Ed.). (1987). *Les mutations de la radio en Aquitaine, 1981-1986.* Talence: Presse Universitaire de Bordeaux/Maison des sciences de l'Homme.

9

Revista Mea: Keeping Alive
the Romanian Community in Israel

GABRIEL BAR-HAÏM

Introduction

When my family arrived in Israel in 1963 and settled in one of the developing towns of Galilee, the Agency for the Jewish Absorption and Welfare of Immigrants gave us four rough metal beds, a gas stove, and some money. On the day of our arrival, the elderly couple living in the apartment across from ours, who had arrived 9 months earlier, visited and brought with them some food, cakes, blankets, and a few copies of a weekly Israeli-Romanian magazine called *Revista Mea* (*My Magazine*).

For a few months after our arrival, we continued to receive back issues from our neighbors, accompanied by warm recommendations to pay attention to a particular article or picture. Often our neighbors or relatives commented on stories, argued over opinions, recited some of the satirical verses, and reminded one another of the veiled meanings of the cartoons. The features and contents of this popular magazine were also the center of conversation when out-of-town relatives came to visit, and sometimes they settled many family squabbles using—allusively— characters in the stories, gossip about celebrities, or the suggestive lines of cartoons.

Almost half a year after our arrival and after Mother had been working for several months, we started to buy *Revista Mea* every week. It became one of the small indulgences, like challah bread and ice cream, that was pleasurably consumed on the sabbath. By then, in comparison with the newcomers who continued to pour into the town, we were considered established. Among other things, we could afford to buy *Revista Mea,* organize now and then an occasional party and even purchase a tape recorder—a commodity much desired by my brother and myself. Like every Romanian housewife around us, Mother would place a pile of back issues of *Revista Mea* on the shelf beneath the radio or under the coffee table. When guests or new immigrants arrived in the neighborhood, they would be offered these issues as a gesture of goodwill, presumably to take their minds off the pressing problems of adjustment.

The tasks of buying the magazine and of making public use of its contents were mainly done by women, whereas men only read it furtively. Because the magazine featured so many activities relegated to women's traditional responsibilities, health, cooking, and education as well as containing short love stories and gossip, it was identified with the women's world and with what men jokingly called women's "weaknesses." Although my father regularly read the magazine, he always harbored *Viata Noastra* (*Our Lives*) in the living room, the only daily Israeli-Romanian newspaper that concentrated on political and international news.

This short biographical reminiscence has been given not only to relate the subject of my analysis to its human context and thus to indicate how I came to examine it but also to illustrate that the value of the magazine, though emanating from its content, goes beyond the meanings and significance produced in one individual consciousness. The magazine became an artifact collectively used as an exchange commodity, a spiritual resource, and a means to create a rite of passage and was a collectively recognized object signifying gender distinctions. Although the Romanian community in Israel was in a sense a captive audience because of its limited access to the Hebrew press, the centrality of *Revista Mea* in the life of this community can be explained only by its undisputed popularity.

The subject of this chapter is why this magazine is popular. The argument is that the popularity of a magazine requires a correspondence between its contents and the collective identity of its readership, thus making the readers receptive to accept familiar cultural elements as well as elaborate on them. In this chapter I shall first briefly describe the main characteristics of the Romanian community in Israel, highlighting its cosmopolitan orientation in a situation of perceived marginality. Next, I will describe the contents of *Revista Mea*. The popularity of the magazine will be conceptualized not only as a cultural index of an ethnic identity (as would be true of any widely read ethnic magazine) but also as a self-commentary on the community's cultural orientations with respect to those of other communities.

Knowledge of the magazine and its popularity comes first and foremost from my own personal exposure. I have reread back issues and compared various periods of time, looking for changes, innovations, and repetitions in features, content, and illustrations. To complement my own knowledge and that which came to me from relatives, friends, and neighbors, I interviewed its present editor and some of the contributors. The editor and his colleagues were interviewed in July 1988 in Tel-Aviv. In July and in August of the same year, I interviewed approximately 20 elderly people, almost all of them from Nazareth Elit, a community founded by Romanian Jews, who settled there in the late 1950s and 1960s. Clusters of questions that were addressed to the interviewees focused on two complementary issues central to the concerns of this study. The first cluster of questions concentrated on the characteristics of the Romanian-Israeli community as these people perceived them, while the second cluster was directed to obtaining what could account for the popularity of the magazine. Based on the answers given by the subjects, I have distilled the four cultural orientations described below as well as analyzed the homology between the text of the magazine and the perspectives of the readers.

The Collective Identity of
the Israeli-Romanian Community

There are not many published sources for describing the ethnic identity of the Romanian settlers in Israel. By all accounts, the community numbers approximately 300,000 people and represents the second largest Eastern European immigration to Israel after World War II. Most of the members of the Israeli-Romanian community immigrated from medium- and large-size cities. Their style of life and expectations were typically urban, although some kind of inner differentiation could be made between those who originated from the large cities of Bucharest, Iasi, and Cluz and those from smaller cities. The majority of those older than 40 at the time of immigration in the 1950s and 1960s were likely to have had only a high school or vocational education at the most. Their occupational status reflected the constraints on the Jewish population in Romania before World War II when the immigrants were young. Most of this generation were managers, shopkeepers, artisans, and clerks. A minority, however, were professionals.

As the social and political reality of Romania before the war defined the education of this generation, so the context of the newly socialist Romania defined their occupational functions. The majority of the male Jews under the socialist regime held high-level managerial positions, both locally and nationally, positions that exceeded their educational qualifications. The number of Jews holding such positions was greater than the percentage of Jews in the national population. The reason for this discrepancy can be attributed to the fact that the new regime urgently wanted to develop a modern economy. The Jewish population, being urban and secular, tended to be better educated than the rest of the population, which by and large was still rural, often illiterate, and therefore, less flexible in responding to new opportunities. Jews were better prepared than the gentile population to fill the managerial positions of the newly centralized economy.

Regarding the new regime as a unique opportunity for changing the constraints imposed on the Jewish community by the previous regimes, many people were highly motivated to upgrade their social status and to improve their economic condition. Some young, professional Jews were even active members of the new socialist bureaucracy, occupying party and government positions until they either became disillusioned or fell out of grace. As happened in most of the socialist countries of Eastern Europe, a certain period of openness toward the Jewish population was followed by a revival of nationalism and anti-Semitism. The party and government positions occupied by the Jews were transferred to gentile Romanians who, by that time, were more motivated to climb the new social ladder.

The immigrants who arrived in Israel before the age of 40 were better educated than the older generation. Many held professional degrees, especially in technical fields and had, by and large, better social positions. Those under 40 also felt more rooted in Romanian culture and better integrated in the indigenous social structure than previous generations. Although the older Romanian Jews were relatively more knowledgeable about Jewish customs and religion—they spoke or at least understood the Jewish lingua franca, Yiddish—the younger generation was thoroughly ignorant of their heritage. However, *Jewishness* was for both, beyond anything else, an ethnic-cultural awareness defined more by external constraints, that is by Romanian society, than by internal cultural activities.

Contrary to the Jewish community in Poland, the Romanian Jewish community was in the early and mid-20th century in the process of being rapidly assimilated. It did not have a large population polarized into two groups, the religiously orthodox and the secular nationalists (such as the nationalist-revisionists or the Yiddish socialists). The Jewish community in Romania lived to some extent a life more integrated within the larger indigenous culture than their counterparts in Poland, who developed a self-contained, parallel culture. The two communities differed also in terms of their use of languages. The reliance of the Polish Jewish community on the Yiddish and Hebrew press and literature was dominant in their cultural life, whereas there was no such preponderance of the two languages among the Romanian Jewry.

By virtue of sheer numbers and the diversity of groups, the Jewish community of Poland had been the center of European Jewry. Consequently, the community was well organized with a strong central structure that promoted Jewish education and encouraged political expression. Both the Jewish education, on the one hand, and a certain political militancy, on the other, became assets for members of this community when they eventually immigrated to Palestine. Thus by the time of the major Polish immigration to Palestine in the decades preceding World War II knowledge of the main languages as well as political organizational skills and connections made the Polish Jewish community the predominant one.

The contrast between the two communities is important, because they became the largest European populations in Israel. The Polish community undoubtedly remained the most influential ethnic group in the newly proclaimed nation. Its members held leadership and middle-level positions in government institutions, whereas the Romanian community was, and still is, marginal. This marginality, and the cultural handicap carried by Romanian Jews, encouraged and motivated a quick adjustment to their new life. There have been feelings of resentment among the Romanians toward the power held by their Polish counterparts.

Very early, the Romanian community felt frustrated with the reality of Israel, alienated from the centers of power and culturally isolated. Feeling that their potential was not being realized, many argued that they had made great sacrifices in emigrating and yet the professional, spiritual, and cultural aspects of their new life in Israel were unsatisfying. Those who emigrated from the large cities of Romania, where there was an intense cultural life, especially complained of cultural isolation. They were cut off, having no public figures to reflect and comment on the new and difficult life they were encountering in Israel. Geographical isolation also contributed to this feeling because many Romanians were forced by bureaucrats to settle in developing towns where cultural activities were either not yet in existence or considered inappropriate.

A digression is in order here, because the reader might be compelled to ask what motivated the Jews of Romania to immigrate en masse to Israel. The motivating conditions also form the main references of their collective identity and, therefore, are central to the thesis that the popularity of *Revista Mea* is connected to the collective identity of its audience. The three conditions are (a) the fresh memories of the atrocities of World War II, (b) the disillusionment with the Communist regime and the uncertainty it generated, and (c) the creation of the state of Israel in 1948 and the promises of this historic event.

Although the Romanian Jews had not been sent to Nazi death camps as the Polish Jews had been, the plight and suffering caused by anti-Semitism left its scars on their collective identity. During the war, the Fascist regime mobilized most of the men into forced labor camps, and several devastating pogroms in Iasi and Bucharest still remain unforgettable in the memory of the community. In spite of the events preceding and during World War II, most of the Romanian Jews co-existed relatively peacefully with their gentile counterparts. The result of their integration has been a general attitude affirming that it is possible for modern Jews to maintain their own ethnic identity while, simultaneously and without short-term contradictions, be part of the local society. The democratic societies of Western Europe were assumed to be the reference, especially by educated Jews in Romania after the war. No grudges against these countries or the United States were held, and no bitter feelings of betrayal for their inaction and apathy toward the mass extermination of Jews, as existed among the Polish Jewish community.

The rapid disillusionment with the Communist regime turned Romanian Jews further away from ideological partisanship such as socialism or Jewish nationalism, two dominant ideological currents in the political scene of Israel. The lack of political or social militancy, the presence of apathy, compounded by the constraints of adjustment to the new country, forced the Romanian Jewish immigrants to develop a practical individualism that might have been self-defeating in a highly politicized environment such as the state of Israel. Beyond anything else, the permanent need of these immigrants was the overwhelming quest for security, and such a need was mirrored in an emphasis on domesticity, family life, and the acquisition of modern commodities.

Being neither overly religious nor highly politicized, the Jewish community of Romania regarded the establishment of Israel as a major historical event that could provide a haven in the aftermath of the devastating world war and the Communist regime. They did not entertain either biblical-religious dreams or ideological ideals of secular redemption. Their aspirations were for a place where they could secure a certain material comfort as well as assert their cultural identity as Jews. In general, these people did not aspire to radical changes in their style of life; just the contrary, they desired to preserve their previous cultural life and ethnic tradition.

This community's motives for immigration, coupled with its lack of resourcefulness in translating its considerable size into political power, also paved the way to its marginal location in the Israeli ethnic mosaic. The cultural isolation and, by and large, a certain cosmopolitan outlook in the community was a disadvantage in the context of the newly created state. Nationalistic-folkloristic orientations, on one hand, and religious-traditional orientations, on the other, have dominated the local cultural scene for at least three decades. Only lately has there been an upsurge of Americanization. Between these dominant orientations, the newly immigrant Romanian Jews, given their outlook, could hardly find a cultural niche.

Two other ethnic groups that might be used to illustrate the characteristics of the collective identity of Romanian Jews are the Moroccan and Russian Jews. Each became a reference for the Romanian community. The Moroccan Jews emigrated to Israel at the same time as their Romanian counterparts. They underwent the same process of adjustment, sharing together the difficulties of living in temporary encampments and then in developing towns. They have shared the problems of finding employment and appropriate educational settings for their uprooted children. They learned to understand how the bureaucracy works, what leisure facilities were available and what spiritual comfort could be offered to them by the surroundings.

Although comrades bound together by hardship, the Romanian Jews felt themselves superior to their Moroccan counterparts by virtue of their European education and were better equipped to cope with the demands of a new modern society. Yet the Moroccan Jews could turn to their cultural resources to cope with the new life and its pressures. Moroccan Jews could speak either French or Arabic, often both, giving them access to a wider variety of media, both in Israel and the surrounding Arab countries. Due to their traditional religious education, many Moroccans knew enough Hebrew to feel comfortable or confident in the language. Furthermore, their religious knowledge and commitment to traditional festivals plus having large extended families provided continuity with their previous way of life. For a majority of adult immigrants, the synagogue remained the central institution in the community and its elders and rabbis their spiritual leaders.

Before the Russian immigration of the 1990s, the bulk of Russian immigrants had arrived in Israel in the 1970s, 10 to 20 years after the Romanians. Although much smaller, the Russian community was incomparably more visible, militant, and nationalistic. The Russian immigration was more dynamic, internally better organized, and had a more public image in Israel as a whole. Less isolated geographically, most of its members established homes in major Israeli cities; they were better prepared because of their knowledge of the Hebrew language and the intricacies of the Israeli political system. Consequently, the new Russian immigrants were less isolated culturally and often better off materially than their Romanian counterparts.

A major difference between these two communities concerned their attitudes toward the Western world and toward Israel. The Russian Jewish community, living for many years in isolation from Western culture, developed an internal network of support and a secular, nationalistic orientation that became important resources in the process of adjustment to Israel. The Zionist idealism and anti-Communist militancy of the internationally known *refusniks* provided a respected leadership that brought prestige and lent weight to the entire community of Russian immigrants.

Revista Mea

The magazine *Revista Mea* was founded in 1960 as a commercial venture. It invariably runs 66 pages (on a 9×25 cm format) printed on a low-quality paper and with low-quality photographs. The only color picture is the cover, which is almost exclusively of female models. Published every Friday, the magazine presently costs approximately $2 US and has a distribution of about 13,000 copies. According to the editor, this number should be multiplied by three or four, because every purchaser shares it with family members or friends. A recent decrease in sales can be attributed to the death of its increasingly older readership.

The print media in Israel aimed at Romanian readers is relatively sparse. The only daily newspaper, *Viata Noastra,* features local and international news and political commentaries. *Facla* is a weekly paper 7 or 8 years older than *Revista Mea* and has a distribution of 9,000 copies a week. It features mainly in-depth original reports on current topics, although there are many translations. *Facla* and *Revista Mea* share similar journalistic features and are the property of the same owners.

The weekly *Revista Familiei* (*The Family Magazine*) has a format similar to *Revista Mea,* but lacks its features on political, social, and cultural topics. In its early years in the 1970s, *Revista Familiei* attempted to attract the readers of *Revista Mea.* Even though the former was successful for a while, it lost the competition and then began to develop an identity as a diversified family and variety magazine, displaying many pictures of tourist sites and movie stars. Its 50 pages contain romantic and detective stories, comic features (similar to those of *Revista Mea*) as well as medical, nutritional, and cosmetic columns. *Revista Familiei* uses the same format as *Revista Mea,* although the pictures on the cover alternate between young female models and pictures of mothers with their children. Recently, a new magazine, *Minimum,* has attempted to be the educated readers' equivalent of *Revista Mea.* *Minimum* has more literary articles and uses a more elaborate and sophisticated style. It, too, is filled with pictures (although in this case of classical musicians, artists, and politicians), short memoirs, and fiction.

In fact, all of these magazines easily succumb to the structural formula that *Revista Mea* best epitomizes: short, varied, and diversified features, punctuated with attractive or suggestive pictures, cartoons, puzzles, and advertisements. As far as I was able to discover, and as the editor of *Revista Mea* confirmed, no other similar type of magazine can be found among the other ethnic media in Israel or among the Romanian press of the gentile Romanians in exile in Western Europe or America. A recent commercial attempt to imitate the success of *Revista Mea* has been made by founding a somewhat equivalent magazine in Russian called *Krug* and aimed at the Russian immigrants in Israel. As expected, the Russian community has several magazines, however, that seem to emphasize political and ideological articles rather than leisure and social topics.

It may be that the visible lack of political positions of all the Romanian magazines is consistent with the apolitical attitude (and even apathy) that the Romanian Jews display. The tradition of little civic involvement and disgust toward politicians has emerged over many years of disillusionment with various political parties and regimes, and this is evident in the profile of these magazines. On the other hand, the readers hold an almost sacred image of the state. The result is that in order for the magazine to be popular, it understandably must not over-emphasize the ideology of any political party nor take sides in any factional conflict. The magazine must hold the state in reverence, its institutions, its office holders, and its national and religious celebrations. The editor of *Revista Mea* was explicit in arguing that because he does not want to insult anybody he has decided not to publish material that deviates from the community's political consensus. In an interview he argued:

> The average Romanian that I know has a lot of equilibrium. Extremism of any kind is something rare among these people. Romanians do not have political ambitions. They are working hard all week long and at the end of the week they prefer to relax and enjoy life.

When asked who were the readers of the magazine, the editor replied: "The readers are clerks, shop workers, dentists, and housewives. They tend to be older; many of them are grandparents. Sixty percent of these readers are women that worked hard all their life and sacrificed a great deal for the family." Because the mortality rate among men between 60 and 80 is higher than among women of the same age, one would indeed assume that the readers are now more likely to be women, a character-istic that would have been somewhat different in the recent past when men were still likely to be avid readers even though women usually bought the magazine.

The Successful Formula

One might describe the character of *Revista Mea* as the opposite and the complement of the daily *Viata Noastra*. While the latter presents news and commentaries reflecting the mainstream politics of the Labor party, *Revista Mea* aims more for the optional aspects of life, for leisure as well as for certain types of liminal reflections that suspend taking political positions. From this viewpoint, the magazine shares its char-acteristics with similar genres of popular culture that by definition are reactions to ideological pressures (Bar-Haïm, 1990).

In a sense, there is a built-in formula for success in this magazine: culturally isolated readers with no access to other media, a general spiritual void filled by a medium aimed at allegorically or directly commenting on daily life. The formula assumes not only a diversity of topics and accessibility but also a balanced mix of practical topics; escapist articles that suspend the pressures of daily life such as romance, mystery, and detective stories (Cawelti, 1976); and social and international commentaries—treated from a broad political consensus—on such matters as anti-Semitism, the Arab-Israeli conflict, elections, Soviet-Israeli relations, and so on. Also significant is the extensive number of humorous cartoons, anecdotes, and epigrams. *Revista Mea*'s uniqueness consists not only of having the practical, suspenseful, and relaxing features that can be found in many magazines of a general nature but of combining these with original pieces and translations tailored to fit the interests of the Romanian readership.

Such a formula never seems to go wrong, because the material published does not antagonize anyone; nor does it aim at the problematic or conflicting aspects of social life. The reflective pieces do not convey existential angst or suggest doubts about the present social order. The success of such a formula is based on the perception among readers that the material and generally the policy of the magazine is above partisan ideologies, group conflicts, and the internal dissensions of Israeli society. Nonetheless, the magazine can easily be categorized ideologically. The avoidance of controversy and the concentration on leisure convey an impression of a nonengaged magazine that serves only ethnic and individual needs.

This formula is shared by many magazines, not necessarily connected with ethnic groups. For instance, the most popular Israeli magazine for women, *L'Isha,* possessing more resources to provide journalistic profiles and investigative reports, follows a similar pattern. *L'Isha* must, in fact, adopt the same quasi-noncontroversial, nonexplicit positions, presenting diverse and balanced material, because it tries to appeal to a group of readers whose only similar characteristic is their gender. In the case of women's magazines, there are other publications that aim to subvert the popularity of *L'Isha.* No such alternatives exist for the Romanian community. Hence, the more elite groups as well as the more politicized and those with a different set of values are held hostage.

It can be argued that the range and limits of the features in *Revista Mea* are compatible with the general collective identity of the community. The avoidance of civic activity and political confrontation, on one hand, and the escape to a world that has practical bearing on daily life, on the other, results in a lack of sociopolitical awareness. The avoidance assumes a disconnection between the individual and the society.

It is difficult to imagine a comparable format for the Moroccan or Russian readers. Due to their emphasis on family, synagogue, and entrenched traditional routines, the former would be uninterested in individualistic flights into secular leisure. Likewise, it is hard to imagine a similar magazine becoming a popular and attractive medium for the majority of Russian readers because of their politicized and militant world view. Although this generalization would hold for the majority of the Moroccans and Russians, it would not apply to those groups within these communities that resemble the Romanians: those that are secular, urban, and non-nationalistic. Marginal groups, especially among the immigrants from non-Russian republics, such as Moldavia (previously part of Romania), share similar characteristics with their Romanian counterparts. The newly established Russian magazine *Krug* seems to tap such readers.

Ethnic Cultural Orientations

To make sense of the homology between a magazine's content and the collective identity of its readers, I propose a conceptual scheme that draws on the major features of an ethnic community's identity. It should be stressed that the framework being suggested is applicable to all ethnic groups in Israel as well as elsewhere. Two major features highlight the general traits of the Romanian collective identity: the first is continuity versus newness and the second is cosmopolitanism versus localism.

The first feature refers to time. It assumes that most of the adult readers have been influenced by past events that shaped their cultural interests, tastes, values, and worldview. One would assume that many, although not all, of these interests—as well as many of the practical daily activities and habits that came to form their identity while in Romania—are transferred to the new homeland. Much effort would be invested by an ethnic magazine in identifying and articulating these elements of continuity.

However, the readers presently live in a very different sociocultural reality. Despite being Jewish and living in a Jewish state, the reality of Israel is quite different from what they were accustomed to in Romania.

Therefore, the adjustment to the new society requires that these people learn new skills and appropriate new habits and values while simultaneously suppressing the previous patterns of behavior. Often the present reality is so radically different that an analytical distinction between continuity and newness is warranted (Even-Zohar, 1979).

The second feature refers to place. Members of a community may regard themselves as part of a broader cultural entity—a cosmopolitan orientation. In the case of Israel, the broader entity may be European, American, Slavic, or Arabic cultures. Alternatively, immigrants may regard themselves primarily as part of the local culture—a local orientation (Merton, 1957).

The interaction between these four features produces four cultural orientations that should exist in the written and visual material of any ethnic magazine. The logic of the structural scheme has semblance with Mary Douglas's (1982) scheme grid versus group, which also aims to elicit four universal categories of perception. The four cultural orientations can be drawn as shown in Table 9.1.

Cosmopolitan-Continuity Orientation

Among the four categories of content, it would appear that the cosmopolitan-continuity orientation is the most frequent. Regular features in *Revista Mea* concerned with worldwide events include the following titles: "Meridians," "Modern Actualities," "People and Facts," "Files of Famous Crimes," "Chronic of the Bizarre," "Curiosities," "Fantasies," and "Variétiés." The amount of coverage devoted to these topics when they occur anywhere in Western Europe, particularly in France, or in the United States is disproportionate to the coverage given local Israeli or worldwide Jewish topics. *Revista Mea* continues the traditional cultural connection between France and Romania. The editor of the magazine, answering a question about what guides the profile of the magazine, succinctly argued, "France is the capital of the world and we are Francophones and Europeans."

In general, the perception among the Romanian-Jewish readers that they are Europeans and, therefore, should be knowledgeable about what takes place there is continued by *Revista Mea*. The magazine also provides information about the British royal family, Italian fashion, and not surprisingly, prosperity in Germany. Even the female models featured on the cover embody typical Western European notions of beauty, contributing iconographically to the readers' perception that *Revista Mea* resembles a European magazine. The readers' perception is thus

TABLE 9.1 The Four Cultural Orientations

| Cultural Orientations Related to Place | Cultural Orientations Related to Time | |
	Continuity	Newness
Cosmopolitanism	1	3
Localism	2	4

maintained that they continue to be concerned with the same issues and have the same taste and standards they had earlier while living in Romania.

Western Europe has been in the past and continues to be the cathartic and escapist reference of romantic love stories and suspenseful stories involving the bizarre. The reference to Western Europe and the genres of romance and suspense are exactly what these readers used to read in the Romanian magazines of the period before the Communist regime. The overwhelming preoccupation of the magazine with the bizarre, the extraordinary, the deviant, and the paradoxical—often treated in a whimsical and entertaining fashion—implies that the unpredictable and the uncontrollable exist only in a fantasy world, one the readers should not take too seriously. The improbability of the stories proves the rule, most people live most of their lives in subdued familiar routines. The tone of the fantasies implies that what counts is the basic European ethos that produced the readers' values and on which they can rely for understanding their surroundings. The basic, everlasting Western values are assumed to provide predictability, order, and control, and although there are exceptions, these values should apply in Israel as they applied in Eastern Europe. Continuity of Western values and the connection with the countries in which they were embedded ensure that civility, especially in the Middle East—which abounds with people who are profane to these values—continues to persist. The tone of the journalistic material in this category sometimes implies a certain taken-for-granted familiarity ("Because we are Westerners . . .") and a patronizing subtle note (the superior Western taste).

Localism-Continuity Orientation

The second most frequent category seems to be localism-continuity. Two major clusters of material can be regarded as bridging the community's past traditions and its local Israeli life. First, some of this material can be clustered under the category "advice on personal, community, and family practices." This personal and family-oriented material is in fact either transferable cultural practices and daily customs or universally recognized practices appropriate for the local context. Such features include "Matrimonial Courier," "Bon Appetit," and "Physician's Advice." Other features are concerned with child care, women's fashion, puzzles, and cartoons. Whatever the practical usefulness of these articles, their symbolic virtue is to bestow a sense of universality, continuity, and perpetuation. Symbolically, the daily personal and family practices encourage observing life in a longer perspective by forcing consideration of the human universality of practical routines, valid for the new local context as well.

Ultimately, these practices confirm and sanction the existing cultural order as it is reduced to personal and family life. They bestow security in that the local context can at least be partially understood through the same daily, practical manifestations that can be recognized everywhere in the world. The cartoons, a favorite feature for many readers and a prominent one, are overwhelmingly dominated by the themes of family life and gender relationships. Cartoons aiming at the political scene, international events, and ethnic-cultural relationships are rare.

Second, another major cluster of material includes information on secular issues related to Judaism and Jewishness. Thus the magazine maintains a permanent column about or by Jewish Romanian writers who treat Jewish themes, review new books on Jewish affairs, or report on events that affect the Jewish condition. There is also a column titled "The Little Judaic Encyclopedia" and historical commentaries called "Critical Times in Jewish History." Topics related to the Holocaust, anti-Semitism, Jewish freedom fighters during World War II, and renowned Jewish figures and their contribution to either Zionism or global history abound throughout all the issues. Commentaries and reflections are treated from the perspective of secular Judaic values and are underlined by a tone of cynicism implying that, in spite of changes, the fundamental animosity and hostility of the gentile world toward Jews continues in the present despite the state of Israel.

Topics that by their nature assume a continuity with the new local context of the Romanian immigrants are highlighted. One such theme concerns the history and cultural life of various Jewish communities scattered all over the world, which not only, by their disappearance, reinforce readers' beliefs that the sacrifices of living in the land of Israel are worthwhile in some kind of historical perspective but also contain reminiscences of the rich life of the Jewish communities in the Diaspora. A different topic, common in various kinds of journalistic writings, is the theme of Yiddish culture: language, theater, and music. Because the Romanian Diaspora has been an important center of Yiddish theater, many of the articles reminisce about various aspects of the Yiddish theater. There are many personal articles on Jewish family celebrations, such as the traditional Passover, or the emotionally charged fast of Yom Kippur (Day of Atonement). Reminiscences abound concerning famous Jewish community leaders of Romania before World War II as well as non-Jewish personalities whose activities affected the Jewish life of the time. The abundance of memories and reminiscences is fundamental in that it bridges the past and the present both in terms of topic and the underlying tone of the articles.

In most cases, the author who reminisces makes an explicit link between the present Israeli life and whatever is the subject of his or her article, often indicating similarities and dissimilarities between past and present. The tone underlying most of the material falling in this category is mild cynicism and familiarity, as if it stated that much of what is happening here and now also happened there and then and has its roots in the past. Memoirs and reminiscences are a quintessential genre for conveying such an attitude.

Cosmopolitan-Newness Orientation

This orientation is emphasized less in the pages of *Revista Mea* than the two preceding orientations. Articles in this category are concerned with the connection between Israel and the world at large. The establishment of the state of Israel produced among all Jews, including the Romanians, a feeling of a secular millennium with great expectations. Much energy was channeled into trying to create a society radically different from what the Jews had previously experienced. The late 1940s and the 1950s and 1960s were decades infused with hope and pride, the collective aspirations of Israelis and Zionist Jews had been to make Israel a normal country, like any other nation on the globe. The Romanian Jews, as all Jews living the unique historical events of those decades, were both enthusiastic and proud of the new state. They looked with awe and wonderment at its achievements as well as with puzzlement and anxiety at the difficulties and dangers.

Some material in *Revista Mea* still echoes this mood. Often one can find articles whose central idea is the uniqueness of the new state in comparison with other countries with longer traditions. The cosmopolitan dimension comes into the picture when the state is described as an equal of other national states or when it is discussed in the context of the global integration of nations. There are commentaries explaining the geopolitical importance of Israel and the contribution of the newly created nation to the aspiring countries of Africa. Other articles are concerned with the vital role of the state in defending Jews in various totalitarian countries, such as the Soviet Union, Argentina, and Syria, or the dignified visit of one of the Israeli prime ministers to Romania.

Alongside these sociopolitical commentaries are regular stories that attempt to prove that Israel is like any other secular Western country, such as those describing New Year's Eve parties in Tel Aviv, courses for flight attendants (an occupation based on appearance, manners, and service skills that are viewed with awe and pride), the success of the Israeli candidate for the crown of Miss Universe, the new rise in popularity of an Israeli rock group, and the booming Scandinavian tourism in Eilat.

Almost invariably the tone of such articles is pride about the achievements of Israel for its role in the world and Jewish affairs. Although radically new issues and new types of people are formed by the new social context of their present life, the assumption of *Revista Mea* is that the new context can be understood if it is seen in perspective with other societies. Thus it provides both a sense of uniqueness as well as an impression of the normality of the new Israeli society.

Localism-Newness Orientation

The localism-newness orientation is the least frequent in the magazine, because the material that might contain it is least appealing to the readers. This orientation is more problematic and ambivalent than the others, at least for the Romanian Jews, because it assumes a concern with a totally new and radically different reality that is hard to comprehend. However, it is the same new reality that dominates local life and that forms the uniqueness, for better or worse, of Israeli society. It is the same new local sociocultural processes that belie both the vision for some and the disillusionment for others. For those who do not actively realize their vision through political participation (most of the Romanian Jews), the unique character of local life is often a source of anxiety and alienation. Thus typical of the range of issues covered by the magazine in terms of this orientation are such subjects as the character of the Israeli political parties, the extremism of the ultraorthodox religious factions, the Israeli-Arab conflict, the nature of the Israeli army, immigration and emigration, and the cultural-political power struggle for domination between various ethnic groups.

The Zionist revolution aimed first and foremost at creating a new type of person that was supposed to become eventually the embodiment of the normality of the Jews in their own land, after 2,000 years of being a dispersed nation without a country of their own. Those born in the land of Israel, the so-called Sabras, were regarded with a certain amount of awe and wonderment, for they were the symbol of newness in Israel. The normality of the Sabras is in essence an ostentatious disregard and irreverence for the daily customs and manners brought by the immigrants from their lands of origin. The behavior of the Sabras and the local culture in general have been both a source of irritation and pride among all immigrants.

Thus many of the commentaries concerning the local cultural and social events exude an ambivalence toward the Sabras' candid behavior and their youthful culture. Often, however, as if it understood the collective feelings of the readers, the magazine scornfully comments on the Sabras' lack of respect for other people who do not have the advantages of knowing the Hebrew language as fluently as they do, but whose achievements nevertheless deserve reverence. Often the lack of politeness and etiquette in the Sabras' culture seems to exasperate the new immigrants and these emotions are definitely carried in the commentaries of the magazine.

The magazine dutifully marks the secular celebrations and holidays, emphasizing their importance as reminders of the new life of optimism and hope that can be achieved by the Jewish people only in the land of Zion (Caspi, 1986). In keeping with the attitude of ambivalence toward the local newness, the underlying tone of the journalistic content is also a mixture of admonition and didactic explanation as well as moderate nationalistic pride.

Concluding Remarks

Successful magazines are cogent examples of how the status quo is cultivated. Consequently, research on successful magazines ultimately becomes a study of the perception of how they guide their readers in coping with present social life, in escaping from it, and eventually making the best of it. The assumption made by successful popular magazines is that the average reader should be soothed and pacified rather than educated to develop new understandings of himself or herself and the surrounding social world. Such an assumption lends itself to transforming popular magazines into a major instrument for entrenching conventional social arrangements. In other words, any magazine, or any cultural medium, that does not assume that readers should be provoked and takes for granted that social conventions should be cultivated, concerns itself with the reproduction of the present social modalities. But as so often happens, the publishers of these magazines argue that they provide readers with what they demand.

Yet, the goal of becoming a successful magazine is more complex than just employing a recognized formula that includes short light pieces, many attractive pictures, and diversified material aimed at a broad readership. Particularly when it involves a specialized readership, as is the case for ethnic, youth, humor, or women's magazines, it becomes necessary to adjust the content of the magazine to fit the dominant cultural orientations of the targeted readership. Although one would assume that an editorial board would use a sensible approach to the material to make it attractive to the readers, there is still a correspondence that is required between the content of the magazine (its latent assumptions, linguistic discourse, signification, and connotations) and the dominant cultural orientations of the readership.

The dominant cultural orientations of a defined population can be roughly constructed by relating the basic structural features of that population to the context in which they live. In other words, by distilling the major structural parameters of a group, one is likely to define the *weltanschauung* of that group, at least within a certain context (Douglas, 1982), that is, a cultural universe that sets out the competing alternatives and shapes the group's sensibilities. For a researcher the next task at hand is to observe how the magazine's content is selected and directed to correspond to the group's cultural orientations that are perceived to be dominant among the available alternatives. This should provide an empirical way of understanding how ideological hegemony asserts itself and consequently how popular culture reproduces the social. The challenge for a student of the mass media, however, is not only to prove that successful popular magazines reproduce and even reinforce social arrangements but to describe and analyze how it is done, especially at the semiotic level that becomes taken-for-granted mythology (Barthes, 1983).

I have summarized the traditional arguments of the critical sociology of culture regarding the way commercial culture reproduces the status quo. It has been implied as well that the manipulable reader is lulled by the very culture—and even pays for it—that reinforces oppressive social conditions from which he or she should desire to escape (Horkheimer & Adorno, 1988). But rather than uncritically accepting these ideas, one might seriously consider an altogether different interpretation of the actions of readers.

Perhaps it is not true that readers are enticed into cultural anesthesia, but are consciously interested in discovering how culture is created, fascinated by the endless ingenious formulas for encoding familiar yet problematic social relations as cultural mythology. Thus they obtain some kind of satisfaction from discovering the transparent social through the veil of culture. The satisfaction of discovering the tricks through cultural deconstruction may also be a form of resistance. One might carry the idea further, arguing that what takes place is a sort of dialogue; readers buy the magazine not as a vehicle of escape but to be a partner in a continuous dialogue with the magazine concerning the social. The magazine inventively prepares the mask of society, to use a metaphor from the theater, while the reader takes pleasure in catching a glimpse of the makeup process. Often, the magazine, by now an entity with its own life rather than the product of a mere organization, suggests without being aware of it ideas about the nature of society and how it functions. The magazine facilitates a collaboration with the reader in his or her self-induced delight in unveiling the infinite range of cultural deceptions aimed at enticing him or her to affirm social relationships.

In other words, although the magazine presents society as a given, the reader makes it problematic. The dance has its own arrangement: The popular magazine encodes the social in simple codes, and the reader takes joy in decoding them. If the codes were complex and the discourse critical, society would naturally be represented as problematic, and therefore, decoding a magazine would not be a source of contemptuous gratification for the reader.

This idea of a dialogue between readers and the reified society represented by popular magazines puts forth a worthwhile alternative interpretation of the question why some magazines become more successful than others. The topic deserves further study. The interaction between a society represented by magazines, on the one hand, and readers, on the other, has been ignored while the passivity of readers, who in reality have their own agenda, has presumptuously been overestimated (Inglis, 1990). This alternative interpretation can also be applied to explain the success of an ethnic magazine. The position of marginality of an ethnic group is carried through a tacit dialogue that can find its echo in the commercial success of an ethnic magazine.

References

Bar-Haïm, G. (1990). Popular culture and ideological discontents: A theory. *International Journal of Politics, Culture, and Society, 3*(3), 279-296.

Barthes, R. (1983). *Mythologies.* New York: Hill & Wang.

Caspi, D. (1986). *Media decentralization: The case of Israel's local newspapers.* New Brunswick, NJ: Transaction Books.

Cawelti, J. G. (1976). *Adventure, mystery and romance: Formula stories as art and popular culture.* Chicago: University of Chicago Press.

Douglas, M. (1982). *Essays in the sociology of perception.* Boston: Routledge & Kegan Paul.

Even-Zohar, I. (1979). The emergence and the crystallization of the local Hebrew language in the land of Israel, 1882-1945. *Katedra, 16*, pp. 60-82.

Horkheimer, M., & Adorno, T. A. (1988). The cultural industry: Enlightenment as mass deception. In M. Horkheimer & T. A. Adorno, *Dialectic of enlightenment*, pp. 5-84. New York: Continuum.

Inglis, F. (1990). *Media theory, An introduction.* Oxford, UK: Basil Blackwell.

Merton, R. (1957). *Social theory and social structure.* Glencoe, IL: The Free Press.

10

Minority-Language Broadcasting and the Continuation of Celtic Culture in Wales and Ireland

W. J. HOWELL, Jr.

Communication is the essence of culture, and language is the primary symbolic code on which all human communication, be it personal or mediated, is dependent. But a language—any language—must be spoken by people in everyday situations if it is to remain alive. In technologically complex societies, however, interpersonal usage is a necessary but less than sufficient condition for the survival of a language unless it is also disseminated by the prevailing channels of the institutions of mass communication.

It is thus recognized by proprietors of culture and national policymakers in today's world that telecommunication technology can be an ally rather than an enemy in the task of saving minority languages and authentic cultures from extinction. The fact that languages have intrinsic value as the primary source of ethnic identity and cultural expression for groups and individuals alike make their continuation an especially emotional problem for the "stateless nations of the Fourth World" (Mackey, 1979, p. 48), those minority cultures that exist within countries but whose ancestral languages are threatened with extinction by the dominant culture of the majority of the national population.

Despite diligent efforts by parents and teachers to speak and teach an ethnic dialect within the home and school, living languages have become critically dependent on broadcasting for their continuation and survival. Among the mass media, radio and television are the most powerful vehicles for transmitting national as well as popular cultures from generation to generation. Broadcasting seems to invest its content with status; therefore, languages used on the air have legitimacy and gain credibility in the minds of audiences. This prestige factor is particularly important to children and minorities, because they hold the key to a minority language's future.

It is, therefore, easy to understand why cultural minorities throughout the world place a high premium on gaining access to their nations' airwaves and cable systems as practical and effective means of helping their beleaguered native tongues to survive. This has become a critical issue of language policy in bicultural nations where competing language groups co-exist and where their two languages enjoy equal status as official languages of state.

The Principality of Wales and the Republic of Ireland represent two interesting models of bicultural societies that have enlisted broadcasting to assist in the revival and continuation of their traditional Celtic languages within dominant English-speaking contexts. The mutual preoccupation by Wales and Ireland with bilingual broadcasting matters is perhaps the most conspicuous manifestation of their shared heritage of nationalism and their strikingly similar histories, cultures, and physical circumstances.

Although a political component of the United Kingdom, Wales regards itself as a nation in cultural and geographical terms. And although all of its 2.7 million people speak English, 20% prefer to use Welsh as their first language. Put another way, 80% are English monoglots and 20% are bilingual. Those who speak Welsh are known as the *Cymry Cymraeg* and are most salient as a cultural force in the North.

Following a decade of bitter political turmoil, activists were successful in having Britain's new Channel Four television service operated under an autonomous body in Wales and its output there dominated by programs in Welsh. Ireland, too, experienced a similar controversy during the 1970s over striking a suitable balance between programming in English and Irish, and imported versus domestic production levels, on its new radio and television networks.

Today, only about 5% of the Republic of Ireland's 3.5 million residents speak Irish exclusively, although it is estimated that roughly 12% are fluent in the ancestral tongue. The Irish monoglots, the *Gaeltachti,* are concentrated in the western counties of Donegal, Galway, and Kerry—a region known as the *Gaeltacht*. Another 20% are bilingual in the sense that they have competence in Irish but, with little opportunity to use it, rely mainly on English. The remaining 66% of the Irish speak English almost entirely, although most know some expressions or words in Irish.

This study compares and contrasts the minority-language broadcasting policies and practices of Wales and Ireland by tracing their parallel pasts and examining their present bilingual radio and television services. It will draw from official studies and recommendations; current publications by broadcasting organizations in the two countries; correspondence with executives from the BBC, HTV, Channel Four in Wales (S4C), and Ireland's RTE; the public positions taken by prominent language groups and government bodies; contemporary programming data; press clips from Welsh and Irish newspapers; and my previous field research in Wales and Ireland.[1]

Parallel Pasts as Cultural Cousins

The ancestral Welsh and Irish languages sprang from the Celtic group's two companion branches: *Goidelic*—Irish, Scotch Gaelic, and Manx—and *Brythonic*—Welsh, Cornish, and Breton (Thomas, 1980). Today, both vernaculars enjoy legal parity with English as co-equal and official languages of state, but such was not always the case. Welsh had no official status until passage of the Welsh Language Act of 1967, even though it is the oldest language spoken on a daily basis in Europe (H. P. Jones, 1982). The 1967 law formulated the principle of *equal validity,* which guarantees each citizen of Wales the legal right to communicate in the language of his or her choice and to be responded to in that same language, in writing if need be (Broadcasting Council for Wales, 1975). The act also brought about bilingual official forms and public signs, a renewed interest in all-Welsh schools, the establishment of language camps (*wulpans*), and an impetus to organize a lobby for bilingual broadcasting issues. The Irish language received its official endorsement 30 years earlier. Article 8 of the Irish Constitution of 1937 cites in its first clause that Irish is the national language and the first official language.

So, too, do the histories of Wales and Ireland parallel one another. Both are marked by economic exploitation and social subjugation by Anglophonic Britain, whose ethnocentric laws governed each for centuries. Both Celtic cultures have rich oral traditions, replete with indigenous storytellers and poets. Religion has also played signal roles in the evolution of their two peoples from pre-Roman civilization to the present—albeit Irish Catholicism vis-à-vis the Nonconformist Protestantism of Wales. But several differences exist between Wales and Ireland that have required each to develop unique bilingual broadcasting policies and implement services that address the specific needs of their respective minority cultures.

Parallel Problems With Domestic Distinctions

Coincidentally, Wales and Ireland share a number of geographical features that have plagued the development of their respective broadcasting systems. Among these are mountainous terrains that impede domestic patterns of coverage by their broadcast transmitters, television spillover from English stations the signals of which reach the majority of their households, and national television services with programming schedules that are dominated by Anglo-American productions in English. Accordingly, Welsh and Irish nationalists have demanded and won some concessions from their broadcasters for proportionate programming in their own native languages.

One important distinction is geopolitical. Because Wales is part of the United Kingdom, it is by definition a nation in cultural and geographic terms only. It is, therefore, served by the regional services of a national network duopoly composed of the public service British Broadcasting Corporation (BBC) and the private commercial federation known as the Independent Broadcasting Authority (IBA). Ireland, however, is an autonomous political entity with sovereign control over its own broadcasting monopoly, *Radio Telefis Eireann* (RTE)—a semistate corporation commissioned by the Irish Parliament (the *Oireachtas*) and dependent in roughly equal measure on license fees on television receivers and advertising sales for its operating revenue.

Next is the disparity in degrees of bilingualism between the two countries. Whereas about 20% of the Welsh and Irish people are bilingual, Ireland has a small segment of people (5%) who speak no English. Because everyone in Wales is conversant in English, the Welsh language movement historically has been at a distinct disadvantage in its attempt to influence the programming policies of the BBC and the IBA. On the other hand, language guardians in Ireland have been able to cite the small but determined contingent of Irish monoglots in its negotiations with RTE. However, in terms of fluency and daily usage, more people in Wales have chosen Welsh as their lingua franca than is true of the Irish-language speakers in Ireland—by ratios of 20% and 12%, respectively.

Last, a uniform Welsh idiom has been disseminated from pulpits throughout the country since the Bible was translated into Welsh in the 16th century, whereas each of the three Gaeltacht areas in Ireland has its own distinctive Gaelic dialect. This makes it nearly impossible for

RTE to reach the Gaeltachti with a standard form of Irish, because technically none exists.

Bilingual broadcasting in Wales and Ireland evolved through three parallel stages of development. Both began by integrating limited amounts of minority-language content into their English-language radio broadcasts. Next, each scheduled blocks of bilingual and culture-specific programs on their national television systems. Finally, the broadcasting organizations serving Wales and Ireland established official language policies and guidelines for Welsh and Irish programming.

The Development of Welsh-Language Broadcasting Policy and Practices

Guardians of the Welsh language have struggled to gain access to the airwaves since the early days of radio in Britain. However, the first broadcasts in Welsh came not from England but from Ireland, a bitter irony that was recognized in a 1927 report issued by the former Welsh board of education:

> We regard the present policy of the British Broadcasting Corporation as one of the most serious menaces to the life of the Welsh language. . . . It is a rather pathetic comment on the position of Welsh in its own country that the only regular Welsh programme is that given once a week from the Dublin station by the Irish government. (Jones, 1982, p. 26)

The BBC responded to such criticism in 1929 by initiating occasional broadcasts of major cultural events in Welsh, like the annual *Eisteddfod* arts festival. Welsh-language broadcasting was formalized in 1932 through the BBC's Welsh Religious Advisory Council, and 5 years later it created the Welsh Home Service radio network in recognition of "the social and cultural aspects of regional broadcasting" (Briggs, 1965, p. 322). It took several more decades and the arrival of television before broadcasters in the UK formulated Welsh-language policies. The 1952 BBC charter established national broadcasting councils for Scotland and Wales to supervise radio and television programming for the two regions.

The BBC's operative Welsh policy was first defined in Article 10 of its 1964 charter, which vested the Welsh Broadcasting Council with full authority to provide programming to Wales that expressed "full regard to the distinctive culture, language, interests and tastes" of the Welsh people (British Broadcasting Company [BBC], 1980, pp. 257-258). This policy mandate was implemented through the BBC Wales, which commenced a new television operation for the region on an opt-out basis from the national BBC-1 network in 1964. Later it was augmented with Radio 4 Wales, a bilingual service that split into separate stations—Radio Wales in English and *Radio Cymru* in Welsh—during 1977.

The market structure of British broadcasting changed from a monopoly to a duopoly with passage of the Television Act of 1954, which introduced the BBC to competition in the form of Independent Television (ITV). ITV was subsumed by the Independent Broadcasting Authority (IBA) in 1973 when IBA added Independent Local Radio to its charter.

The new authority assigned Wales its first commercial franchise, Television West and Wales (TWW), in 1958. A second ITV company, Wales West and North (WWN), began providing a largely redundant service to populated areas in 1962 and subsequently failed. The TWW station eventually aired 5 hours of weekly programming in Welsh via its *Teledu Cymru* service, but was persistently chastized by Welsh nationalists. The 1960 Pilkington Committee on Broadcasting reprimanded both the IBA and the BBC, charging that "the language and culture of Wales would suffer irreparable harm" unless more programs in Welsh were forthcoming (Howell, 1982, p. 43). These criticisms resulted in the original TWW franchise being replaced by Harlech Television (HTV) in 1968. HTV expressed public concern about the "erosion of the language," referring to the Celtic tongue as the "cornerstone of national identity" (Howell, 1981, p. 125).

Broadcasts in Welsh increased in air time and quality via both radio and television during the 1970s. By the beginning of the 1980s, the BBC Wales was providing 7 hours of television programming a week in Welsh and 6 in English. Its Radio Wales and Radio Cymru outlets were each on the air 65 hours a week in English and Welsh, respectively. But HTV also had grown, airing more than 7 hours weekly in Welsh and 4 in English. Two Independent Local Radio stations in Cardiff and Swansea also were broadcasting several hours in Welsh on a daily basis. In sum, Wales was receiving an average of greater than 14 hours of television programs and nearly 70 hours via radio in the Welsh language from the BBC and IBA (Howell, 1981).

Despite this, a controversy was brewing in Wales relative to the Welsh programming policy for Britain's impending fourth television channel. Activist groups like the Welsh Nationalist party (*Plaid Cymru*) and the Welsh Language Society (*Cymdeithas Yr Iaith Gymraeg*) voiced strong arguments for having all Welsh-language programming placed on the new channel. The English monoglots and both broadcasters favored having television programming in Welsh spread over several channels, as had been the practice for nearly two decades. Eventually, the fourth network was awarded to the IBA and placed under the control of its newly created Channel Four Television Company. To assuage the unique language issue in Wales, the new service would be known as *Sianel Pedwar Cymru* (S4C) and run by a separate body, the Welsh Fourth Channel Authority.

The idea for a fourth television channel in Britain was hatched in the 1960 Pilkington Committee on Broadcasting (1960), whose report 2 years later cited the special programming needs of the Welsh and gave impetus to the establishment of the BBC Wales services (p. 229). The November 1974 Report of the Committee on Broadcasting Coverage (1974) went a step further and recommended that a fourth channel be allocated to Wales "as soon as possible" and ahead of the rest of the UK, noting that "Welsh language programs should be given priority" (p. 79) and thus placed entirely on the new service. The Labour Government of the day accepted these findings and empowered the Working Party of the Fourth Television Service in Wales, chaired by J. W. M. Siberry, to plan its implementation. The 1975 Siberry Report proposed that a transmission network be developed and that the BBC and HTV Wales contribute a combined total of 25 hours of weekly programming in Welsh for the new channel.

The conclusions and recommendations of these and other bodies were later reviewed by the Committee on the Future of Broadcasting, a 16-member group headed by Lord Noel Annan and charged with the broad mandate of preserving yet accommodating Britain's public service model of broadcasting in the wake of emerging technologies like cable, teletext, home video, and satellites. The Annan committee deliberated from April 1974 to March 1977. Its findings, as they pertained to Wales, endorsed the idea of starting a fourth television channel in Wales but rejected the demands of the language nationalists and the Siberry Report to place all Welsh-language programming on the new channel. The Annan Report caused a stir in Wales but was to become moot as the 1979 general election neared.

The Conservative party's Election Manifesto for Wales called for all BBC and HTV Welsh-language programming to be scheduled on a new IBA-controlled fourth channel. However, when the Tories came to power they abandoned their Welsh on Four stance. New Home Secretary

William Whitelaw declared in a 1979 policy speech before the Royal Society in Cambridge that the IBA and BBC should each concentrate all of their respective Welsh-language programming on just one of their two channels. Such a scheme would, in his judgment, be the quickest and most cost-effective way of satisfying demands for more Welsh content during peak viewing hours and also maximize the choice of programs in English by the viewing majority.

The issue galvanized nationalist opinion in Wales and became more contentious as the attitudes of speakers and nonspeakers of Welsh hardened around what the Broadcasting Council for Wales (1975) termed "rival concepts of language" (p. 4) meaning language as a means of communication versus language as an expression of cultural identity and heritage. Likewise, the controversy surrounding the fourth channel's language policy in Wales came down to two conflicting positions. The so-called Welsh on Four proposal called for all programming in the Welsh language, whether produced by the BBC or HTV, to be placed on the new service in Wales. The other plan called for a bilingual programming mix on both BBC channels as well as on both IBA channels (HTV and S4C) so as to better approximate the way the two languages naturally co-exist in Welsh society. Nationalists and most bilingual people supported the former scheme, whereas the English monoglots and the broadcasters favored the latter.

The Welsh Language Society (1979) carried the banner for an all-Welsh television service in order "to preserve, restore and promote" the indigenous language as a basic aim of Welsh broadcasting policy, because television had become such a "crucial factor in forming people's attitudes toward the world around them" (p. 3). However, the Welsh on Four arrangement also drew support from those viewers who only spoke English, because the idea of banishing all Welsh-language programs to the new channel would end the annoying local preemption of their favorite programs in English from the national BBC and ITV networks. In fact, many English monoglots believed that the Welsh-language policy was being enforced at their expense. In retaliation, many had pointed their home antennae in the direction of television transmitters in bordering England to avoid unwanted Welsh content via the BBC Wales and HTV stations.

The Tory postelection turnabout on its Welsh on Four campaign promise infuriated Welsh nationalists and language loyalists. Representatives from more than 100 Welsh volunteer organizations and local government formed the National Council on Broadcasting and implored the home secretary to reconsider his Cambridge pronouncements. They reiterated their demands for an all-Welsh channel, funded by the BBC and IBA yet operated by a Welsh broadcasting authority. The government chose to ignore these pleas and issued its broadcasting bill in February of 1980, sanctioning a second commercial television service to commence in 2 years.

The Conservatives' breach of promise concerning the Welsh channel fueled one of the worst outbreaks of civil disobedience in modern-day Britain. Violent and nonviolent protests escalated during the spring and summer of 1980 as Welsh extremists bombed television transmitters, Conservative party offices, and dozens of English-owned vacation homes in Wales. More than 2,000 Welsh viewers refused to pay their television license fees, and others threw eggs at the queen and prime minister on state visits to Wales. The most ominous pressure, however, came from Dr. Gwynfor Evans, president of the Welsh National party *(Plaid Cymru)* and a respected leader of public opinion in Wales, who threatened to fast until death if the Welsh on Four proposal was not reinstated. The issue was also an important factor in the movement for political independence from Britain, but cessationist demands for a sovereign Welsh assembly were defeated overwhelmingly by the voters of Wales in a March 1979 referendum.

The new Conservative government was subsequently warned by Lord Cledwyn and the archbishop of Wales that if Evans's hunger strike led to his death it would very likely lead to widespread violence throughout Wales. Eventually, the realization by Tory leaders of their untenable position led Home Secretary Whitelaw to restore the plan for a minority-language channel in Wales (Howell, 1981).

The Development of Irish Language Broadcast Policy and Practices

Discussions about broadcasting in the Irish language can be traced back to 1926 when Ireland's first station, Radio Eireann, began interspersing some minority-language programs into its national English-language schedule. Ironically, most attempts to mix programming in the two languages have provoked chronic criticisms from both language communities—Gaelic groups wanting more and better programs in Irish, and the English-speaking majority calling for less. History shows that the programs in English have always been more popular than the Irish-language broadcasts. But it was not until television came on the scene that a formal language policy was established for broadcasting in Ireland.

The Irish government formed two committees during 1958 to study separate aspects of the language issue. One was the Commission on the Restoration of the Irish Language, which deliberated until 1964 but somehow never recommended that an all-Irish radio service be created to encourage usage of the ancestral tongue. Another, the Television Commission (Report of the Television Commission, 1959), charged with planning Ireland's first national television system, advised in its 1959 report that the nation's radio and television services ought to "provide for the use of the Irish language and for the adequate reflection of the national outlook and culture" (p. 2). The Irish Parliament codified similar wording in Section 17 of the Broadcasting Act of 1960, which required the national broadcaster to pursue "the national aims of restoring the Irish language and preserving and developing the national culture" (Howell, 1986, pp. 211-212). Ireland's first television channel, Telefis Eireann, was initiated 2 years later and merged with the radio service in 1966 to form a new national broadcasting organization, renamed Radio Telefis Eireann.

The Radio Telefis Eireann (RTE) Authority translated the minority-language mandate of the 1960 act into a self-imposed goal of producing at least 10% of its television programming in Irish. This bilingual broadcasting effort was bolstered during the 1970s by four events. The first of these came in 1972 when RTE inaugurated *Raidio na Gaeltachta*, an exclusively Irish-language station targeted to reach the monoglot population in the three Gaeltachti strongholds along the western seaboard with 4 hours of culture-specific programming each evening.

Next, the government-appointed Broadcasting Review Committee set forth the most complete articulation of an official language policy to guide RTE in its 1974 report. Four objectives were identified:

> 1) To present programmes in Irish over the full range of output; 2) to present programmes, in English and Irish, aimed at creating an awareness in the public mind of the philosophy and significance of the Irish language; 3) to encourage in the broadcasting staff an appreciation of the vital contribution they can make towards the national objective of language restoration; and 4) to seek to implement this policy by providing (a) programmes for those competent in the language, (b) bilingual programmes for those with a limited knowledge of Irish, (c) programmes, in English and Irish, analysing and explaining the philosophy of Irish language, culture and tradition. (Broadcasting Review Committee, 1974, pp. 85-91)

The third benchmark occurred with the passage of the Broadcasting Authority (Amendment) Act of 1976, which superseded the 1960 law and broadened the cultural mandate of Section 17 by suggesting that it encompass the whole island of Ireland and give "special regard" to the republic's distinguishing characteristics—especially the Irish language. The Broadcasting Review Committee had heard many conflicting views about the purpose and proportion of Irish-language programming on RTE. Nationalist groups charged that the authority's bilingual policy had failed by not instilling "language loyalty and self-esteem" among the Gaeltacht population because programs in Irish "were too few and too rare" (BRC Report, 1974) and because a substandard form of the language was used. This led some critics to demand that RTE establish a standard Irish dialect for the whole nation and a set of performance criteria to guarantee quality control and accountability.

The English-speaking majority, on the other hand, claimed that radio and television were guilty of overemphasizing Irish to the point of creating public hostility toward the native language as well as RTE itself. Other critics suggested that autonomous services like Raidio na Gaeltachta precluded the Irish language from becoming a living component within a genuinely bilingual culture by making it culturally irrelevant to Anglophones while simultaneously stigmatizing it in the eyes of many speakers of Irish. Still another similar argument maintained that attempts to integrate programs in Irish with those in English have inevitably led minority-language shows to be scheduled at unattractive times, tuned out by most viewers, and compared unfavorably with English language broadcasts (Howell, 1982).

Finally, RTE added second television and radio networks during 1978 and 1979, respectively. The RTE-2 television service was meant to provide viewers in the western and southern counties of the republic, who up to that time could receive only RTE's sole domestic channel, with a choice of television programming more closely approximating that of their fellow countrymen living along the northern border and east coast in the so-called multichannel region, which was blessed with British television signals from the BBC and ITV stations in Belfast and Cardiff (Howell, 1979). RTE Radio 2 was created mainly to quell demands by younger listeners for more Anglo-American music in stereo. However, because these new nationwide services multiplied programming options by relying on imported television productions and recorded music in English, they may have actually hurt the cause of Irish-language broadcasting.

Present Welsh and Irish-Language Broadcasting Services

The Welsh and Irish languages are alive and well and on the air today at levels that demonstrate an earnest commitment to their survival in both Celtic cultures. But this is not to suggest that everyone is satisfied or that there is no room for improvement. Television output in the two languages has leveled off in both Wales and Ireland as financial woes and popular tastes conspire against future endeavors in cultural continuity through broadcast communication.

An examination of minority-language programming in Wales and Ireland over the past two decades reveals trends that are encouraging yet also sporadic. Welsh-language radio broadcasts, for example, have grown from only 14 hours per week via the BBC's Radio 4 Wales in 1965 to the current weekly level of more than 6 times that amount weekly on the all-Welsh Radio Cymru. By 1991, the BBC's Radio Cymru was transmitting 4,680 hours in Welsh annually—an average of about 90 hours a week. This amount represents roughly half (46%) of the total radio output produced by BBC Wales each year (BBC, 1986). Likewise, television programming in Welsh has increased from less than 10 hours a week of combined output from the BBC Wales and TWW's Teledu Cymru service in the mid-1960s to 3 times that amount today on S4C—Channel Four's autonomous operation in Wales.

S4C has an organizational structure that is unique, as is its programming mission. The air product it receives weekly from the BBC Wales is free of charge, because it is covered by the license fee revenue. IBA, on the other hand, gives S4C an annual grant from a percentage (20%) of the Fourth Channel Subscription Fee the authority collects from the net advertising proceeds of its 15 franchises to defray the expenses of Channel Four's UK-wide operation. S4C in turn buys programming from HTV Wales/Cymru and from independent producers in Wales. This arrangement is special in the sense that it is a cooperative business and creative venture, which results in programs from public and private broadcasters, as well as freelance producers, that are aired on the same channel (Sianel Pedwar Cymru [S4C], 1987b).

Yet even S4C's impressive performance shows signs of vacillation. To illustrate, the new channel initiated its service during 1982-1983 by producing 1,144 hours of programming in Welsh (averaging 22 hours per week) for just greater than £18 million; 3 years later S4C's annual output in Welsh had risen to 1,375 hours (26.4 hours a week) at a cost of nearly £32 million. By the 1986-1987 season, however, S4C was producing 43 hours less Welsh-language programming for even more money (Betts, 1987).

S4C is currently on the air 4,364 hours a year, an average of 84 hours each week. More than one third (35.7%) of this programming is Welsh-language programming—an annual total of 1,560 hours or 30 hours weekly (Coopman, 1991). S4C has relied on three suppliers for all its programming—the BBC, HTV, and freelance producers. Each has a contract with S4C to make specific amounts and kinds of programs in Welsh. In 1987, the BBC Wales produced 542 hours (41%) free of charge—an average of 10.5 hours per week. (In fact, all of S4C's Welsh-language news is produced by the BBC Wales, which draws heavily on the resources of its Radio Cymru news department.) HTV contributed another 455 hours (34%), or 9 hours weekly, under its HTV Cymru banner and sold it to S4C. The remaining 335 hours (25%) were commissioned by S4C at an hourly rate of £35,799 from 35 independent production companies then flourishing in Wales and who collectively made about 6 hours of the channel's Welsh-language content each week (S4C, 1987a).

In Ireland, the picture is even less clear and the trend more volatile. RTE aired very little regularly scheduled Irish-language programming on radio until Raidio na Gaeltachta was established in 1972 and began offering 4 hours nightly in Irish. This amount grew to 38.5 hours a week in its first decade. Today, Raidio na Gaeltachta broadcasts 65.5 hours a week nationally in Irish only (*World Radio TV Handbook* [WRTH], 1991).

But RTE television has a less impressive record. In 1970, for instance, 6.5% of RTE's home-produced programming was in Irish. After 5 years the figure had dropped to 2.8%. At present, RTE is airing a total of 6,106 hours of television programming on its two channels, 57% of which is imported. Although home-production was increased from 34% in 1986 to 43% in 1987, Irish-language programs still account for less than 5% of RTE's total output and expenditures.

Ironically, the launching of a second television channel by RTE in 1978 has made things both better and worse for Irish-language broadcasting in the republic. Several reasons account for this. First, to fill a full schedule of programming at the outset of RTE-2, the Irish government authorized RTE to import up to 80% of the programming for the new service. This decision had the positive effect of nearly doubling the total amount of RTE's television air time while also creating more program options for viewers in all parts of the republic. But it also brought about several negative effects in terms of home production in general and Irish-language content in particular. For example, during the last year of single-channel service (1976-1977), RTE imported 60% of its television programming (1,892 hours) and produced 40% (1,340 hours). After the second channel was added, RTE's total imports rose to 67.5% (3,929 hours)—all of it in English and most of it from Britain—while its home production dropped to 32.5% (1,890 hours). Therefore, even though RTE produced more hours of programming in both English (527) and Irish (59) with two channels in 1979 than with one channel in 1976, Irish-language programming as a proportion of total air time actually declined from 4.1% to 3.3%. The net result is that the Irish public has received more programming hours and options in both languages with the addition of a second channel, but at the expense of (a) doubling foreign programming in English only, (b) further reducing domestic production as a proportion of the total broadcast schedule, and (c) gaining little additional Irish-language programs while the English-Irish content ratio languished in the range of 10 to 1 (Howell, 1982).

Wales and Ireland also have employed remote broadcasting units to help keep their authentic cultures alive by being responsive to local concerns. Since its inception in 1975, RTE's mobile radio service, Nationwide Community Radio (*Raidio Pobal na Tire*), has visited 100 remote areas for short stays of less than 1 week. Because the service operates only about 120 hours a year, its contribution to the Irish-language broadcasting mission is negligible. The experiment may be useful in helping RTE establish permanent local radio stations throughout the country to compete with the 70-odd unlicensed broadcasters in the republic who now operate stations illegally (Radio Telefis Eireann [RTE], 1987). The BBC was so impressed with Ireland's model that it adapted the concept in Wales. The service there is called Neighborhood Radio (*Radio Bro*) and is composed of several mobile studios that tour the Welsh countryside, staying in small communities for a few days or even months, and broadcasting locally produced programs daily in English and Welsh (BBC, 1986).

Minority Language Programming in Wales and Ireland

Radio Cymru shifted its programming emphasis in 1986 from satire to situation comedy, resulting in the Runyonesque series *Tipyn o Annwyd,* and *C'Mon Mid Ffild,* which followed the fortunes of a losing football team. The all-Welsh station also mounted its own "live-aid" show, *Arian Byw* (*Quick-Silver*).

S4C offers a breadth of program genres in Welsh, including documentaries, agriculture and rural life features, light entertainment, drama, music and fine arts, religion, sports, news and public affairs, education, and shows for children and young people. The channel acted on a report on children's viewing patterns—compiled by the Welsh Language Research Unit of University College, Cardiff—by increasing the number of hours of children's programs, and scheduling them in the late afternoon to accommodate better their school responsibilities and family lives. Approximately 30 to 60 minutes of air time are targeted to children at 4:00 p.m. during winter months and 4:30 p.m. in the summer. Weekends included, children receive about 7 hours of programming in Welsh each week, year round, from S4C. Teenagers, too, have a block of time on S4C devoted to their interests. Chief among these programs—which air Thursday evening, 9:00 to 10:00—are dramas and pop music performances such as *Roc Rol Te* and *Enka,* which reflect the current Welsh-language rock scene (S4C, 1987b).

A rock group from Bangor called Fflaps has been praised by the press in Wales for singing in Welsh and damned for also singing in English. The switch from English to Welsh was seen by purists as an attempt to recoup from claims by some critics that the band has an anti-Welsh attitude. Fflaps's leader said the charge "is simply untrue." His explanation points out what many see as the no-win situation of trying to be bilingual: "We have always sung in both languages since our very first gig. Part of the point of this group was to break down the apartheid that exists in the music scene in Wales, and we object most strongly to being used by those people who want to propagate that apartheid" (cited in Lewis, 1987, p. 8).

The BBC Wales makes television productions in Welsh for S4C that cover a wide spectrum of subjects. These include radio plays by Rhydderch Jones; a 1985 Michael Povey drama, *Sul y Blodau;* a musical series, *Byd Cerdd;* concerts by Welsh choirs; documentaries; and regularly scheduled newscasts (BBC, 1986).

The cornerstone of BBC Welsh-language programming, however, is its 7:00 nightly newscast on S4C, *Newyddion Saith* (*News at Seven*). This ambitious effort not only covers events in Wales and the rest of Britain but now offers reports in Welsh from Washington, Beirut, Geneva, Cuba, the Philippines, Zimbabwe, and China. Presenting contemporary news coverage in Welsh via the medium of television has required the ancient Celtic language to adapt to present-day vocabulary and technology. Because many English-speaking subjects are interviewed, producers have been faced with practical questions about dubbing and subtitling their comments into Welsh. An ideal balance in using these means of translating has yet to be achieved, but audience response and preferences are being measured in hopes of pleasing most viewers (S4C, 1987b).

The BBC's programs in Welsh are among the most popular on S4C. The highest audience rating for Welsh-language television shows is about 90,000 viewers. The *News at Seven* typically reaches 50,000 plus, as does *Rhaglan Hywel Gwynfryn,* a talk show, and *Pobol y Cwm,* a weekly drama series. Other popular BBC productions are a sports magazine feature (*Y Maes Chwarae*), a sitcom (*Hafod Henri*), and *Bilidowcar,* a children's show (M. Brooke, personal communication, December 11, 1987). In comparison, the BBC's evening newscast in English on S4C draws around 300,000 viewers. Research indicates that nearly three quarters (72.8%) of the television households in Wales watch S4C on a weekly basis (BBC, 1986).

HTV Wales/Cymru also produces a number of successful programs in Welsh for S4C from its studios in Culverhouse Cross (Cardiff), Pontcanna, and Mold. Those most popular with audiences are *Y Byd ar Bedwar (The World on Four),* a twice-a-week current affairs forum that won a top award at the 1987 Celtic Film Festival in Inverness, Scotland; *Ffermio,* a farming feature that airs fortnightly; and *Dinas,* a weekly drama. *Chiz,* featuring Welsh entertainer, Huw Chiswell, won a silver award at the 29th International Film and Television Festival in New York in 1987. It was the first time that a Welsh-language program won an international award at a North American ceremony. HTV Wales also supports such cultural events as the Royal National Eisteddfod, the Llangollen International Musical Eisteddfod, and the *Urdd* (Welsh League of Youth) National Eisteddfod (Harlech Television [HTV], 1987).

Perhaps the most exciting and innovative Welsh-language productions are coming from the burgeoning number of freelance producers and filmmakers. By 1988, some 60 independent production companies had set up offices and facilities in Wales. In the south, Cardiff has become the second largest center of filmmaking activity in the UK. Caernarfon, the capital city of North Wales, has been nicknamed "the Welsh Hollywood," because of the area's explosion of television and film production, most of it in the Welsh language and all of it due to the creation of S4C. Independent producers, who employ 300 people directly and another 300 indirectly, netted £6 million in television production contracts in 1987 alone (I. W. Jones, 1987).

Animation is one of the most acclaimed activities in the Welsh independent sector. To date, more than 100 animators are now based in Wales. Cartoons from Wales, many in Welsh, have won international praise for their quality and already have been sold to broadcasters in 70 nations—including the United States' Disney Channel and Gosteleradio's Central TV in Russia. The best known and most commercially successful Welsh cartoon in the international programming marketplace is SuperTed, a Welsh-speaking teddy bear with heroic capabilities that Siriol Animation made in its Cardiff studios for S4C and Channel Four. It won the top award from the British Academy of Film and Television Arts (BAFTA) for best animation work of 1987. Siriol has also produced two other animated specials that have gained critical and financial reward. *Wil Cwac Cwac* has been booked and renewed on television systems in France, Scandinavia, Italy, and Canada. *Sion Blewyn Coch* (*A Winter Story*), a Christmas special, was aired on S4C and Channel Four and sold to Finland, Ireland's RTE, and TF1 in France ("Sell Out," 1986).

Much of the independent production output has been in the form of feature films. Broadcasters in Britain have rejuvenated the nation's film industry, and again, Channel Four has taken the lead with its *Film on Four* showcase and its distribution arm, Film Four International. S4C has played a similar role as a catalyst for Welsh-language filmmaking for television and theatrical exhibition. *Boy Soldier* (*Milwr Bychan*), about a Welsh soldier accused of murder in Northern Ireland, won three major awards at film festivals in Mannheim and Cannes (Robinson, 1987). Also featured at Cannes was the social comedy *Coming Up Roses* (*Rhosyn a Rhith*), made for S4C and later released to the movie-house market by the ex-patriot American director Stephen Bayly. His Red Rooster company has made several television films in Welsh with financial backing from S4C, including *And Pigs Might Fly, The Works,* and *Joni Jones,* the latter shown with subtitles on New York's public television station, Channel 13 (Forsberg, 1987). The Welsh Film Foundation (*Ffilm Cymru*), jointly backed by the BBC Wales and S4C to the tune of $11.5 million, was created in 1990 and charged with producing six feature films in Welsh over the following 3 years (Coopman, 1991).

In Ireland, minority-language production is more limited in scope, variety, and quality than the vibrancy being experienced in Wales. All entertainment shows in Irish are scheduled on RTE-1, including *Eureka,* a 30-minute quiz show seen Saturdays at 5:30 p.m.; *Iris,* a popular life-style feature on Sunday evenings; and several short productions aimed at children—*Dilin O Deamhas, Futafota, Baile Beag,* and *Maister Mhic Cheo*—and aired as part of the weekday after-school series, *Dempsey's Den.* By the 1987-1988 season, children's programming in Irish averaged roughly 40 minutes per week for an annual total of 17.3 hours.

The news in Irish (*An Nuacht*) airs seven nights a week from 8:00 to 8:10 and is usually followed by a half-hour strip of informational programming like *Suil Thart,* a weekly news review seen on Mondays, and *Cursai,* a public affairs presentation seen the rest of the week. All programming except the news is produced on a production schedule running between 26 and 32 weeks of each year. Thus the only Irish-language program that is broadcast 52 weeks a year is the Nuacht newscast. Together, RTE-1 and RTE-2 were responsible for approximately 125 hours of Irish-language programming by 1988—averaging close to 5 hours a week from October to April each television season (RTE Guide, 1987).

Looking Ahead

Several changes in minority-language broadcasting occurred during the late 1980s in both Wales and Ireland. Private broadcasting finally arrived in Ireland with the formation of the Independent Radio and TV Commission (IRTC) to oversee two new commercial radio networks (Atlantic 252 and Century Radio) and to license two dozen local radio stations. A new privately owned commercial network, TV3, was also approved for operation in 1991 (WRTH, 1991).

The Welsh Fourth Channel Authority announced in late 1987 that it would invite all interested program producers to tender proposals and bids for supplying the 14 hours of programming in Welsh and English that HTV has been providing to S4C each week since 1982. IBA's contracts with its 15 television franchises run through 1992, but the steady growth of cable and satellite programming services makes the whole ITV contractor scheme uncertain beyond that date. In fact, the entire telecommunications environment was rendered uncertain by the government's 1988 white paper—"Broadcasting in the 90s: Competition, Choice and Quality"—the framework for the Broadcasting Act of 1990. The new law required that all ITV franchises be auctioned off to the highest bidders and subsequently become Channel 3 in place of ITV.

Channel 4 will sell its own advertising but will also retain its public service status and alternative programming mandate.

S4C has surprised friends and skeptics alike with its success in marketing Welsh-language television and film productions outside the borders of Wales. Its distribution subsidiary, the Mentrau Group (S4C Enterprises), sold more than $1 million worth of programming in fiscal 1987, 35% of which was in the form of overseas sales of Welsh-language television programs and another 8% coming from the publication of books based on S4C productions in Welsh (S4C, 1987a). Some of the credit for S4C's marketing success story must go to computer-assisted technologies like teletext that make translation easy and cost-effective. But the fact that some Welsh purists object to the inclusion of English words within the dialogue of Welsh-language dramas attests to the well-known tenacity of the *cultural lag phenomenon.*

Across the Irish Sea, the ministers of the Gaeltacht and the Department of Communications decided in March 1986 to set up the Working Group on Irish Language Television Broadcasting to examine and report on ways in which RTE could present a television programming service that would satisfy Irish-speaking viewers and also make the best use of the television medium in promoting the native language. Seven members of Irish-language organizations and media organizations were appointed to the body. The working group considered three topics:

1. What would constitute a satisfactory range of programs in Irish on RTE's channels in terms of content and amount of output.
2. The effects that an increased range of Irish-language programming would have on other [meaning English-language] output, advertising revenues, technical capacity, and the finances of RTE.
3. The feasibility of establishing a third television network with exclusively Irish-language programming.

The working group set about (a) analyzing a wide range of previous reports on broadcasting in Irish and compiling technical and financial data from RTE and the Department of Communications, (b) meeting with representatives from the major Irish-language organizations as well as advertising practitioners and broadcasting executives, (c) reviewing official documents concerning the rights of lesser-used languages in Europe, and (d) consulting with the Welsh Fourth Channel Television Authority in Cardiff (Working Group on Irish Language Broadcasting [Working Group], 1987).

Nearly a decade ago, the RTE Authority appointed the Advisory Committee on Irish-Language Broadcasting to help set guidelines for meeting its statutory responsibility to fashion a schedule of radio and television programming in Irish. The committee's ensuing 1979 report recommended that a full range of programming types be made available to the public in Irish, including entertainment, current events, sports, and agricultural specials. Specifically, the report called for at least one "worthwhile" television show for adults and another for young people each day of the week, more programs broadcast with either Irish or English subtitles, an increase in home production in Irish for children, and a nightly Irish-language newscast comparable with the one in English to be aired between 7:00 and 10:00 p.m.

At the government's request, the Bord na Gaeilge prepared an action plan for Irish to be implemented between 1983 and 1986. The objective of such a plan was to provide a "comprehensive radio and television service in Irish [as] a necessary and basic condition for the community as a whole to progress toward a viable bilingual situation" (Working Group, 1987, p. 3). The first step called for one "substantial program" in Irish for adults each evening and a "comprehensive range" of regularly scheduled broadcasts for children and teenagers.

RTE responded in 1983 by setting a target for 1986 of 20% of its home-produced television output in the Irish language, with particular attention paid to children's programs. In fact, RTE had announced these same goals 3 years earlier and had also promised one major program in Irish nightly, a new recruitment policy favoring program makers conversant in Irish, and new instructional programs for teaching the Irish language to adults via radio and television (Howell, 1982). As for adding a third television service completely in Irish, RTE believed it would not be financially feasible but that extending the hours of Raidio na Gaeltachta was affordable. The authority also committed itself to increasing the level of Irish used in programs through "bilingual narratives" (in which Irish would be integrated into English-language scripts) and through dubbing popular imported shows into Irish (Working Group, 1987, p. 4).

By the end of 1985, it was a matter of record that RTE had not met its 20% Irish-language quota in home production. One reason cited is that Irish-language programs have not proved attractive to advertisers, who do, after all, account for 50% of RTE's annual income. In fact, RTE now questions the whole notion that television is the answer to saving, let along resurrecting, the Irish language. The official broadcaster has charged that it "is a somewhat simplistic approach . . . [to believe that producing] a certain number of hours of Irish language programming would lead to a renaissance in Irish language broadcasting. Nothing could be further from the truth" (Working Group, 1987, p. 5).

A new thrust in the demands being placed on RTE by language forces is for it to promote the increased involvement in independent television production companies in developing entertainment programs in Irish for use on RTE channels. To achieve this would require that RTE overcome a historic defect by creating a new structure within its corporate body, one that will ensure a stronger voice for Irish-language programming interests on both policymaking and day-to-day operational bases. The S4C model has devised a management control mechanism for scheduling programs in English and Welsh in such a manner as to maximize audiences while simultaneously maintaining that channel's Welsh ethos. Many in Ireland believe it is time for RTE to follow S4C's example.

The Working Group recommended that a graduated approach be taken, from 1988 through 1991, in an effort to improve the amount, types, and quality of Irish-language television programming. This would culminate in 14.5 hours of air time in Irish each week—or 2 hours per day, 7 days a week, 365 days a year—for a grand total of about 750 hours annually. This output would be regularly scheduled so that 90 minutes would be aimed at adults during peak viewing hours (7:00 to 10:00 p.m.) and children would receive 30 minutes of age-specific content earlier. Programs would be formatted entirely in Irish or bilingually or dubbed into Irish (as in the case of domestic or imported television shows and films in English or a foreign language).

A sample weekly schedule of Irish-language programming was envisioned by the working group as follows: news (seven programs of 15 minutes), current affairs (two programs of 30 minutes), sports (one program of 60 minutes), interviews (one program of 30 minutes), children's programs (seven programs of 20 minutes), magazine programs (two programs of 30 minutes), drama (four programs of 30 minutes), religion (one program of 30 minutes), entertainment (three programs of 30 minutes), shows for teenagers (one program of 30 minutes), cartoons (seven programs of 10 minutes), and miscellaneous (two programs of 30 minutes). The potential audience was characterized as small but eager to see programs in Irish. The cost of producing this amount of Irish-language programming was estimated to be £18.5 million Irish —45% of it for additional equipment and the rest for producing 750 hours of programming annually (2 hours × 365 days).

It was also recommended that RTE or some other agency set timetables, targets, and standards for purchasing independently produced programs in both Irish and English. Furthermore, RTE, in association with Irish-language groups, was supposed to assist freelancers through funding, facilities, and advice about appropriate subjects. Finally, a unit was to be established within RTE that would guarantee a strong commitment to the gradual phasing in of a separate Irish-language television channel within clearly defined time limits.

The Working Group cautioned against starting such a service too quickly for fear that the Irish language might become ghettoized. The strategy favored by them was to have 2 hours of programming in Irish each night on one of the existing television channels to serve those who now speak the native language while cultivating enhanced interest and competence in Irish among the general public.

At the same time, it was assumed that RTE would put into place, over a 5- to 10-year period, the necessary financial, technical, and human resources to commence a third television channel exclusively in Irish. This would require that a pilot television service in Irish be implemented using RTE 1 and 2 transmitters until a full-scale terrestrial network could be integrated with cable systems and satellite services providing near universal coverage of the Republic's population by RTE 1, 2, and 3 (Working Group, 1987). The cost of building the transmission network and additional studio facilities for a third channel was believed to be £40 million. Another £15 million would be required to program it for a year (Working Group, 1987).

Conclusions

Broadcasting in Wales benefits more than it is harmed by its affiliation with Britain's BBC and IBA giants. S4C has the most autonomy in terms of programming decisions and scheduling and has used it wisely, but also receives substantial tangible support and professional expertise from the London-based broadcasting establishment. RTE, too, enjoys autonomy in that it is Irish owned and controlled, but it is chronically plagued with in-fighting among language zealots and also lacks the commitment and funds to provide adequate television programming in Irish.

The fifth of the population who choose to speak Welsh are united by a common version of the language and by locale, concentrated mostly in North Wales. These factors make them better connected to each other and to power centers in South Wales than is the case with Ireland's linguistic minority vis-à-vis itself and Dublin. The Cymry Cymraeg also have demonstrated a more vociferous commitment to their language cause than the Gaeltachti have to theirs. The comparatively small number of Irish speakers is fragmented by competing dialects and scattered over the most remote regions of the republic—making them far removed from Dublin, physically and psychologically, where most national decision making is centralized. Nor have the Gaeltachti found a unifying leader or force to match Dr. Gwynfor Evans and the Plaid Cymru of Wales.

S4C offers 10 times more minority-language air time than does RTE television, and for a smaller population. And viewers get 30 hours of programming in Welsh 52 weeks a year, contrasted with RTE's 5 hours in Irish weekly for only half a year. Newyddion Saith airs 30 minutes of news daily in Welsh whereas Nuacht is essentially a 10-minute headline service. Wales devotes nearly 1 hour of air time weekdays to its children, plus highly creative cartoons daily; the children of Ireland receive 30 minutes in Irish a week for half a calendar year and virtually no language instruction via television. In fact, the only instructional programs in the Irish language are those broadcast in Northern Ireland by the BBC's School Television unit, which also provides academic instruction in the Welsh medium to secondary schools in Wales (BBC, 1986). The strongest broadcasting commitment to the Irish language is made through Raidio na Gaeltachta, but its signal covers only 75% of the country, and it loses listeners because of its split transmissions (signing on and off during midday hours). Radio Cymru is on the air an average of 13 hours daily (4 hours more than Raidio na Gaeltachta) and enjoys 98% nationwide coverage.

S4C has shown a great deal of business acumen in marketing its Welsh-language productions in Anglophonic Britain and throughout the world and in terms of its television advertising in Welsh. RTE, and most language enthusiasts in Ireland, are imbued with antibusiness attitudes when it comes to the subject of Irish-language broadcasting. There is also a clear resistance to change, which results in an unimaginative approach to alternative types of funding and to relevant themes and formats in programming. In Marshall McLuhan's (1964, p. 19) perspective, the Irish are inclined to look at the future through a rearview mirror. Nothing exemplifies this more than officialdom's lack of will or ability to come to grips with the rampant growth of pirate broadcasters, a state of affairs that hurts the credibility of RTE in its dealings with both language groups.

Gauging the effectiveness of broadcasting in promoting the use of minority languages in Wales and Ireland is difficult at best. An executive at the BBC Wales is optimistic:

> On the use of Welsh by children, there is a good deal of anecdotal evidence from families and teachers that the provision of television programmes in Welsh is of considerable help in supporting the use of the language in the home and in schools. But it would be impossible to separate out the effect of radio and television from, for example, the fundamental changes in education which have occurred with the emergence of linguistically-segregated schools in most parts of Wales. By far the most reliable information on the extent of Welsh-speaking comes in the official census figures which are produced every 10 years. I should add that in the 1981 census there were signs of a slight increase in Welsh-speaking below the age of 20, so the foundation for a revival may already have been laid. (M. Brooke, personal communication, December 11, 1987)

Another media researcher in Wales has suggested "a 40% increase in the numbers of children speaking Welsh since 1971" (Jones, 1982, p. 28). The Linguistic Institute of Ireland surveyed the population in 1976 and 1983, and reported some improvement in the use of Irish—with about 20% showing competence in the language but having little chance to use it (Working Group, 1987).

Broadcasters in societies endowed with more than one official language and competing ethnic cultures face an uneasy dilemma when having to decide between offering radio and television services in one dominant language or providing minority cultures with programming in their own lesser-used vernacular. Broadcasting in one language is cheaper, easier, and presents the population with a standard communication currency and unified identity that helps the cause of nationhood. But ignoring the desires and needs of ethnic minorities for broadcasts that reflect their cultural identities and heritage is often a prescription for alienation, political strife, and separatism. And, of course, the two options are not mutually exclusive, only mutually expensive.

Minority-language broadcasting, therefore, can bolster the pride and integrity of minority cultures and, as is the case in Wales and Ireland, can also resuscitate, preserve, and ensure the continuation of their ancient idioms. Such policies and practices may prove wise—when minority languages are saved and loyalty to the government fosters national unity—or counterproductive—when broadcast pluralism backfires by fueling the fires of tribalism and disunity, leading to the formation of cultural ghettos and the stigmatizing of minority languages (Howell, 1986).

Authentic folk cultures like those of the Cymry Cymraeg and the Gaeltachti find it difficult, but not impossible, to adapt to modern technologies such as television, the story-telling medium in today's world. But to be alive in today's world is to want relevant entertainment and credible news in one's own language via the telecommunication media, regardless of whether one belongs to a minority culture or a dominant culture. In effect, access to the airwaves has become an expected birthright of humankind, irrespective of cultural status.

Note

1. Some of the background understanding of these issues was gleaned firsthand through interviews I conducted with broadcasting personnel in Ireland (1977) and in Wales (1980). Through correspondence I have attempted to keep abreast of developments and nuances in both places. Among those I met with are Elwyn Jones, religious programs director, BBC/Radio Cymru, Bangor, Wales; Louis McRedmond, head of information, RTE Dublin; Wyn Thomas, head of Welsh programming, Swansea Sound, Ltd.; T. R. J. Williams, head of administration, BBC Wales, Cardiff; Muiris MacConghail, controller of television programs, RTE; Tony Fahy, head of audience research, RTE; Huw Davies, director of programs, HTV Wales, Cardiff; and Geraint Stanley Jones, head of programs—television, BBC Wales.

References

Betts, C. (1987, November 12). S4C "confident" as output drops. *Western Mail,* p. 9.

Briggs, A. (1965). *The golden age of wireless.* London: Oxford University Press.

British Broadcasting Corporation. (1980). *BBC handbook and annual report.* London: BBC Publications.

British Broadcasting Corporation. (1986). *BBC handbook 1987.* London: BBC Publications.

Broadcasting Council for Wales. (1975). *The committee on the future of broadcasting, 1974: Memorandum from the broadcasting council for Wales.* Cardiff: BBC.

Broadcasting in the '90s: Competition, choice, and quality. (1988). London: HMSO.

Broadcasting Review Committee. (1974). *Report 1974.* Dublin: The Stationery Office.

Brooke, Michael. (Dec. 11, 1987). Secretary, BBC Wales. Letter to author.

Coopman, J. (1991, January 21). Welsh-lingo web spurs prod boom. *Variety,* p. 43.

Forsberg, M. (1987, August 20). An American director offers a quirky Welsh lament. *New York Times,* p. H-13.

Harlech Television. (1987, October 22). *HTV report and accounts 1987*. Cardiff, Wales: HTV Group P.I.C.

Howell, W. J., Jr. (1979). Ireland's second TV channel: Seeking national culture and viewer choice. *Journalism Quarterly, 56*(1), 77-86.

Howell, W. J., Jr. (1981). Britain's fourth television channel and the Welsh language controversy. *Journal of Broadcasting, 25*(2), 123-137.

Howell, W. J., Jr. (1982). Bilingual broadcasting and the survival of authentic culture in Wales and Ireland. *Journal of Communication, 32*(4), 39-54.

Howell, W. J., Jr. (1986). *World broadcasting in the age of the satellite*. Norwood, NJ: Ablex.

Jones, H. P. (1982). Wales gets its own TV. *Irish Broadcasting Review, 13*, 26-31.

Jones, I. W. (1987, November 9). Why S4C could have 22 million pounds going begging. *Daily Post*, p. A-12.

Lewis, B. (1987, November 13). No sonic apartheid by Fflaps. *Caernarfon Herald*, p. B-12.

Mackey, W. F. (1979). Language policy and language planning. *Journal of Communication, 29*(2), 5.

McLuhan, M. (1964). *Understanding media*. Toronto: McGraw-Hill.

Radio Telefis Eireann. (1987, March 27). *Annual report 1986*. Dublin: Radio Telefis Eireann Authority.

Report of the Advisory Committee on Irish Language Programming (1979). Dublin: The Stationery Office.

Report of the Committee on Broadcasting 1960 (1962). (Chairman: Sir Harry Pilkington). London: HMSO 1962 Cmnd 1753.

Report of the Committee on Broadcasting Coverage (1974). (Chairman: Sir Stewart Crawford). London: HMSO 1974 Comnd 5774.

Report of the Committee on the Future of Broadcasting (1977). (Chairman: Lord Noel Annan). London: HMSO 1977 Cmnd 6753.

Report of the Television Commission (1959). Dublin: The Stationery Office.

Report of the Working Party on the Welsh Television Fourth Channel Project (1975). (Chairman: J. W. M. Siberry). London: HMSO for the Home Office.

RTE Guide. Radio Telefis Eireann publications (weekly), Dublin.

Robinson, D. (1987, January 30). Challenge from Wales. *The Times of London*, p. 25.

S4C. (1987a.) *Annual Report, 1986-87*. Cardiff: The Welsh Fourth Channel Authority.

S4C. (1987b.) *Television in Wales—The New Industry: 1982-87*. Cardiff: The Welsh Fourth Channel Authority.

Sell out for S4C animation. (1986, December). *TV World*, p. 62.

Sianel Pedwar Cymru. (1987a). *Annual report, 1986-87*. Cardiff: The Welsh Fourth Channel Authority.

Sianel Pedwar Cymru. (1987b). *Television in Wales—The new industry: 1982-87*. Cardiff: The Welsh Fourth Channel Authority.

Thomas, W. (1980). *A brief introduction to the Welsh language*. Unpublished program script, Swansea Sound.

Welsh Language Society (Cymdeithas Yr Iaith Gymraeg). (1979). *A Welsh Fourth Channel: The only answer*. Mimeographed position paper. Cardiff: WLS.

Whitelaw, William. (Sept. 21, 1979). Policy speech before the Royal Society, Cambridge, England.

Working Group on Irish Language Broadcasting. (1987). *Report to the ministers for the Gaeltacht and communications*. Dublin: Author.

World radio TV handbook. (1991). (edited by Andrew G. Sennitt). London: Billboard Ltd.

11

The Postcolonial Policy of Algerian Broadcasting in Kabyle

ZAHIR IHADDADEN

Algeria has a single national broadcasting corporation that consists of three channels. Channel number one broadcasts nationwide in Arabic, the official national language; *Kabyle,* a minority language, is used for the second channel; and the third broadcasts in French and other European languages, particularly English and Spanish. Although this situation might seem abnormal in a developed country, it reflects the complexity of the linguistic problem in Algeria. Broadcasting in three principal languages is a remnant of the colonial era, which still lingers after nearly 30 years of independence. Furthermore, there is an actual audience in the country for each of these channels and any attempt to modify this structure is met with more or less open opposition that has consequences on the political and cultural levels (Chevaldonné, 1981, 1988; Taboury & Taboury, 1987).

In this study it will not be possible to tackle all of the problems that this brief introduction evokes. Instead, this chapter will focus on the radio channel that broadcasts in Kabyle. As the title of the chapter suggests there will be two parts to this chapter: The first is devoted to the historical context of the Kabyle language, and the second will be a description of this channel.[1]

History of the Kabyle Dialect

Without dealing in depth with complex linguistic problems, it might be sufficient to mention that Kabyle is a dialect of the *Berber* language that was used throughout historic times by the population dwelling in

EDITORS' NOTE: English translation by Stephen Harold Riggins and Paul Bouissac.

North Africa (Gellner & Michaud, 1972). Its area is geographically delineated by Egypt on the east, the Subsahara on the south, the Atlantic Ocean on the west, and the Mediterranean on the north. The population of this area, which used to form a single people, spoke the same language, generally designated by the term *Berber.* This is an improper term but one that permits, for the time being, some relevant generalizations. The Kabyle dialect is used by a population living in a geographical area called Kabylia in the north of Algeria. The term *Kabylia* is a transcription of the Arabic word *Kabā'il,* which means "tribes." The French used it in the 19th century to designate a specific region of Algeria. Before that time this area was a part of a greater geographical entity that historians called al-Maghrib al-Awsat (Central Maghreb) and, previously, Numidia (Montagne, 1973; Wilkin, 1900/1970).

Kabylia was inhabited by two large tribes, the Ketamas and the Zwawas, whose Berber origin is common with other neighboring tribes, particularly the Sanhadjas in the north and the Zenatas on the high plateaux and in the west. These tribes occupied the territory that presently forms Algeria. Although they all once spoke the Berber language, today a vast area within this region is inhabited by speakers of Arabic. Berber is spoken only in isolated but important areas such as Kabylia, the Aurès, and the M'zab as well as smaller areas such as the Chenoua, the Snassen, the Hoggar, and the Adrar. Kabylia is situated in the north of Algeria, between Algiers and Tijel. The Aurès is in the southeast of the country, the M'zab at the border of the desert, occupied by the regions of the Hoggar and the Adrar in the extreme south of Algeria. The Chenoua is located to the west of Algiers and the Snassen to the west of Oran. These regions constitute islands that stretch over the whole Algerian territory. The land is generally mountainous or desert (e.g., see Desfois, 1964). The Kabyles do not form an ethnic minority in the full sense of the term because they come from the same ethnic group as other Algerians. Their uniqueness comes solely from the fact that they continue to use a Berber dialect.

Historical studies make it possible to distinguish two phenomena that have contributed to the current situation: the arrival of the Hilālī Arab tribes on the one hand and the deliberate will of the Berber tribes to become Arabized on the other hand.[2] The Hilālī phenomenon has been the object of several contradictory studies. In general, historians (and French historians in particular) credit the Hilālīs for the Arabizing process of Algerian populations (Golvin, 1957). However, this may be a mistake, because it appears that the presence of the Hilālīs only facilitated a process that had begun before their arrival and whose dynamic factor was religion and the will of the Berber kings.

The arrival of the Hilālīs occurred in the 10th and 11th centuries. But at that time there already existed centers of Arabization everywhere, such as Kairawan, Mehdya, Tunis, Tolbna, Kalaa, Bejaïa, Tiaret, Tlemcen, Fez, and Marrakech, to mention only the most important centers. Teaching was provided there in Arabic, and several poets had written in Arabic, although they were from Berber origin. Moreover, Hilālīs remained nomadic for a long time and could not have formed a center from which an Arabization movement could have spread. For more than four centuries, from the 11th to the 15th century, they lived in perpetual conflict with the royal dynasties and with the surrounding populations in spite of a few ephemeral alliances. For the most part they were harassed and dislocated. 'Abd al-Nu'mān, the successor of Ibn Tumart, was the founder of the Almohad dynasty, which reigned over the Maghreb in the 12th and 13th centuries. 'Abd al-Nu'mān repelled them from all of Algeria and Tunisia after their defeat in a decisive battle near Constantine. Later, he used them as a reinforcement for his army. In the 14th and 15th centuries the dynasties that succeeded the Almohads, that is the Hafsids, the 'Abd-al-Wādids, and the Marīnids, continued to call on the Hilālīs whenever their inner conflicts necessitated the reinforcement of their army.

This tumultuous presence of the Hilālīs in the Maghreb created many ties through marriage and politics. Assimilation and integration among the populations were facilitated by the fact that they held the same Islamic religious beliefs. The Hilālī Arab tribes, whose importance is the object of controversy, blended through the centuries with the Berber populations. Consequently, as early as the end of the 16th century it was difficult to distinguish a Hilālī from a Berber. Some fractions of Hilālī tribes became Berberized and used the Berber language; the reverse also happened (L'Africain, 1958). But generally speaking, this phenomenon has favored the Arabization of Algerian populations more than their Berberization. Moreover, it is important to emphasize that the Hilālīs had not come to the Maghreb to Arabize the populations, but to revenge the Fatimid King al-Mu'izz. The role they played in the expansion of Arabic was not voluntary and still less determining.

The Arabization of Algeria comes primarily from the will of the Berbers themselves to speak Arabic. This desire reveals the degree of sincerity with which the Berbers embraced the Muslim faith. The practice of Islam requires familiarity with Arabic. Learning verses for prayers, making the pilgrimage to the Arabic peninsula, attending Friday sermons, and taking the theological or law courses are conducive to an intense contact with the Arabic language. As early as the reign of Caliph 'Uthmān, around the year 25 of the Hijrah, a Berber delegation lead by King Izmar who reigned over an area delineated by the high plateaux of today's Algeria, paid a visit to Mecca to express to the caliph their desire to become Muslims and to work toward the expansion of Islam. This commitment remained intact.[3] The famous conquest of 'Uqbah ibn Nāfi', which took place several years later, in the years 67-70 of the Hijrah, can only be due to the fact that he went through regions that had been Islamized for about 50 years and consequently encountered little resistance.[4] Ten years later, it is these areas that provided the Berber Tariq ibn Ziyād with the strong troops that conquered Spain.

Fluency in Arabic developed with the expansion of Islam in the Maghreb. As a consequence, when the first Muslim Berber kingdoms were formed the working language was already Arabic. The Rustamids in Tiaret in the 9th century, the Zayyānids at Kairawan and Mehdya, and the Hammadids at Kalaa in the 10th century aided the spread of Arabic-Muslim culture. The same is true for all the dynasties that reigned in the following centuries.

The Berber language remained the language of everyday communication, however. Ibn Tumart translated the Koran into Berber and wrote theological and legal works in the language. He also preached in Berber. Yaghmorassen, the founder of the dynasty of the 'Abd-al-Wādids in Tlemcen at the end of the 14th century, always spoke Berber in his *diwān*. But these efforts for the consecration of Berber were not sustained. As the same dynasty became more powerful, Berber floundered to the advantage of Arabic. The successors of Ibn Tumart wrote in Arabic, those of Yaghmorassen wrote poetry in Arabic, and their capital cities increasingly became centers of intense diffusion of Arabic-Muslim culture. Ibn Khaldun, the famous historian, and Ibn Rushd, the famous philosopher, lived in Berber capital cities.

Thus it can be said that the Berbers themselves facilitated the development of Arabic in the Maghreb to the disadvantage of the Berber language. Obviously, this was reinforced by other factors such as the Hilālī phenomenon, mentioned earlier, and the Andalusian refugees, who fled Spain from the end of the 15th century until the 17th to settle in Maghreb cities, particularly Tlemcen, Oran, Mostaganem, Ténès,

Algiers, Bejaïa, Annaba, and Tunis. It should also be emphasized that these Andalusian refugees were for the most part Arabized Berbers.[5]

All these converging factors resulted in an acceleration of the Arabization of Algeria in the 17th and 18th centuries. From the cities, Arabic spread to the countryside, first in the plains, then in the lower hills. In the 19th century isolated and relatively inaccessible areas, such as the high mountains and the deep south, had not yet been touched by this expansion. The process was stopped by the French colonization of Algeria beginning in 1830. After the resistance organized by the Emir 'Abd al-Qādir was defeated in 1847, the colonial army was able to conquer, in spite of serious losses, all the more inaccessible regions by the end of the 19th century. Throughout this period of colonial invasion, Algerian populations turned inward to organize resistance; contact among themselves was severed and the Arabization process did not progress, limiting itself to the maintenance of several Zāwiyas ("monastic complexes") particularly in Kabylia where teaching in Arabic was offered with great difficulty.

French colonial policy took an interest in Kabyle uniqueness and used it to help weaken the unity of the country and to promote the politics of Franco-assimilation (Lustick, 1985). This policy aimed at curtailing the teaching of Arabic and substituting French through the creation of schools. At the University of Algiers a chair in Berber was established that emphasized Kabyle. This insidious policy did not produce outstanding results. One can even call it a failure because the radical nationalist movement recruited a large proportion of its leaders and militants among the Kabyles (Harbi, 1980; Quandt, 1969). For example, between 1926 and 1937 the Kabyles formed the majority of the membership of the dissident organization the North African Star (Kaddache, 1980). The reform movement of the Ulemas, which struggled for the renaissance of Arabic and the purification of Islam, also found many supporters in Kabylia. During the war of National Liberation, Kabylia and Aurès, the populations of which are Berber speaking, were the most ardent centers of support for the revolution.

The Berber colonial policy was questioned even among certain Kabyles who graduated from French schools and considered the Kabyles to be different from the other Algerians. But this difference is not founded on ethnicity or on a particular history, as all historical evidence that has been summarized here tends to prove. The only uniqueness of the Kabyles is that they have preserved a Berber dialect as did other regions of Algeria.

The Kabyle Radio Channel

French colonial policy toward the Berbers did bring about one positive result: the creation of a radio channel in Kabyle. However, it is important to emphasize that this policy did not have the defense and restoration of the Berber language as its main goal. The channel broadcast only in the Kabyle dialect, totally ignoring the other Berber dialects. Its object was nothing other than exacerbating the uniqueness of the Kabyles to create antagonism between them and the other Algerian populations. Moreover, radio was merely a means of communication for the administration, which wanted to convey its messages in the service of colonialization in one language that was spoken throughout this region while at the same time practicing a policy of cultural deprivation because 90% of the population in this area was maintained in total illiteracy. Nevertheless, the Kabyle channel contributed to maintaining the Kabyle dialect as a living language by broadcasting its songs, poems, and tales—in short a whole Berber-Muslim culture. I will try in the following pages to describe this channel and to define its role.

The decision by the French authorities to create this special program at Radio Algiers dates from 1948 (Albert, Tudesq, & Ihaddaden, 1984). From then on there were the three broadcasts mentioned at the beginning of this chapter. A studio was created for the new channel; it had a weak broadcasting power because its purpose was to cover only Kabylia, situated a little more than 100 km from Algiers. In 1954 the broadcasting power of Radio Algiers was 300 kW; in 1968 it was increased to 600 kW. One should remember that in the 1950s radio receivers required electricity and that the areas that had electricity were limited to the main centers, which excluded the rural and mountain populations. The audience for this radio was, therefore, limited: Only the fairly important cities such as Algiers, Tizi-ouzou, Bejaïa, and Bouïra could receive the signals. Consequently, it is difficult to evaluate its audience, but it could not have been very large. The Muslim audience for all three channels of Radio Algiers has been estimated in 1956 to be 157,000, a very low figure considering that the Muslim population was thought to be 8 million. This figure includes the Kabyle listeners whose numbers must not have been more than one third of the total, in all likelihood about 50,000 listeners. Algeria was then experiencing for the first time a public radio network and the existence of this medium was in itself a fairly important political event and a social fact that was to have long-term consequences. For instance, radios were soon installed in cafés and listening to the radio became a collective event with deep repercussions, particularly on the weekly market days. Radio quickly assumed a popular character.

The programs that were broadcast were attractive to a large audience. For the young it was Kabyle music and songs; for the older audience it was poetry and religion. The analysis of the programs shows that in 1953, 57% of the time was devoted to music and song; 19% to religion and cultural programs; and 24% to the news. While playing an important part in the diffusion of the colonial message, the Kabyle channel, through its cultural programs, was bringing a better knowledge of Berber culture to the listeners, not only by the songs that were much appreciated but also through poetry and stories in the very language of their creation, that is, in a language not yet contaminated by the external influence of Arabic or French.

However, this purity was adulterated by the language that was used in the news broadcasts; indeed journalists who did not master the Kabyle dialect and had no knowledge of its syntax, morphology, or creativity chose an easy solution by merely adding Kabyle endings to French or Arabic words. They even used ordinary French words because the language of the news was mainly inspired by French. At the time of independence in 1962 this was still the situation of the Kabyle channel.

During the first years after independence, the Algerian government was principally preoccupied with the problem of the written press, which was overwhelmingly colonial and had to be nationalized and Algerianized. The radio, which changed its name to Radio-Télévision Algérienne (RTA), was already a state monopoly. All that had to be done was to appoint new directors and to change the contents of the news broadcasts. The rest, particularly the programs, remained as it was before. The Kabyle channel continued to broadcast in that dialect. Some modifications were introduced in 1967 in the administrative structures of RTA and the Kabyle channel (which then became channel number two) lost its autonomy and its role was increasingly questioned (Lahlou, 1983).

Until the last reorganization, which occurred in 1987 and which has not yet been completed, channel two was managed by a subdirector reporting to a radio director who was himself under the authority of the general director of RTA. Channel two consisted of two departments, one for the news and another for the production of programs. Organizationally, channel two has always appeared to be an extension of the first channel. Even though its head was an assistant director, bearing the same title as the head of channel one, channel two seemed to be marginalized as far as the general director was concerned, who usually did not speak or understand Kabyle. In 1984, the budget for channel two was 1,519,515 DA. The number of its journalists was reduced, and their exact number was difficult to establish because of their frequent mobility from channel to channel. From RTA sources it appears that channel two employed 7 full-time journalists and 50 who worked on a freelance basis. The development of its technical installation was minimal. Its broadcast power was not changed; it is still exclusively oriented toward Kabylia. Channel two possesses two middle-wave transmitters, one situated at Algiers and the other at Ain-el-Hamam in the Djurdjura Mountains, as well as another short-wave transmitter. The power of these transmitters is 100 kW. The broadcasting time of channel two is 12 hours on workdays and 17 hours on Thursdays and Fridays, which constitute the Algerian weekend. The division of the programs is still the same as before independence. The three main categories are also still news and political commentaries (14.89% of the totality of the programs); Kabyle music and songs (57.95%); and finally, cultural and religious broadcasts (27.16%). As can be seen, music forms the major part of the programs. This includes Kabyle songs, totally ignoring the other Berber songs; however, for the last few years some broadcasts are devoted to Andalusian songs the melodies of which are undoubtedly of Berber origin. The impact of such a program is noticeable but the choice of singers is biased by political criteria much of the time.

During workdays, the programs of channel two in Kabyle are divided into three periods: 6:00 a.m. to 9:05 a.m., 1:00 p.m. to 3:00 p.m., and 5:00 p.m. to 11:00 p.m. This division has not changed since the colonial era. The longest period of time is during the evening, but channel two must then compete with television in Arabic. The division of the third period in 1985 was the following:

5:00 to 5:15: Opening and Koran.

5:15 to 6:30: Songs and music mixed with information bulletins.

6:30 to 7:00: Programs for the handicapped.

7:00 to 7:05: News bulletin.

7:05 to 8:00: Songs.

8:00 to 8:15: News report.

8:15 to 9:00: Songs.

9:00 to 10:00: Cultural programs: music, theater.

10:00 to 10:50: Songs.

10:50 to 11:00: Koran.

The categories of programs are subdivided into the following:

1. Information (14.89%):
   News (7.44%).
   Sports (4.25%).
   Commentary and interviews (3.20%).
2. Variety and Music (57.95%):
   Songs (28.15%).
   Audience requests (15.15%).
   Morning greetings (7.44%).
   International music (0.44%).
   Miscellaneous (6.77%).
3. Cultural Programs (27.16%):
   Religion (10.50%).
   Art and literature (7.25%).
   Education (6.64%).
   History (2.30%).
   Science (0.56%).

The cultural programs remain relatively important. Although the proportion has not changed, the content has been considerably enriched. Naturally, it includes poetry and theater, but also scientific, medical, and artistic programs. A fairly important portion of it is devoted to history. It represents 9.46% of the cultural programs. These deal mainly with the history of the Algerian revolution or with the history of the Muslim era of Algeria, overlooking earlier times, as can be expected. However, the great Berber kings of classical times, Massinissa or Jugurtha, for instance (Berber kings of the 2nd and 1st centuries B.C.), are sometimes evoked in the context of great historic figures or in the form of theatrical plays.

It is certain that the audience of channel two is now much more important than it was during the colonial period. But it can be heard only in the north of Algeria, in an area that is between Cherchel to the west, Jijel to the east, and Mehdya to the south. In other words, it covers Kabylia and a large part of the district around Algiers. The Berber-speaking population of this region has been estimated at more than 3 million out of the 6 million Berber speakers in the whole of Algeria

(25% of the nation's total population). No survey has ever been done to estimate the audience of channel two, but the wide diffusion of transistor radios would encourage one to believe that it is important in Kabylia and in Algiers, especially for Kabyle songs, which are almost never broadcast on television. Kabylia now has a fairly high level of electrification. Even out-of-the-way villages have electricity, as a result of the government's ambitious program for rural electrification. On the other hand, the market has been inundated by radios that are imported or in most cases manufactured by the factory at Bel-Abbès. The use of transistors and batteries has facilitated the penetration of radio in the most remote areas. Almost one out of two people in the global population owns a radio. It was estimated in 1987 that more than 10 million radios existed in Algeria in a population of 24 million. This means that all Algerian families own at least two radios. The density of listening is very high within the region covered by channel two, keeping in mind that its broadcasting power is weak. It is also broadcast in France for the Algerian immigrants among whom a large majority is of Kabyle origin.

It is, therefore, a fact that channel two is widely heard. It plays a role in politics, and the Algerian government is far from indifferent to it. Somewhat neglected until 1975, channel two has since been the object of controversy; 1975 coincides with the time when Arabization became an important issue of national policy. Some considered the existence of this channel to be questionable and did not hesitate to ask for its suppression, but to no avail. The government has indeed no other way to communicate with a population whose rate of literacy barely exceeds 50% and who understand neither French nor Arabic. Channel two allows the government to maintain contact with this population and to convey political messages to it. This is all the more necessary when the Front de Libération Nationale (FLN) party has some difficulty in implementing its leadership in the country.

For these reasons, channel two has been retained, but some people have tried to counterattack from another angle. After the riots that shattered Kabylia in 1980 the culture problem in Algeria became an issue and the central committee of the FLN devoted its seventh session in 1982 to the topic. A recommendation was made to transform channel two into a national channel, specializing in popular culture of which Kabyle would be just one expression among many. This recommendation obviously attempted to drown channel two in a generalized folklore. Obviously, this was an insidious and nefarious proposition. But to date the recommendation has not been implemented. These various attempts reveal, without doubt, that the existence of the channel raises a major problem. Because it seems difficult to repress it completely or even to restructure it, it is given a low profile and it tends to vegetate.

In fact, the problem of channel two is linked to the problem of Arabization, which does not reflect the reality of the country, the motivations for which include dimensions that are not exclusively national. The goal of Arabization is to make a country uniform that does not have that characteristic (Roberts, 1982, 1983). Undoubtedly, Arabization is necessary but it should be made at the expense of the French language whose influence in Algeria is a colonial remnant. It should be made without involving xenophobia toward the French language and culture, which still have their place both in teaching and in the media. Many Algerians, mostly professionals, are soaked in French culture. This is a reality that must be taken into account. But, on the other hand, Arabic must resume its place in education, administration, economic, and daily life, the place of a national language of a sovereign country. This is the goal of Arabization. But the efforts that this objective necessitates should not result in the neglect of the Berber language, which needs aid to survive. It is possible to achieve these two objectives, which must be pursued along parallel lines. Official policy acknowledges and supports this necessity, for example, in the report on cultural policy adopted by the FLN during the fifth session of June and July 1981: "One of the most urgent tasks is therefore to collect methodically the different kinds of the popular national heritage, to record them, to organize their conservation, and to facilitate the access of those who are interested in them. It is necessary for the accomplishment of this task that special organizations be created (p. 30)." Obviously, the Berber language is part of the popular national heritage. However, the implementation of this policy seems to encounter several difficulties (see also Chaker, 1981).

Difficulties come from the fact that not all Algerians are aware of this reality. The ignorance of their history, which was sustained by colonization and which has been somewhat falsified since independence, has resulted in the perception that the Berber language and its dialects are the heritage of a minority. However, as was noted in the first part of this chapter, the historic diffusion of Arabic among the Algerian people did not involve the superposition of two different populations but was voluntary and organized by Algerians themselves. The survival of the Berber language is obvious throughout Algeria in the names of places, cities, and villages and in the Arabic dialects of vast areas like North Constantine and the Algerian west, particularly the Tlemcen region, which are rich in Berber expressions. Even their syntax is influenced by Berber.

The Berber language is not, therefore, the heritage of a minority but of the whole Algerian people. The challenge is to have this reality widely recognized. The existence of channel two works to this effect. It could become a kind of laboratory in which a real renaissance of the Berber language and the Kabyle dialect could occur through the necessary adjustments demanded by modern life and particularly through the information broadcasts. It could also be achieved through the planned broadcast of all the tales, proverbs, poems, and songs that have a classical character (Lahlou, 1983). By increasing the number of broadcast hours and the power of its equipment so that it could be heard in all the regions where Berber is spoken, channel two could become a national channel devoted to all Berber dialects.

The achievement of this goal would coincide with a political necessity. The level of illiteracy still remains high in Algeria (around 50%) in spite of serious efforts to change the situation. The remote areas do not benefit from these efforts, and it is the case that these regions are more Berber than Arabic speaking. Only radio can overcome this inconvenience in a language that this population can understand: In other words, the radio must be in Berber.

Notes

1. *The Annuaire de l'Afrique du Nord* (1981-1982) includes a long bibliography on all the aspects of the Berber language as well as articles about the Berbers that sometimes differ from the thesis developed here.

2. The Hilalis were a large tribe of nomadic Arabs that inhabited the south of Egypt until the 19th century. At the beginning of that century, following disputes between the Zirids of Kairawan and the Fatimids of Egypt, the Fatimid king had the tribe invade the Maghreb (Golvin, 1957).

3. Historians date the wars that took place in the south of the Aurès to a period that ranges from 65 to 80 of the Hijrah. During the fighting, Berber Queen al-Kahinah and Arab General 'Uqbah were killed. But the same historians do not mention any other fighting between the Muslims and the Berbers in any other region of Algeria before or after that period. I interpret this as confirming the thesis of peaceful and voluntary Islamization in all of the central and western regions, especially following the actions of King Izmar.

4. Historians report that 'Uqbah was killed on the return from his famous conquest in an ambush by the Berber Kossayla. But historians fail to emphasis that Kossayla was a Muslim and that his revolt was not a repudiation of Islam but that it was directed against the arbitrary behavior of 'Uqbah ('Abd al-Hakam, 1942).

5. Several Berber tribes, particularly the Maghrawa and the Banu Ifran of Algeria, went to reinforce the power of the Umayyad 'Abd al-Rahman when he took power in Cordova in 75. Later in the 12th and 13th centuries, several other tribes went to Spain and settled in the region of Grenada and were the original founders of the city (Glick, 1979).

References

'Abd al-Hakam, I. (1942). *Conquête de l'Afrique du Nord et de l'Espagne* (A. Gateau, Trans.). Alger: Editions Carbonel.

Albert, P. , Tudesq, A., & Ihaddaden, Z. (1984). *Histoire de la radio et de la télévision.* Algiers: OPU.

Annuaire de l'Afrique du Nord. (1981-1982). Aix-en-Provence: Centre National de la Recherche Scientifique.

Chaker, S. (1981). De quelques constantes du discours dominant sur les langues populairs en Algérie: De la marginalisation à l'exclusion. In *Annuaire de l'Afrique du Nord* (pp. 451-457). Aix-en-Provence: Centre National de la Recherche Scientifique.

Chevaldonné, F. (1981). *La communication inégale: L'accès aux média dans les compagnes Algériennes.* Paris: Centre National de la Recherche Scientifique.

Chevaldonné, F. (1988). Nationalization, market-economy and sociocultural development—the structures of audiovisual communication in independent Algeria. *Media, Culture and Society, 10*(3), 269-284.

Desfois, J. (1964). *L'Afrique du Nord.* Paris: Presses Universitaires de France.

Gellner, E., & Micaud, C. (Eds.). (1972). *Arabs and Berbers.* London: Duckworth.

Glick, T. F. (1979). *Islamic and Christian Spain in the early Middle Ages.* Princeton, NJ: Princeton University Press.

Golvin, L. (1957). *Le Maghreb Central à l'époque des Zizides.* Paris: Gouvernement Général de l'Algérie.

Harbi, M. (1980). *Le FLN: Mirage et réalité.* Paris: Editions J. A.

Kaddache, M. (1980). *Histoire du nationalisme Algérien.* Algiers: SNED.

L'Africain, L. (1958). *Description de l'Afrique.* Paris: Adrien-Maisonneuve.

Lahlou, M. A. (1983). *La RTA et le langue en question.* Tizi-ouzou: Tafsut (special series).

Lustick, I. (1985). *State-building failure in British Ireland and French Algeria.* Berkeley: University of California, Institute of International Studies.

Montagne, R. (1973). *The Berbers: Their social and political organisation.* London: Ernest Gellner.

Quandt, W. (1969). *Revolution and political leadership: Algeria 1954-1968.* Cambridge, MA: MIT Press.

Roberts, H. (1982). The unforeseen development of the Kabyle question in contemporary Algeria. *Government and Opposition, 17*(3), 312-334.

Roberts, H. (1983). The economics of Berberism—The material basis of the Kabyle question in contemporary Algeria. *Government and Opposition, 18*(2), 218-235.

Taboury, E., & Taboury, M. (1987). Berber unrest in Algeria—Lessons for language policy. *International Journal of the Sociology of Language, 63,* 63-79.

Wilkin, A. (1970). *Among the Berbers of Algeria.* Westport, CT: Negro University Press. (Original work published in 1900.)

12

Spanish-Language Media in the Greater New York Region During the 1980s

JOHN D. H. DOWNING

Introductory Issues

The aim of this chapter is to provide an overview of Spanish-language media in New York City. The introductory sections discuss some of the issues related to minority empowerment, one of the goals of ethnic minority media, as well as the implications of defining minority audiences in terms of either class or culture. The concluding sections of the chapter analyze the character of two UHF television stations, two AM radio stations, and two daily newspapers serving the region.

Ethnic media are a long-established feature of American culture. New York alone boasts 20 or more Jewish newspapers (in English, Yiddish, and Hebrew), 6 Chinese newspapers, 2 or 3 Russian newspapers, 2 black newspapers and 4 national black magazines, and 2 Greek newspapers, to name only the most salient. The Latino media surveyed in this chapter are not the only sources of information available in Spanish. Papers from San Juan, Puerto Rico, such as *Vocero,* are also on sale, and there are two other radio stations (WSKQ and WKDM), and programs broadcast by several university radio stations (Columbia, Fordham, Seton-Hall, and

AUTHOR'S NOTE: This research was initially presented to a UNESCO conference in Ilkley, UK, in 1985, and then in a revised version at the annual convention of the Applied Anthropology Association in Oaxaca, Mexico, in 1987. I would like to thank Jeannette López for her assistance in the earliest phase of this research, and Richard Pérez and Saskia Sassen-Koob for their help at certain key points. The work and assistance of Federico Subervi-Vélez, my valued departmental colleague whose knowledge of this area is encyclopedic, has been of the greatest help, especially in updating a number of my observations. Responsibility for this chapter is entirely mine.

Medgar Evers College). It is clear that Latino media are thriving throughout the United States, in contrast to the relative doldrums of the black press (Downing, 1990; Garland, 1982; Subervi-Vélez et al., 1992).

This immediately raises the question of how far the Spanish language is being retained in the United States. This has been, of course, one of the hottest political issues in education, practically replacing bussing as a racially charged topic of school policy. Neither this policy issue nor its ramifications can be addressed here,[1] but certain observations are relevant. First, language in a multilingual environment is normally contextually specific. If someone works at home, or in an ethnic store within an ethnic neighborhood, there is no need to develop a facility in a second language. Even if someone works in a different linguistic environment, at home they may prefer to retain their mother tongue. I write *may,* because in the New York region and elsewhere many younger Latinos function by preference either in English or in *Spanglish,* a mixed language code in which users may switch back and forth between both languages within a single sentence, depending on the utility of particular terms and expressions (similar phenomena are readily observable in educated middle-class conversations in India, *mutatis mutandis*).

Furthermore, there are indications that in the realm of public communication certain strata within Latino communities may place more confidence in both commercial and political advertisements if they are in English. The Republican strategy in 1984 worked on this assumption (Subervi-Vélez, Herrera, & Begay, 1987), as did the largest single print medium targeted at Latinos, the insert magazine *Vista,* which had a distribution of 1.1 million copies weekly in 1987. *Vista* was edited from Coral Gables, Florida, and was entirely in English. (It was inserted at the time of writing only in one small New Jersey newspaper, and so does not form part of this study.) At the same time, other studies showed that the rate of retention of Spanish was highest among the Puerto Rican segment of the Latino community nationally, with Mexicans coming next and Cubans last (Nelson & Tienda, 1985).

For this study of the New York region, these findings have varying significance. They suggest a priori that Spanish-language media would be most needed and most used in that region precisely because of the dominant demographic position of Puerto Ricans (see below). At the same time, they suggest that print media may be less in demand among the young, and that combined perhaps with a contextually specific use of language among more affluent strata, the long-term future of Spanish-language media—rather than English-language media addressed to Latino audiences—*may* depend on fresh immigration rather than any other single factor. At the same time, all indications are that such immigration will continue.

These media also require that we consider the concept of *empowerment*. In the specific context of ethnic and/or immigrant-worker communities, the term implies a substantive gain in the community's ability both to determine what happens to its members and to alter structures that hitherto have adversely affected them. It presumes that structurally determined power and powerlessness are at the root of many specific problems experienced by the community. Empowerment through media would imply, therefore, the expansion of needed information and the opportunity to debate issues of moment to the community. It might also, in this context, imply the cultural reinforcement of a community under threat from various forms of cultural invasion or domination—including linguistic subversion—from a powerful majority culture.

In studies of radical alternative media in a number of countries (Downing, 1984, 1988), I proposed that their roles could usefully be seen as overcoming atomization among the currently powerless and as providing the basis for autonomous political communication and organization—without presupposing success in any given case. In particular I proposed that the gradual integration of sometimes diverse concerns of nationality, race, gender, age, and still other differentiating factors into a multiple common political agenda was a task particularly appropriate to such media. Without necessarily assuming that ethnic minority media *should* adopt the role of radical alternative media, a basic question in this research was how far Latino media in the New York region have acted as agents of empowerment in any of these senses.

There are three excellent survey articles covering ethnic minority media, one is a cross-national study (Husband, 1986); another examines ethnic media, assimilation, and pluralism in the United States (Suberví-Vélez, 1986); and the third examines the general situation of Latino media in the United States in the early 1990s (Suberví-Vélez et al., 1992). In the present context, however, a major issue emerges from all three essays. How far do various terms—*worker, migrant, ethnic, language-group, integration, assimilation,* and *pluralism*—denote aspects of the social reality that must be considered and/or constitute concepts adequate to that reality? For example, what relation, if any, should be considered to exist between assimilation and empowerment? Does not assimilation imply submersion, disappearance as an identifiable group, and therefore, loss of a community to empower? In a different way, if the issue at stake were to be entirely collapsed into the category of *workers,* then once again there would be a kind of disappearing act. Finally, the converse, a solely cultural/ethnic definition of the situation also flattens the issues into a shape barely recognizable to most people who, let us say, regularly travel the New York subway at rush hour.

In this research I have endeavored to maintain a multiple focus on the variety of dimensions involved and, as far as possible, on their interpenetration. For example, to take one aspect not mentioned so far, rates of unemployment among Latino youth simultaneously demonstrate their dependence on a wage, their location within the age group hardest hit by joblessness, and forms of active discrimination against them, including the long refusal of the federal government to organize decent educational facilities rather than the production of machines of destruction.

Two dominant responses during the 1980s to the position of Latinos in the United States demand some comment. One is economic and implies the trouble-free absorption of these minorities into the conventional consumerist processes of American society. This is the *Spanish-language market* theme. The second is political and consists of plans to tame what it envisions as the *Latinization* of the United States, although less on narrowly cultural than on political grounds.

In the former case, flurries of articles in advertising magazines about a market supposedly worth $60 to 70 billion a year in the mid-1980s were evidence of a widespread corporate desire to cash in on the process, with likely implications for the character of Spanish-language media dependent on advertising revenues. *Advertising Age,* for example, the leading American magazine in its field, ran an article in which the writer observed: "It is little wonder that marketers who understand how to address them [Latinos] directly are finding out just how rewarding this market can be" (Strand, 1984, p. 56).

The Latinization debate included both a scare-mongering campaign designed to underpin the Reagan administration's support for the status quo in Central America and a sustained attempt to woo Latino voters to the ranks of the Republican party (Suberví-Vélez et al., 1987). The scare campaign was based on the assertion that atheistic Marxist tyranny would somehow engulf Mexico from Central America and then sweep triumphantly across the Rio Grande. This was stated by both President Reagan and his associates, was dramatized in the film *Red Dawn* (1984), and was perfectly exemplified in the license allowed ex-Colonel Oliver North to bypass Congress. At the local level in California and elsewhere, *English only* campaigns, directed against bilingual education policies and multilingual public notices, represented a less global but equally visceral reaction to the growth of Latino communities.

At the same time, the Republicans spent far more money wooing the Latino vote than the Democratic party did, and both parties spent more money wooing the Latino vote than the black vote. This was clearly aimed at establishing a bridgehead for the future in this fast-growing community, especially among the more affluent Chicano components, most elements of the Cuban expatriate community already being firmly within the Republican fold. The dual *scare-and-woo* strategy was, it seemed, aimed at severing the ties and sympathies of as many U.S. Latinos as possible with Latin American concerns about the domination of their countries by the United States and thus at establishing hegemony over Latino political opinion.

All in all, therefore, Latinos found themselves in the 1980s both an economic and a political target, with community empowerment definitively taking a backseat. How did their media fit within this context?

The Nationality and Social Class of Latinos in Greater New York

I have defined greater New York in census terms as the five boroughs of the city itself, together with Putnam, Rockland, and Westchester countries to the north and Bergen county to the south in New Jersey. This area is termed the New York Standard Metropolitan Statistical Areas (SMSA). I have also included three areas in New Jersey, namely Jersey City, Newark, and Paterson-Clifton-Passaic. Less technically, this is the built-up region anyone can see from an airplane circling to land.

The Latino proportion of the population in this region is difficult to determine with precision because of widely differing estimates of the numbers of undocumented aliens (Table 12.1). These estimates vary from 2 to 12 million for the country and about 1 million for New York alone (Briggs, 1984; Keely, 1982; Passel & Woodrow, 1984). It is generally assumed that the largest proportion of such illegal migrant workers is Latino. This aspect of the enumeration is extremely slippery, not least because high estimates—for example, from the Immigration and Naturalization Service—are sometimes suspected to be founded either on the attempt to increase the agency's bureaucratic numbers and power or on nativist paranoia so typical of immigration control officials the world over. The issue of undercounting various ethnic minority

TABLE 12.1 Census Figures on Latino Nationalities in Greater New York[a] (1980)

Total greater New York	12,000,000
Total Latino population	1,831,000
Puerto Ricans (New York SMSA only)	898,000
Dominicans	139,000
Cubans	114,000
Colombians	61,000
Ecuadoreans	53,000
Mexicans	10,000

SOURCE: The figures are derived from the 1980 Census of the Population, (U.S. Department of the Census, 1983a, pp. 251-252, Table P7; 1983b, pp. 34-39, Table 195; 1983c, pp. 133-134, 151-153, 157-158, Table 206A, pp. 1041-1042, 1075-1076, 1083-1084, Table 229). The *Detailed Population Characteristics* series is based on 10% samples and may underestimate Latino populations. In general, however, the 1980 census is widely regarded as much more accurate in this respect than the 1970 census was.
NOTE: a. The numbers have been rounded to the nearest thousand.

groups in the 1990 census rapidly became a major political battle-ground, in part because of the factors mentioned and in part because urban governments frequently anticipated federal aid to their cities being lowered on the basis of low census estimates.

In turn, the number of people who can be classified as migrant workers within the Latino population—and it is often forgotten how far back the roots of the Latino community go in New York (Vega, 1984)—are equally obscure, not only because of undocumented workers but also because there is a well-established phenomenon of reverse migration to both Puerto Rico and the Dominican Republic (Center for Puerto Rican Studies, 1979; Ugalde, 1979). Indeed, in the case of Puerto Rico, because of the absence of passport controls, moves back and forth during an individual's lifetime are quite common (similar to the actions of black migrants to northern cities).

In terms of labor-force location, the census indicated that the primary form of employment is in manufacturing, despite the overall decline in the region's industrial base. Sassen-Koob (1985) has argued that there has not been a flight of industrial capital from the region as much as a recomposition of capital in favor of certain sectors, notably the garment industry, which is hardly a newcomer to New York, but which certainly employs many undocumented immigrants (Campos & Bonilla, 1981; Grasmuck, 1984; NACLA, 1979; Sassen-Koob, 1980, 1981, 1984b). The other major area was in personal and business-related services, as will be evident below. In general, expansion was within the so-called secondary labor market, namely low-paid, insecure employment of the kind to which migrant workers and women have generally been consigned.

Within industry, the main employers for males are in apparel; printing, publishing, and allied trades; the electrical goods industry; and fabricated metals. For women, the main sectors were apparel, electrical goods, and printing. In the New Jersey section of the region there was more emphasis on chemicals, textiles, and food processing, although apparel still ranked first. The total number, rounded to the nearest thousand, was 228,000.[2]

Taking the next largest category, private and government professional labor, which accounted for 134,000 (the two categories are separated in census statistics), a note of caution is in order. The main institutions involved were schools and hospitals, and the figures showed about one third more women than men employed in this category. Given what is known about the normal distribution of women's labor in such settings, it is fairly safe to conclude that most were employed in low-paid nursing, clerical, and service work. The term *professional,* therefore, should not be allowed to mislead analysts.

The third, fourth, fifth, and sixth largest employers were the retail trade (86,000); finance, insurance, and real estate (57,000); personal services (50,000); and transport and communications (45,000). In finance, insurance, and real estate it is plausible that mostly clerical labor was involved, and in personal services it is probably principally domestic labor, home nursing, and similar activities. Transportation and communications had a much higher ratio of males to females than the other categories.

By contrast, the numbers self-employed in retail or construction—standard avenues of economic mobility for workers without good educational certification—were much smaller (5,100 and 1,400, respectively, rounded to the nearest hundred). This figure may, of course, understate the true numbers, because construction is an area where it is easy to work in the second economy. However, the 20,000 working in public administration, another apparently middle-class sector, are also quite likely to have been engaged in low-paid clerical tasks. Thus even the most accessible middle-class employment sectors offered very little evidence of Latino advancement.

If we examine figures for economic distribution, rather than employment, an even worse picture emerges. Among U.S. urban centers the New York–New Jersey SMSA (a slightly smaller area than the one I have been analyzing) ranked 12th in terms of Hispanic median family income, 2nd for the proportion below the poverty level (39%), and 13th for those aged 25 and over who had graduated from high school (35%). These figures are from Sassen-Koob's (1984a) analysis of materials generated by the Population Research and Analysis Unit of the Human Resources Division of the City Planning Department of New York City. New York Latinos also have an exceptionally low rate of telephone ownership, a valid index of economic deprivation in the United States: 68% compared with 89% in Miami and 85% in Los Angeles (Juárez, 1984).

If these rankings and percentages are put in the context of the very large number of Latinos involved (second in size only to the Los Angeles-Long Beach region), then it is clear that poverty is a very real experience for a considerable number of Latinos in the greater New York region. It is no doubt because of generally low wages that such a high proportion of Latinos are in paid employment. Officially, 267,000 women were registered as paid employees in greater New York as compared with 369,000 men. Given that the dominant segment within the Latino population is Puerto Rican, it must be kept in mind that as early as the mid-1980s, 40% of Puerto Rican families nationally were headed by women, and that the true unemployment rate among Puerto Ricans was in the region of 30% to 40% (Pérez, 1985).

Putting all these data together, and in light of the major recession that began to strike New York City from the time of the 1987 stock market crash and that made the situation of ethnic minority communities even harsher, it is clear that empowerment on a variety of levels, not least the economic, is an urgent need for Latino communities in New York. It is a legitimate question to ask in what ways any of the six media institutions examined in this chapter were concerned about promoting such empowerment.

El Diario-La Prensa

The circulation of the daily newspaper *El Diario-La Prensa* is in the region of 54,000 to 58,000, and its editorial staff claimed a readership approaching a quarter of a million. It has three daily editions, one of which goes to Chicago, Philadelphia, and Baltimore by truck; the second goes to New Jersey; and the third is for New York City. Its editorial staff in 1991 numbered a little more than 40, with another 80 people assigned to nonjournalistic tasks, excluding printing, which is done in New Jersey but transmitted electronically from the New York office.

The paper's title represented a 1963 merger of two earlier newspapers, one started in 1913, the other in 1948. In 1981, the paper was taken over by the Gannett Corporation, which in 1985 ranked 203rd in *Fortune* magazine's list of the 500 largest American corporations. In that year it owned 85 newspapers, including the third largest selling paper in the country, the ultramodern (and ultrabland) *USA Today* (McNicol & Carlson, 1985; Seelye, 1983). In that same year, Gannett started a satellite advertisement service for 37 of its own operations and 27 other organizations. It owned six television stations and 16 radio stations, it operated the Gannett News Service for its affiliates, and it owned the Lou Harris polling organization and the largest billboard advertising operation in the country. However, in 1989, Gannett sold *El Diario-La Prensa* to a consortium of Anglo businesspeople and the Latino publisher of the newspaper since 1984.

Gannett's purchase of *El Diario-La Prensa* resulted in changes in both personnel and editorial policy. For example, in the past any Latino candidate running for public office was automatically given space in the paper; now it began to be more selective, basing its coverage on candidates' positions on major issues. Politicians used to come in simply to be photographed; now they had to do something deemed newsworthy to be covered. Edward Koch, New York's mayor for the entire 1980s, was now criticized from time to time in the columns, a previously unheard of practice. Similarly, reporters were expected to cover stories in person, rather than simply taking down details over the telephone from their sources.

Official editorial policy on relations with Latino communities was to give Puerto Ricans the largest coverage, being the largest community in the region but also to emphasize Dominican and Colombian community news. As regards foreign news, *El Diario* kept permanent correspondents in San Juan and Santo Domingo and would sometimes send a special correspondent out of the country to cover a particular event (for example, the Mexico City earthquake of 1984). Otherwise, it depended on the international wire services, including the Spanish news agency EFE, which maintains a network of correspondents in the Hispanic and Lusophone world. One of the paper's most popular features, however, was a section titled *"Nuestros Paises"* ("Our Countries"), which covered Latin America, the Spanish-speaking Caribbean, and the Iberian peninsula. In 1985 this section was expanded from three to four pages daily. The paper also brought out special issues for particular national days of Latino countries.

Noticias del Mundo

Noticias del Mundo, a 24-page daily newspaper, began publication in 1980. It has a journalistic staff of 30 and another 50 workers for noneditorial duties. Its editor in 1985 proudly claimed 19 different nationalities among its employees. It is a sister paper to the *Washington Times,* owned by Time Tribune Corporation, formerly News World Communications. In turn this parent company is directly controlled by the political-religious organization of the Reverend Sun Myung Moon, of the Unification Church. This body's self-proclaimed mission to reverse any trend toward communism in the Americas and to develop media to this end has been solidly documented (Abas, 1984; Anderson, 1984; Boyer & Alem, 1985; Rothmyer, 1984), as have its connections with some of the least savory elements in the international Far Right (Clarkson, 1987). Reverend Moon's financial empire is a considerable one, based on sales of ginseng, weapons, and other artifacts, and is said to garner in the region of $50 million a year just from street sales of flowers by his unpaid U.S. adherents. This in turn helps to explain how the Moon newspapers in the United States, technically well produced and designed, can continue to operate at what seems likely to be a considerable loss (the highest estimates of the *Washington Times*'s circulation, for example, were below 130,000 for much of the 1980s). Moon's own oft-stated conviction is that World War III will be—and is—the battle of ideas with Communism.

A reading throughout the 1980s of the Moon organization's main American monthly publication, *Causa USA Report,* reveals the standard obsessions of the American Far Right: subversion in the hemisphere by Soviets, Cubans, and Nicaraguans; impassioned support for the Central American status quo outside Nicaragua; Soviet "disinformation" tactics; Communist "fronts"; the importance of religion; and more in the same vein. The language was often quite violent, the humor heavily sarcastic, and the analysis laden with vitriolic personal attacks on Marxist leaders.

Yet at the same time, strenuous efforts were being made to present Moon's followers (*Moonies*) as a multiracial and multicultural group. Far to the political right as the organization may be in many respects, its goals are different from the traditional Far Right (e.g., the Klu Klux Klan). As well as having close links to the Reagan and Bush administrations, it also vigorously pursued stronger ties with the Vatican and with conservative elements in the Latin American Catholic hierarchy.

It would be most unwise to write the Moonies off because of their slightly comic name or the checkered financial career of their leader.

We may also note that the editor of *Noticias,* José Cardinali, was invited to dinner at the White House on a number of occasions during the Reagan administration, and Phillip Sanchez, former U.S. ambassador to Honduras and Colombia and a person invited to become a member of Reagan's first administration, joined the newspaper as managing director in spring 1987. Cardinali had previously been editor of *Crónica,* a mass circulation Buenos Aires newspaper selling about a million copies daily. The newspaper had not been a mouthpiece of the Videla-Galtieri dictatorship but was very close to the bureaucracy of the *peronista* labor unions, which in turn had been supportive of the dictatorship. Arguably, the character of the editorial policy in *Noticias del Mundo,* given such personnel and political associations, was fairly sophisticated. A certain kind of populism was much in evidence—how else would one reconcile Reverend Moon with the paper's daily inclusion of horse-racing information?

The paper's circulation in the New York metropolitan region was difficult to determine with precision. At the time of writing it was not audited by the Audit Bureau of Circulations, so that only the newspaper's own claims of circulation were available and were not independently verifiable. In the mid-1980s about 55,000 copies a day were claimed, and a readership of 150,000. In 1987 it was producing three local editions: one for Brooklyn and Queens, a second for the rest of New York, and a third for New Jersey. Since October 1984 there had also been a *Noticias del Mundo,* in Los Angeles, with an apparent circulation of 30,000. Half of the paper was produced in New York, and then transmitted to the West Coast via satellite to be joined with the other half. In 1985 there were rather grandiose plans to expand this arrangement to cover Miami; Chicago; Texas; Boston; Philadelphia; Washington, DC; and San Francisco, but by 1990 only New Jersey and Boston could be numbered, and between these cities less than 10,000 copies were actually sold.

Although its readership was more concentrated among Dominicans than Puerto Ricans, editorial policy was to avoid targeting any one group in particular. Editorial policy was tilted strongly toward community news. An example cited to me by the editor (José Cardinali, personal communication, May 16, 1985) was the front page coverage given to the airport arrest of a Puerto Rican father (on an immigration charge), whose child was receiving emergency medical care in the city, rather than to a terrorist bombing in Lebanon, which was covered on an inside page. The activism and presence of *Noticias* reporters in various community confrontations was something noted with a certain disquiet by a number of Latino political activists, who were concerned that these reporters might become too well informed about the identity of those who were involved in the grass-roots political life of the city and might act as unwelcome communication channels to police Red Squads.

Noticias del Mundo also gave regular coverage to the various Latin countries, often assigning a whole page to each country. It kept one full-time correspondent in Santo Domingo but otherwise used stringers in other capitals, as well as the wire services of UPI and EFE.

Indicative contrasts between *El Diario* and *Noticias del Mundo* included the following. The former sharply attacked a coverup of the violence meted out by prison guards to *marielitos* (Cuban criminals deported from Cuba in 1980) in the Brooklyn Navy Yard jail and the proposed gentrification of the *Marqueta* area in Spanish Harlem. *Noticias* made no reference at all to the first and covered the second in terms that presumed no other issue to be at stake than progress. On contentious foreign policy issues, *El Diario* ran an interview with a priest sympathetic to the Sandinista revolution and in the same issue an interview with the then president of Costa Rica saying that co-existence with the Sandinistas was impossible. No such balance was visible in *Noticias,* which featured events such as "Solidarity Week with Nicaragua" (i.e., with the contra rebels) and devoted more than a page to a Cuban anti-Castro group under a heading such as "The Voice of Free Cuba."

Radio WADO

Under one ownership or another, Radio WADO has been broadcasting since 1934. Its 1992 owner was a small family-owned chain based in Dallas, Texas, named Tichenor Media Systems, Inc. It broadcast 24 hours on AM and had a normal reach of 50 miles. Between 6:00 a.m. and midnight its average weekly audience 12 years of age and older was estimated by Arbitron as a 1.4% share of the market, or 36,800 people in fall 1986.

WADO's own sense of its audience was that they were older members of the Latino communities, together with a small segment of younger people interested in discovering once more the earlier heritage of Latino popular music and its often strong lyrics. The index of WADO's impact that the station's staff preferred to cite was the file-past at the funeral of one of its announcers in the 1970s, a man known by his voice alone to most people. About 70,000 attended, some praying, some in tears. In the 1980s there were 21 members of the production staff, with another 15 in administration. Two of the reporters on *El Diario* at that time acted as stringers for the station, phoning in reports that were then broadcast. The station had no full-time reporters.

The station's offerings to Latino communities took various forms. The morning and evening commuting to work, the prime time of Anglo commercial radio, was not very important for Latinos in New York because so few drove to work. The WADO staff considered their most important contribution to be between 10:00 a.m. and 3:00 p.m. in the day, when on weekdays there was a talk show hosted by the very popular announcer Gilda Mirós titled *No Solo Para Nosotras (Not Just for Us Women)*. This was claimed to be popular with women in factories and at home and dealt with a whole range of topics, varying from personalities in the news, medicine, health, and psychiatry to the Immigration and Naturalization Service. On one occasion the program put the Colombian consul on the air to face a wave of criticism for his agency's failure to deal appropriately with Colombian citizens in New York. WADO claimed to have helped to get about 140,000 people registered to vote over the previous few years on a nonpartisan basis—although it had backed Reagan for the presidency in 1984. The station also carried frequent news from Latin countries. It used correspondents in San Juan, Santo Domingo, Bogot, and Miami (the latter for the Cuban connection). Its other main international news sources were the Associated Press wire service and the British World Service in Spanish.

On Fridays, for 24 hours beginning at noon, WADO aired what it had found to be one of its most popular programs, *Viernes Para Recordar (Fridays for Remembering)*. This consisted of songs and music of yesteryear, performed by the artists who first made them famous. Later in the day on Saturdays, WADO aired *Canto a Las Américas (The Americas in Song)*, during which the folkloric and traditional music of Latin cultures was broadcast, with a focus on an individual country if its national day happened to be close in time.

Thus the audience for WADO can be presumed to be fairly stable, well established in the United States, and at the older end of the spectrum, perhaps rather respectable in tone and a little traditional in style.

Radio WJIT

Radio WJIT dates back to 1930 and was owned in the 1980s by Infinity Broadcasting, a small independent radio network that had another English-language station in New York (in the same suite of offices on Madison Avenue), and a further 12 AM and FM stations across the United States. The broadcasting radius, like WADO's, was about 50 miles. Its staff numbered 48. Arbitron figures for fall 1986 gave it exactly half the listenership of WADO, i.e., a 0.7% market share, or on average 18,400 weekly listeners aged 12 and older between the hours of 6:00 a.m. and midnight. To give some sense of comparison, the equivalent figures for one of the largest New York stations, WHTZ, were 5.8% and 151,000.

WJIT's programming was that of a typical all-music 24-hour station, with the single exception being that its output was practically all salsa and merengue (typically but not necessarily Puerto Rican and Dominican in origin, respectively). Practically the only alternative to music was spot news bulletins together with morning weather and traffic reports. One member of the management staff said there was a news and talk program, sometimes including advice to immigrants, at 4:30 a.m. on Sundays. By contrast, WADO offered 1 hour a day between 8:00 a.m. and 9:00 a.m., covering local, national, and international news (especially from Latin America).

WXTV (Channel 41)

The executive offices of WXTV, like those of the two radio stations, are in Manhattan, but its studios are in Secaucus, New Jersey. Its broadcasting range is similar to that of the two radio stations, but it also had translator stations in Hartford, Connecticut, and in Philadelphia. Arbitron figures for February 1987 gave it an audience of 542,000. It is owned by Univisión, which until January 1987 was known as the Spanish International Network (SIN) (Critser, 1987; Gutiérrez & Schement, 1984). Currently with 409 affiliated stations, Univisión is the giant of Spanish-language television in the United States. Until the time of writing, it had provided Mexican and other Latin national broadcasting, mainly in the form of *telenovelas,* to U.S. audiences. Its takeover by Hallmark Cards began to lead to more programs originating from inside the

United States, and indeed its policy came to be one of modeling itself more and more closely on the three main American television networks.

WXTV's programming certainly depended heavily on telenovelas: 7 hours a day, at varying points in the day. They originated from a variety of countries, including Mexico, Venezuela, Brazil, and Puerto Rico. Talk shows ran for 90 minutes a day, comedy for a further 90 minutes, and news (local, general, and a Mexican news program) for a further 3.5 hours a day. On weekends, news was only programmed for 1 hour on Sundays. In the early morning the station ran religious programs.

Channel 41 had four reporters. As with *El Diario* they relied fairly frequently for news items on spontaneous contacts by members of Latino communities, and on United Press International for national and international news. The station's policy was to try to include news not only from the more established centers of Latino settlement but also from more isolated Latino communities, such as the one in Yonkers. Information for recent immigrants was sometimes included in local news programming but did not seem to be a major priority. At times the station had also worked with various agencies on nonpartisan voter registration. On the other hand, as Subervi-Vélez (1992) notes, the SIN news program *Noticiero* had for a number of years given considerable attention both to Latin American election news, and to elections particularly relevant to Latino voters around the United States.

A word on the telenovelas (Rogers & Antola, 1985) is in order at this point. They tend to revolve around similar themes, as some of the titles indicate: *Tres Destinos* (*Three Destinies*), *Un Solo Corazón* (*Only One Heart*), *Te Amo* (*I Love You*), and *Tu O Nadie* (*You or No One*). The synopsis of another, *La Traición* (*Betrayal*), gives an impression of the genre's content: "So great was her love that she followed him to Paris, only to discover that he was deceiving her. Betrayed, she swears vengeance in this story of intrigue, ambition and above all, love." Suffering, scheming, and deception in love are the staple fare. Women are portrayed as self-sacrificing martyrs or as evil and deceptive.

One Venezuelan telenovela centered on a woman physician, Rafaela (the title of the series), who was in love with another doctor, who, in turn, was very unhappily married. The wife would not grant a divorce but instead feigned a psychiatric breakdown to gain sympathy. The ruse fails, and the wife becomes the target of everyone's dislike. Rafaela nobly goes off into the countryside to give birth to her doctor-lover's child, leaving the scene. At a later point, when everyone meets again, the wife tries to throw the baby off the roof in a fit of jealous rage but is unsuccessful. In the end the lovers achieve their goal: marriage.

It is easy for academics to pour derision on these telenovelas, or at least some of them. Some of the Brazilian series are said to be much better constructed (Lasagni & Richeri, 1986). At the same time, cultural analysts currently argue that they should not be written off simply as cultural pabulum or as celebrations of sexist social structures (Modleski, 1986; Zipes, 1984) but rather should be seen as texts communicating a mixture of messages, some of them stimulating fantasies (in a quasi-Freudian sense) of liberation. In this sense, they may be overpowering, not merely escapist in the sense of mind numbing.

WNJU (Channel 47)

WNJU, with executive offices in Manhattan and production studios in Ridgefield Park, New Jersey, has been in existence since 1965. Its broadcasting area was similar to the others so far surveyed. Its programming was mainly Latino, but in the earlier 1980s this audience competed for attention with many other language groups. Thus the station also rented time slots to other groups, from religious fundamentalists to ethnic minorities (Italians, Greeks, Japanese, Koreans, and East Indians). Its staff numbered 120. In 1987 it was purchased by Telemundo, which already owned a station in Los Angeles and bought stations in Puerto Rico and Miami in the same transaction. Telemundo was owned by the advertising firm John Blair and Co., which in turn was owned by Saul Steinberg's Reliance Capital Group (Berry, 1987). Interestingly, the former news division of SIN/Univisión in Miami joined Telemundo in a news operation called *Noticiero Telemundo* following internal divisions within Univisión.

As with Channel 41, telenovelas constituted a very large slice of programming time, occupying 9 hours a day; they were drawn from Venezuela, Argentina, Chile, Peru, and Colombia. Music and variety shows were another important component in WNJU's programming. Until the change in ownership, news seemed to take more of a backseat on this channel than on Channel 41, being confined to spot news on the hour and a half-hour news program at 11:00 p.m. Before the takeover, community news was not much in evidence, although what was broadcast tended to focus on the Puerto Rican community first and foremost, with Dominican news taking second place. As the change in ownership began to take effect, however, the professionalism of the news operation came to be much more in evidence. In 1988 Telemundo developed a cooperative relationship with CNN, and this also stimulated a higher quality news service. The February 1987 Arbitron figures gave WNJU a larger share of the audience than WXTV—671,000 versus 542,000. Both were small in relation to WNBC's audience, estimated at 5,956,000.

Conclusions

A major reason for the vigor of Latino media—and this is a point that goes to the heart of the issue of empowerment—is the discovery of the Spanish market (Berry, 1987; Critser, 1987). The magnates who bought SIN/Univisión and have created Telemundo were vocal in public about the huge sums of money they expected to make from the investment. Supposedly, in an information society such an investment might be thought to herald progress. Yet if we examine the messages that constitute *information* in this case, it is hard to suppose that this is or will be so.

An initial impression of advertising on these channels, for example, indicates their similarity to Anglo advertising, with certain exceptions. Cosmetics advertisements are even more exaggerated. During the telenovelas advertisements are frequently broadcast for creams, pills, and lotions that will cleanse the skin and reduce fat or weight. Examples are *El Demoledor de Grasa* ("the Fat Grinder") and *Fruta Que Quita Grasa* ("Fruit That Gets Rid of the Fat"). There are also some religious/superstitious ads, such as *la cruz de buena suerte con agua milagrosa* ("the good luck cross with miracle water"). On the radio, some firms will advertise that their staff are bilingual. A law firm, for instance, advertised in Spanish that it specialized in accident compensation cases and in quick divorces, repeatedly presenting a woman's voice relating how she got her divorce in 6 weeks without having to go to court. Just occasionally there are public service announcements advising what to do, *if* you think you *may* have been the object of discrimination.

Admittedly, the existence of Spanish-language media contributes to some sense of community and cultural identity. What stands out about their operation in the greater New York region, however, is the extraordinary opportunity their operation presents for community empowerment but that is largely wasted—and that in the light of recent media empire developments, looks highly unlikely to change. Even the community interest of *Noticias del Mundo* is politically ambiguous, given the character of the parent holding company. The interests of immigrants, especially, seem very low on the agenda of these media, with information about their various homelands prominent in a way that specific advice on dealing with the Immigration and Naturalization Service is not. Latino media in the New York region, with the exception of *Noticias* on the subject of Cuba and Nicaragua, do not produce the strident ultrarightist rhetoric of their counterparts in Miami (Rothchild, 1984), but this can only be classed as a negative virtue. Overall, what we see is a major opportunity missed.

Notes

1. See McCarty and Willshire-Carrera (1988) for an outstanding recent treatment of these issues.
2. These figures and those cited below are drawn from the United States Department of Commerce (1983b, pp. 34-39, Table 195; 1983c, pp. 1041-1042, 1075-1076, 1083-1084, Table 229).

References

Abas, B. (1984, November-December). Inside the paper God wanted. *Columbia Journalism Review, 23*(4), 46-49.

Anderson, J. (1984, August 16). CIA, Moonies cooperate in Sandinista war. *Washington Post*, p. E15.

Berry, J. F. (1987). The new order of Blair. *Channels, 7*(4), 53-56.

Boyer, J. -F. & Alem, A. (1985). L'internationale Moon. *Le Monde Diplomatique, 1*, 18-20.

Briggs, V. (1984). Methods of analysis of illegal immigration into the United States. *International Migration Review, 18*(3), 623-641.

Campos, R., & Bonilla, F. (1981, July). *Bootstraps and enterprise zones: The underside of late capitalism.* Paper presented at the Symposium on the United States Today, Universidad Nacional Autónoma de México, Mexico City.

Center for Puerto Rican Studies. (1979). *Labor migration under capitalism.* New York: Monthly Review Press.

Clarkson, F. (1987). Moon's law. *Covert Action Information Bulletin, 27*, 36-46.

Critser, G. (1987). The feud that toppled an empire. *Channels, 7*(1), 24-31.

Downing, J. (1984). *Radical media.* Boston: South End Press.

Downing, J. (1988). An alternative public realm. *Media, Culture and Society, 10*(2), 163-181.

Downing, J. (1990). Ethnic minority radio in the United States. *Howard Journal of Communication, 2*(2), 135-148.

Garland, P. (1982). The black press: Down but not out. *Columbia Journalism Review, 21*(3), 43-50.

Grasmuck, S. (1984). Immigration, ethnic stratification and native working class discipline: Comparison of documented and undocumented Dominicans. *International Migration Review, 18*(3), 692-713.

Gutiérrez, F., & Schement, J. (1984). Spanish International Network: The flow of television from Mexico to the United States. *Communication Research, 11*(2), 241-258.

Husband, C. (1986). Mass media, communication policy and ethnic minorities: An appraisal of current theory and practice. *UNESCO, RUSHSAP Series of Occasional Monographs and Papers, Mass Media and the Minorities, 17,* 1-38.

Juárez, N. F. (1984, July 6). Researcher debunks myths propagated by self-appointed "Spanish market" gurus. *Marketing News,* pp. 4-6.

Keely, C. B. (1982). Illegal migration. *Scientific American, 246*(3), 41-47.

Lasagni, C., & Richeri, G. (1986). *L'altro mondo quotidiano: telenovelas, TV brasiliana e dintorni.* Turin, Italy: Edizioni RAI.

McCarty, J., & Willshire-Carrera, J. (1988). *New voices: Immigrant students in the U.S. public schools.* Boston: National Coalition of Advocates for Students.

McNicol, T., & Carlson, M. (1985). Al Neuharth's technicolor baby, part II. *Columbia Journalism Review, 24*(1), 44-48.

Modleski, T. (1986). *Loving with a vengeance.* New York: Methuen.

NACLA (North American Congress on Latin America). (1979). [Special Issue: Migrant workers in New York City.] *Report on the Americas, 12*(6).

Nelson, C., & Tienda, M. (1985). The structuring of Hispanic ethnicity: Historical and contemporary perspectives. *Ethnic and Racial Studies, 8*(1), 49-74.

Passel, J. S., & Woodrow, K. A. (1984). Geographic distribution of undocumented immigrants. *International Migration Review, 18*(3), 662-671.

Pérez, R. (1985, June). *The status of Puerto Ricans in the United States.* Paper presented at the Third National Puerto Rican Convention, Philadelphia.

Rogers, E. M., & Antola, L. (1985). Telenovelas: A Latin American success story. *Journal of Communication, 35*(4), 24-35.

Rothchild, J. (1984). The Cuban connection and the gringo press. *Columbia Journalism Review, 23*(3), 48-51.

Rothmyer, K. (1984). Mapping out Moon's media empire. *Columbia Journalism Review, 23*(4), 23-31.

Sassen-Koob, S. (1980). Immigrant and minority workers in the organization of the labor process. *Journal of Ethnic Studies, 8*(1), 1-34.

Sassen-Koob, S. (1981). Towards a conceptualization of immigrant labor. *Social Problems, 29*(1), 65-85.

Sassen-Koob, S. (1984a). The new labor demand in global cities. In M. P. Smith (Ed.), *Cities in transformation: Class, capital, and the state* (pp. 139-171). Beverly Hills, CA: Sage.

Sassen-Koob, S. (1984b). From household to workplace: Theories and survey research on migrant women in the labor market. *International Migration Review, 18*(4), 1144-1167.

Sassen-Koob, S. (1985). Changing composition and labor market location of Hispanic immigrants in New York City, 1960-1980. In G. J. Borjas & M. Tienda (Eds.), *Hispanics in the U.S. economy* (pp. 299-322). Orlando, FL: Academic Press.

Seelye, K. (1983). Al Neuharth's technicolor baby. *Columbia Journalism Review, 22*(6), 27-35.

Strand, P. (1984, July 9). SIN sees strong Latin auto market. *Advertising Age,* pp. 55-56.

Subervi-Vélez, F. (1986). Ethnic assimilation and pluralism: The role of the mass media. *Communication Research, 13*(1), 71-96.

Subervi-Vélez, F., Herrera, R., & Begay, M. (1987). Toward an understanding of the role of the mass media in Latino political life. *Social Science Quarterly, 68*(1), 185-196.

Subervi-Vélez, F., with the collaboration of Berg, C. R., Constantakis-Vélez, P., Noriega, C., Ríos, D. I., & Wilkinson, K. T. (1992). Mass communication and Hispanics. In F. Padilla (Ed.), *Handbook of Hispanic Cultures in the United States.* Houston, TX: Arte Público Press.

Ugalde, A. et al. (1979). International migration from the Dominican Republic: Findings from a national survey. *International Migration Review, XIII* (2), 235-254.

U.S. Department of Commerce. Bureau of the Census. (1983a). *Housing Census, Tracts N.Y., N.Y.-N.J. SMSA* (Section 1). Washington, DC: Government Printing Office.

U.S. Department of Commerce. Bureau of the Census. (1983b). *Detailed Population Characteristics: New York* (PC80-1-D34). Washington, DC: Government Printing Office.

U.S. Department of Commerce. Bureau of the Census. (1983c). *Detailed Population Characteristics: New Jersey* (PC80-1-D32). Washington, DC: Government Printing Office.

Vega, B. (1984). *Memoirs of Bernardo Vega* (Juan Flores, Trans.). New York: Monthly Review Press.

Zipes, J. (1984). *Breaking the magic spell.* New York: Methuen.

The Promise and Limits of
Ethnic Minority Media

STEPHEN HAROLD RIGGINS

Assessing the Problems

This concluding chapter focuses on the contribution the preceding case studies have made to an understanding of the dual role (Subervi-Vélez, 1986) of ethnic minority media. As explained in the introduction, the term *dual role* refers to the fact that it is debatable whether ethnic minority media are tools of cultural preservation or whether they surreptitiously contribute to the assimilation of ethnic minority audiences to the dominant culture within which they are immersed. In other words, it appears that the long-term effect of ethnic minority media is neither total assimilation nor total cultural preservation but some moderate degree of preservation that represents a compromise between these two extremes.

Ethnic minority media might be considered a significant ingredient toward cultural survival but certainly no panacea. There are several reasons for this. First, minority survival cannot depend only on the media; it also requires a critical demographic mass, the persistence of traditional institutions, and a good measure of political conviction and skill. Survival also presupposes, on the part of the dominant culture, a certain willingness to accommodate cultural pluralism for ideological or practical reasons. Modern states control the access to media technology and have the means to efficiently interfere with forms of broadcasting they consider subversive. The crucial importance of the political context of ethnic minority media is evident in all the case studies presented here. Accepting ethnic and cultural pluralism cannot mean that a nation promotes political independence for its minorities. This is no less true when the support for such developments comes from a political or social agency that is antagonistic to the state.

276

In addition, the actual impact of the media on ethnic minority survival remains problematic. One source of ambiguity in assessing the social influence of ethnic minority media comes from the very nature of mass-mediated human communication. The social processes relevant to such an assessment are complex, difficult to measure, and open to varied interpretations. This includes not only the content of the media but also the way it is processed and comprehended by audiences. When it comes to evaluating the durable effects of ethnic minority media on the populations to which they are aimed, it is noticeable that the case studies presented in this book rely mostly on impressions and indirect evidence. But this methodological weakness is not unique to our case studies.

Certainly, the social influence of mass media does not involve a simple direct causal relationship. Some specialists (e.g., Fiske, 1987), who emphasize that audiences actively create meaning in media content, prefer to avoid the word *effect* altogether. In their view the term implies that audiences are passive and lack the critical intelligence to resist the media's manipulative strategies. But audience viewing and reading habits are elusive and leave few objective traces. How mass media messages are actually interpreted by both majority and minority audiences remains largely unknown despite a few excellent studies of mainstream commercial media (e.g., Robinson & Levy, 1986). The theory and methodology of content and discourse analysis are more highly developed now than the scholarly tools needed to investigate audience reception. Consequently, the distinction established by this chapter between the factors that accelerate assimilation and those that delay or prevent assimilation is largely conjectural and should be considered as a working hypothesis for future research.

The ideological complexity of all media content is an additional complicating element. It would be simplistic to conceptualize the content as a unified whole that lends itself to only one interpretation. Any news story contains information that can be interpreted in different ways even though most communications scholars assume journalists slant stories in favor of a particular point of view. One would expect to find in mainstream commercial media both a *dominant ideology*, information consistent with the interests of an elite, and traces of a *counterideology*, information opposing elite interests. The term dominant ideology need not be restricted to content furthering the economic interests of an elite. In a more general sense it may refer to any information that supports an elite's continued dominance. Both ideologies also characterize ethnic minority journalism.

In some respects ethnic minority media provide an oppositional ideology, not in an economic sense because their reporting of economic issues in general appears to be rather cautious and conservative, at least in the present case studies. But as a reaction to perceived neglect and misrepresentation in mainstream media, ethnic journalists tend to be understandably biased. Exercising considerable self-censorship, they concentrate on topics flattering to the minority group. Thus ethnic minority media are characterized by an explicit counterideology in terms of ethnicity. The most obvious level of content consists of information whose function is to empower the minority at the expense of the majority. Empowerment may take the form of a purely symbolic reordering of prestige or the actual pursuit of political or economic power. Empowerment proceeds through content that stresses the differences between minority and majority populations.

But can minority journalists—however militant—escape the influence of the majority culture in which they are immersed? To a large extent it conditions their intellectual life and that of their target audience. As a result, ethnic minority media are characterized by a second level of content, which is the dominant ideology, suppressed to varying degrees, depending on the individual journalist, the social situation of the minority group, and the theme of the news story. Some of this content may be deliberately assimilationist, but much of it is probably unconsciously or inadvertently so. Assimilation is furthered if the shared interests of minority and majority populations are emphasized.

All of the chapters in this volume are based on the assumption that ethnic minority media provide information that prevents or at least delays the assimilation of their audiences to mainstream cultures. There is undoubtedly some evidence that this is indeed the case. Stenbaek, for example, writes that self-government in Greenland would not have been possible without Greenlandic media. According to Valaskakis, satellite broadcasting in the Arctic helped to unite geographically dispersed Inuit communities giving the Inuit greater chances of cultural survival than would be true for small isolated settlements. Howell assumes that in Wales broadcasting has played some role in the modest increase in recent years in the number of people who are able to speak Welsh.

On the other hand, all of the contributors also document the fact that ethnic minority media provide much content—paradoxically and probably unwittingly—that would appear to promote the assimilation of their audiences. The radio station broadcasting to the Mapuches of Chile, investigated by Colle, appears to broadcast as much information about Roman Catholicism as about Mapuche culture and language. Downing believes Hispanic media in New York City contain more information related to American consumerism than information that might empower the local Hispanic community. The articles about international Judaism that appear in the popular Romanian-Israeli magazine, investigated by Bar-Haïm, may reinforce a Jewish identity, but they do not necessarily strengthen a specifically Romanian-Jewish identity.

In view of this complex situation, it may be useful to attempt to untangle the various features that characterize ethnic minority media and to consider them separately. Naturally, it should be kept in mind that these features are always combined in actual cases, such as the ones that have been described in this book, and that they can be isolated only artificially.

Features of Ethnic Minority Media
That May Induce Audience Assimilation

The Implicit Dominant Ideology

The dominant ideology finds its way into ethnic minority media through two sources. First, minority journalists are not in a position to sever all intellectual ties with the surrounding majority culture and are thus bound to create some content with assimilationist implications. My study of the Canadian native press concluded that the more prominent themes in reports on environmental topics were traditional European attitudes that ignore ethical obligations to nonhuman species rather than traditional native attitudes that emphasized such obligations. Second, not all of the content of ethnic minority media is actually created by minority journalists. Extensive use is made of information produced by mainstream journalists, including press agencies, and it is not unusual for minority media associations to hire outside their own ethnic group, especially to fill technical positions. The chapters in this volume show that in terms of their level of professionalism, hiring, financial support, and so forth, most of the organizations producing ethnic minority media are compromising their goals of resisting assimilation. In addition, several contributors describe situations in which majority groups use minority media to communicate directly with minority groups. Downing writes that the Unification Church has established general-interest Spanish-language newspapers to diffuse its religious and political ideas among Spanish audiences. According to Ihaddaden, the Algerian government does much the same through its monopoly on broadcasting to unilingual speakers of Kabyle. A high level of assimilationist content would be expected given such forms of sponsorship.

Borrowed Genres

The term *genre* refers to "a class or category of artistic endeavor having a particular form, content, [or] technique" (*The Random House Dictionary,* 1987, p. 797). Spot news, soap operas, editorials, and adventure shows are mass media genres because they constitute standard formulas for presenting information. For the most part genres are invisible, taken for granted by both audiences and professional journalists, unless their features are combined in unexpected ways. Few minority journalists are consciously violating the rules of the popular genres of majority groups and confronting the dilemmas of how to combine in ways consistent with their own traditions fiction and nonfiction, humor and seriousness, objectivity and subjectivity, linear and nonlinear time, and so on. There are, though, some minor divergences such as exploring spontaneity and group creation. According to Meadows, mainstream media popularize Western literary genres among Australian Aborigines. The ubiquitousness of these models makes it difficult for Aboriginal journalists to imagine alternatives. Meadows believes that some of the stylistic uniqueness of Aboriginal video—features that create intimacy and informality but that also make such videos boring for outsiders—are lost when Aborigines receive training from teachers of European ancestry.

Intellectual Ghettoization

Restricting media attention to one minority group might be termed *intellectual ghettoization.* This practice curtails the possibility of productively interacting on an equal footing with other ethnic groups whether majority or minority. On one hand, intellectual ghettoization may be counterproductive, because the target audience may become bored by content that does not seem to convey new information. It is rare, though, for the content of ethnic minority media to be exclusively about one group, if for no other reason than the fact that majority actions have to be discussed. On the other hand, some minority journalists actively pursue news stories about minorities worldwide perceived to be confronting circumstances similar to those confronting the journalists' own group. They assume that knowledge of shared circumstances strengthens the resolve of their readers or viewers to resist majority domination. However, constant efforts to reach out to other minorities can lead to some forms of universalism or relativism that may be indistinguishable from the cultural pluralism of complex modern societies. The chapter by Bar-Haïm is relevant to the topic of intellectual ghettoization. He writes about a minority in Israel, Romanian immigrants, who perceive themselves as less influential than immigrants from some other Eastern European countries. Bar-Haïm develops a scheme for conceptualizing the cultural orientation that immigrant groups adopt in their new host country, a continuum of two variables: continuity versus newness and cosmopolitanism versus localism. An emphasis on continuity and localism might be one form of ghettoization. The rejection of politics and the drive to acquire consumer goods, themes in the Israeli magazine *Revista Mea,* are by no means unique to this publication. Ethnic activists everywhere are constrained by these widespread values.

An Inclusive Definition of
the Target Audience

An inclusive definition is one that defines the potential minority audience as broadly as possible thus incorporating culturally or linguistically marginal people. Given the small size of many minority groups, an inclusive definition might seem to be the natural one to apply. However, as marginal members are likely to be more integrated into the majority culture, focusing too much attention on them may have the effect of accelerating the assimilation of core members in the minority group.

The Use of Majority Languages

Shared language is a strong source of social solidarity. Language loyalty is also correlated with ethnic identity. Nonetheless, not all ethnic minority media appear in minority languages. For example, the first native newspaper in North America was printed in the Cherokee language in 1831 (Murphy & Murphy, 1981), but English has been overwhelmingly preferred by the native publications that followed. Native languages have lost ground to English partly because of the acceptance of the latter in the media. This has also facilitated the hiring of nonnative journalists.

The Social Effects of Modern Technology

Much research still needs to be done regarding the respective influence on audiences of the medium and the message, to use McLuhan's (1964) concepts. Modern means of communication are probably not as culturally neutral as is generally assumed. For instance, Japanese novelist Jun'ichiro Tanizaki wrote in 1933 in his book *In Praise of Shadows* that the adoption by the Japanese of technical inventions from the West resulted in cultural losses. Concerning the public broadcasting of music, he wrote, "Japanese music is above all a music of reticence, of atmosphere. When recorded, or amplified by a loudspeaker, the greater part of its charm is lost. In conversation, too, we prefer the soft voice, the understatement. Most important of all are the pauses. Yet the phonograph and radio render these moments of silence utterly lifeless" (Tanizaki, 1933/1977, p. 9). In Tanizaki's opinion, it was the Western origins of the radio and phonograph that made them unsuitable to the Eastern character of music and speech. Today, the Japanese in their own country can hardly be construed as an ethnic minority struggling for survival, but the point Tanizaki makes that modern scientific technology and the knowledge required to keep it functioning can be assimilating is shared by other people who remain attached to premodern values or to alternative traditional ways of life.

Features of Ethnic Minority Media That May Counter Cultural Assimilation

The Explicit Counterideology

It is known from ethnographic research on television audiences (Morley, 1986) and from studies of news comprehension (Van Dijk, 1988) that most of the public pays shallow and intermittent attention to the mass media. Although published research on this topic has dealt only with mainstream commercial media, there would appear to be no reason to assume that ethnic minority audiences are different. The conscious goal of associations creating ethnic minority media is to avoid assimilation. This is most obvious in the more superficial levels of the content they produce (the bias in photographs, story topics, headlines, lead paragraphs, disproportionate speaking space, etc.). Minority group members are likely to be depicted in assertive postures as agents of change rather than simply victims of change initiated by others. Thus it is reasonable to hypothesize that ethnic minority media—despite their dual nature—make their greatest contribution in the direction of resisting assimilation. The preference of some scholars to focus on the less obvious layers of media content, as I have done in my own chapter in this volume, may account for the tendency of some past research to come to opposite conclusions.

The Use of Minority Languages

Most of these case studies demonstrate that ethnic minority media are making a substantial contribution to the continued survival of minority languages. The skills of imperfect speakers are improving, languages are being modernized by the addition of new technical vocabulary related to contemporary life, and many groups have been characterized historically by a variety of dialects and orthographies that are being standardized. Ethnic minority media give the young an opportunity to relate to role models speaking their native language. The public validation of minority languages by their use in the media is important for their survival especially in the eyes of the young who would be most tempted to speak exclusively the majority language.

The Establishment of a Minority
News Agenda

The term *news agenda* refers to a ranking of the importance that is attached to public events. Minorities feel not only that they are neglected by the majority's media but that the meager coverage they do receive concentrates on the wrong events or on topics of minor interest. Studies of news retention have concluded that the media may not determine what the public thinks but are influential in determining what the public thinks *about*. To a large extent, audiences accept the media's news agenda (Robinson & Levy, 1986). The possession of the means of media production helps to give a minority the power to set its own priorities in terms of gathering information and thus to allocate resources so that more pressing news stories are kept before the public.

Announcements of Community Events

The publicity ethnic minority media give to community events is a crucial link uniting the group because word of mouth is not an efficient way of informing the public in a modern society. It is not unusual for community participation to decline as a result of the closure of a communications society. In addition, the coverage of social activities may offer some incentives for the socially prominent to participate in community activities. In this respect, the media may increase the interactional density of communities which are spread over large areas.

Advertisements

The effect of advertising on assimilation is naturally related to the ethnic origins and goals of the advertisers. The small size of most minority markets results in relatively little advertising originating from outside the group. For that reason advertising as it presently exists would seem to prevent or retard assimilation. It is not unusual for articles on minority businesses to be in essence unpaid advertisements. Historically, some minority groups have had relatively few professionals and have relied on businesspeople, such as merchants (Li, 1988), to provide noneconomic services. This is an added reason why minorities need a thriving business community.

The Symbolic Significance of Ethnic Minority Media

The mere existence of ethnic minority media may have considerable symbolic significance. Possession of the means of media production could be seen as a public validation of a minority's sophistication or modernity. This in itself would probably be interpreted favorably by many group members as well as by outsiders and may contribute in some subtle way to a determination to resist assimilation.

Activism by Media Organizations and Journalists

As a result of their considerable skills in writing and public speaking, skills that would not be so highly developed without their work in communications, ethnic minority journalists acquire a high profile in their community. It is not unusual for journalists to be energetic workers in various community activities. They may be working to register voters during elections, publicize social injustices such as inadequate health care, disseminate information about ethnic art and music or movements such as feminism and environmentalism. Journalism may be a transitory occupation for many, but the skills of ex-journalists can be lifelong assets for their communities. This could be seen as an indirect consequence of ethnic minority media that would counter assimilation.

Meeting the Challenge:
Policy Implications

It should be abundantly clear that in spite of the productive features listed above ethnic minority media are loaded with dangers. The most obvious danger is the inability to survive long enough to have a significant impact. Many undertakings quickly peter out. Plans may be too grandiose, especially if they involve radio and television, to be sustainable over a period of even 2 or 3 years.

Many amateur minority journalists do not realize all the social implications of modern forms of mass communication that inevitably modify the situation in which they evolve. Any medium of communication creates a culture of its own with its own memory, technical specialization, and social hierarchy. Modern media cannot passively perpetuate a culture but must necessarily interact with it, and a lack of awareness and proper monitoring of this phenomenon can lead to unwanted results.

Another danger is factional bias or elitism. Minority journalists may not be equally responsive to all segments of a community. The opinions of some segments may be overrepresented. Journalists' preferences with respect to programming or their favorite type of media may not correspond with those of many community members, and this can lead to a constituency that is too narrow for sustaining the long-term survival of the media.

There is also the risk that the newness of information can be exhausted quite quickly in small communities. Much of the information presented to the public may already be known to them. Intellectual ghettoization, discussed above, may promote uninteresting repetition and a definite lack of motivation that in turn can encourage practices that unintentionally lead to the demise of the media.

How can these pitfalls be avoided? The case studies presented in this volume do help formulate some practical advice for those considering the creation of ethnic minority media.

It is essential for minorities to have full control over the financing and administration of their own media. Modern communications technology requires a heavy investment. The goal should be the securing of a system of funding with no strings attached other than respect for sound management. If the media are sponsored by an outside organization, as frequently happens, consideration should be given at the outset about how its influence can be held in check.

Minority media should be designed in response to the informational needs and preferences of the community. Giving people the information they want should take precedence over giving them the information that is good for them. A survey should be done, at least informally, concerning the type of media that would be most appreciated, the preferred genres, and the topics people would most like to see at the top of the news agenda. It is counterproductive for journalists to launch into a communications society without a survey—a symbol of democratic intentions—because the whole endeavor is heavily dependent on community goodwill. Surveys should be done at regular intervals so that journalists are aware of the level of satisfaction in the community with their work and can accordingly adjust their program of action.

Long-term planning should be carefully prepared. Spontaneity may be an idealized traditional value, but this need not be interpreted as inconsistent with thoughtful planning. It takes extensive planning to make sure that in 2 or 3 years the media will be able to keep disseminating interesting information relevant to its purpose. Unrealistic planning, raising people's expectations only to disappoint them, may be worse than modest plans that more realistically accept a group's limited resources.

Mutually supportive institutions should join forces. Because mass media alone cannot save a minority language from extinction, journalists should establish ties with the school system. In this way the two institutions can reinforce each other's linguistic and cultural influence.

An explicit policy should be devised with respect to the supply of information. Minority media organizations may want to have a system of scouting the mainstream media for relevant information and story topics. News stories in mainstream media cannot be ignored because they provide a wealth of information for news-starved minority journalists. But some definite mechanism should be in place to reshuffle the mainstream news agenda, to exclude biased and uninformed opinions, and to find appropriate angles for news stories. It may be a good idea to create an extensive network within the minority itself to provide local information on a regular basis. Even in a small community minority journalists may not be in touch equally with all segments of the population. They tend to overrepresent some segments by relying too much on relatives, friends, and acquaintances for information. A more formal network of informants might keep this to a minimum.

Special attention should be paid to the input of media professionals. Preference should be given to hiring minority members, including those who may have more enthusiasm than skill, rather than hiring people primarily on the basis of their professional qualifications. Cultural knowledge and extensive contacts within the minority community seem to be more important than professional experience, which is one avenue for assimilationist content. This principle should apply to everyone, including technicians, because apparently trivial technical features of media such as camera angles, editing, and the pace with which information is presented are actually part of the content. Learning on the job should be encouraged. But the organization should be hesitant about sending employees to other regions of the country for technical training. Instruction that is deemed indispensable might be conveyed by visiting advisers who train a few staff members. In turn, they could serve as intermediaries instructing other minority journalists. Technical information would then be mastered in the context of the ethos of the minority group.

Journalists should aim for excellence with respect to their own culture's standards so that finished products may turn out to be competitive enough to be sold to the mainstream media. It is not enough that minority media are viewed only by minority audiences. Everyone benefits when minority groups are perceived by others and by themselves as valued producers of cultural forms.

The ultimate purpose of ethnic minority media is the peaceful preservation of the linguistic and cultural identity of a population that political and economic factors have put in a threatened position. Naturally, it would be utopian to believe that all of the above requirements can be brought together at once in every case. However, they can inspire goals and function as guidelines even if they can not be strictly followed. It may appear in some instances that ethnic minority media operate as a Trojan horse and bring about the long-term demise of the values they were designed to preserve. But understanding these problems is a first step toward their solution. The wealth of information provided by the case studies in this book should contribute to the creation of more efficient designs for ethnic minority survival in the future. As long as the political context is not overwhelmingly hostile, the successful development of ethnic minority media should be an attainable goal.

288   *Ethnic Minority Media*

References

Fiske, J. (1987). *Television culture*. London: Methuen.

Li, P. (1988). *The Chinese in Canada*. Toronto: Oxford University Press.

McLuhan, W. M. (1964). *Understanding media*. New York: McGraw-Hill.

Morley, D. (1986). *Family television: Cultural power and domestic leisure*. London: Routledge.

Murphy, J. E., & Murphy, S. (1981). *Let my people know: American Indian journalism, 1828-1978*. Norman: University of Oklahoma Press.

The Random House dictionary of English (2nd ed.). (1987). New York: Random House.

Robinson, J. P., & Levy, M. R. (1986). *The main source: Learning from television news*. Newbury Park, CA: Sage.

Subervi-Vélez, F. A. (1986). The mass media and ethnic assimilation and pluralism: A review proposal with special focus on Hispanics. *Communication Research, 13*(1), 71-96.

Tanizaki, J. (1977). *In praise of shadows*. New Haven, CT.: Leete's Island Books. (Original work published in 1933.)

Van Dijk, T. (1988). *News as discourse*. Hillsdale, NJ.: Lawrence Erlbaum.

Name Index

Abas, B. 265
'Abd al-Hakam, I. 255
Abu-Laban, B. 2
Acheson, J. 123
Adair, J. 84
Adorno, T. 215
Akam, N. 170, 182
Albert, P. 248
Alcock, A. 74
Alem, A. 265
Anderson, B. 2
Anderson, J. 265
Annan, N. 223
Antola, L. 270
Applebaum, L. 74

Badger, M. 37
Bar-Haïm, G. 196-216, 279, 281
Barelli, Y. 170
Barthes, R. 214
Bartlett, R. 114
Batty, P. 93
Beckett, J. 99
Begard, D. 170, 182
Begay, M. 257, 259
Bell, D. 87
Bennett, T. 121
Bergman, M. 75-76
Berkes, F. 123
Berry, J. 271-272
Berthelsen, R. 47
Betts, C. 229
Bidot-Germa, D. 187
Black, J. 4
Bogardus, E. 4, 102
Bonilla, F. 261
Bostock, L. 91

Boudy, J. 170
Bouissac, P. 127, 165, 243
Boyer, J. 265
Braudel, F. 165
Briggs, A. 221
Briggs, V. 260
Brisebois, D. 3
Brody, H. 67, 75
Brooke, M. 232, 240
Broudig, F. 194
Browne, D. 99
Brun, E. 51
Buck, E. 157
Burgoon, J. 3
Burgoon, M. 3
Burnet, J. 9
Bush, J. 151

Cagnulef, E. 140
Callicott, J. 105
Campos, R. 261
Cardinali, J. 266
Carey, J. 41, 68
Carlson, M. 264
Caron, A. 77
Carrasco, E. 143
Cashmore, E. 4
Caspi, D. 213
Castedo, L. 129-130
Castillo, E. 141
Catton, W. 107
Cawelti, J. 206
Cazenave, E. 170
Cerda, A. 170-171, 183
Chaker, S. 253
Chapalain, J. 194
Chapman, M. 2

289

Cheval, J. 10-11, 165-195
Chevaldonné, F. 243
Chomsky, N. 121
Clarkson, F. 265
Cochrane, P. 94
Cohen, P. 83
Coldevin, G. 77-78
Colle, R. 11, 127-148, 279
Collin, C. 177-178
Coopman, J. 229, 233
Corker J. 94, 96-97
Coulon, C. 168
Crisp, L. 94
Critser, G. 269, 272
Curran, J. 121

Daley, P. 10, 23-43
Danker, P. 49
Darenco, J. 170
Davies, H. 241
Denton, R. 12
Desfois, J. 244
Diaz, A. 170, 182
Dicks, D. 77
Douglas, M. 208, 214
Dowling, R. 38
Downing, J. 13, 256-275, 279
Drouin, J. 170
Duchasse, R. 170, 182

Edwardsen, C. 23
Egede, H. 45
Eguymendia, Y. 182-183
Elberg, N. 75-76
Encina, F. 129-130
Engels, F. 26
Epstein, E. 121
Erngaard, E. 45, 48
Escarpit, R. 167, 171
Even-Zohar, I. 208
Evans, G. 225, 239
Evans, H. 91

Fahy, T. 241
Fallows, J. 24
Fanon, F. 24
Fenny, D. 123

Ferrer, P. 181
Fesl, E. 99
Fienup-Riordan, A. 13
Finlay-Pelinski, M. 31, 39
Fishman, M. 121
Fiske, J. 7, 277
Fleisher, J. 46
Fleming, A. 65-66
Forsberg, M. 233
Forsythe, D. 2
Foulks, E. 24, 36
Fowler, L. 41
Freire, P. 24, 133-134, 136, 139, 148

Gad, F. 45
Gailey, C. 7
Galdames, F. 129-131
Gallagher, H. 23
Gallagher, M. 14
Gamson, W. 106, 121
Gardy, P. 167
Garnett, E. 45
Garland, P. 257
Gellner, E. 244
Gibson, W. 151
Glick, T. 255
Glynn, F. 92-94
Goldstick, M. 112
Golvin, L. 244, 254
Gordon, M. 11
Graburn, N. 67
Granzberg, G. 7, 77
Grasmuck, S. 261
Grassby, A. 83
Greenberg, B. 2
Grollier, B. 189
Grosclaude, D. 192
Gurevitch, M. 121
Gusfield, J. 12
Gutiérrez, F. 3-4, 89, 160, 269

Habermas, J. 25-30, 36, 40
Haina, K. 154-155, 160
Hamer, J. 7, 77
Harbi, M. 247
Hardt, H. 4
Harris, S. 88

Hay, P. 106
Hébert, J. 74
Heckathorn, J. 152-153
Henningham, J. 10, 149-161
Henry, G. 77
Herberg, E. 2, 11
Herman, E. 121
Herrera, F. 257, 259
Hiebert, A. 42
Hodge, R. 88
Holt, J. 153
Horkheimer, M. 215
Howell, W. 12-13, 217-242, 278
Hudson, H. 77-78
Hughes, E. 2
Hujanen, T. 5
Hurt, R. 118
Husband, C. 9, 258

Idieder, J. 186
Ihaddaden, Z. 10, 243-255, 280
Inglis, F. 215
Innis, H. 41, 67-68
Inukshuk, P. 70
Isaacs, H. 17

James, B. 10, 23-43
Jarvin, G. 78
Jeanneney, J. 179
Johnson, R. 152
Jones, E. 241
Jones, G. 241
Jones, H. 219, 221, 240
Jones, I. 233
Juárez, N. 263

Kaddache, M. 247
Kalakaua, D. 150-151
Kanahele, G. 153, 156, 158
Katz, E. 64, 84
Kealoha, G. 155-156, 160
Keely, C. 260
Kelly, M. 157
Kelly, N. 69
Kelly, W. 69
Kenny, G. 70
Kent, N. 154

Khaki, A. 3
Kimura, L. 152
Klausner, S. 24, 36
Kleinschmidt, S. 46
Korzenny, F 3
Krech, S. 105
Krisol, A. 188
Kroker, A. 68
Kuptana, R. 3, 72
Kuykendall, R. 150

Lacaze, P. 190
Laduke, W. 107
L'Africain, L. 245
Lahlou, M. 249, 254
Lapassade, R. 189
Laplume, Y. 181, 185
LaRuffa, A. 3
Lasagni, C. 271
Lauritzen, P. 49
Law, M. 97
Lawrence, E. 105
Lee, A. 3
Leithner, C. 4
Lenguin, R. 188
Leopold, A. 107
Letamendia, P. 167
Levy, M. 277, 283
Lewis, B. 231
Li, P. 284
Liddle, R. 99
Lieberson, S. 2
Lind, A. 159
López, J. 256
Lorimer, R. 119
Lustick, I. 247
Lynge, A. 52
Lynge, F. 60
Lyons, D. 151

MacConghail, M. 241
Mackay, H. 84
Mackey, W. 217
Madden, K. 77-78
Madigan, R. 24
Malecot, J. 181
Marchak, M. 106
Marcuse, H. 26

Marger, M. 2
Marson, L. 97
Martin, C. 105-106
Martindale, C. 3
Marx, K. 25-26
Mattelart, A. 171
Mattelart, M. 171
Maxwell, M. 45
Mayes, R. 67, 69, 78
McCarthy, W. 90
McCarty, J. 273
McCay, B. 123
McDermott, J. 159
McDonald, M. 2, 13
McLuhan, M. 86-87, 239, 282
McNicol, T. 264
McNulty, J. 119
McRedmond, L. 241
Meadows, M. 6, 82-101, 280
Means, R. 5-7
Merton, R. 208
Meyrowitz, J. 6
Michaels, E. 82, 84-88
Michaud, C. 244
Michener, J. 159
Milbrath, L. 106, 123
Miraldi, R. 121
Mirós, G. 268
Mistral, F. 168
Modigliani, A. 106, 121
Modleski, T. 271
Moller, A. 47-48
Moller, H. 51
Montagne, R. 244
Mookini, E. 150-152
Moon, S. 265-266
Moore, R. 92
Morley, D. 282
Munro, L. 83
Murin, D. 55
Murphy, J. 3, 281
Murphy, S. 3, 281

Nabhan, G. 118
Nelson, C. 257
Nelson, R. 111
Newsom, J. 89

Noble, G. 83
Northrip, C. 28

Obermiller, P. 2
Obijiofor, L. 89
O'Brien, T. 74
O'Connell, S. 77
O'Connor, A. 128
O'Hara, J. 90
Oregi, S. 182
Oshiro, S. 160

Padolsky, E. 3
Park, R. 4, 102
Passel, J. 260
Pérez, R. 256, 263
Peterson, N. 85
Peterson, R. 119
Peterson, W. 24
Petrella, R. 167
Petrone, P. 3
Phillips, A. 66
Platiel, R. 10, 119
Poepoe, J. 151-152
Porritt, J. 106
Prasad, K. 3
Prattis, I. 47
Price, J. 103
Prot, R. 175

Quandt, W. 247
Quirk, J. 41

Rada, S. 14
Ramirez, T. 39
Rasmussen, K. 61
Raudsepp, E. 103
Regan, T. 105-106
Richeri, G. 271
Riggins, S. 1-20, 102-126, 127, 165, 243, 276-288
Rink, H. 45-48
Robbins, R. 73
Roberts, H. 253
Robinson, D. 233
Robinson, J. 277, 283

Rogers, E. 24, 270
Rosing, P. 54, 59
Ross, P. 8
Roth, L. 70, 78, 103
Rothchild, J. 273
Rothmyer, K. 265
Rubio Tió, J. 168
Rupert R. 103
Russell, B. 148

Salter, L. 77
Sassen-Koob, S. 256, 261, 263
Schement, J. 269
Schiller, H. 24, 63
Schudson, M. 119, 121
Seelye, K. 264
Siberry, J. 223
Silva, O. 129-131
Smiley, J. 45
Smith, C. 12
Smolicz, J. 5
Snow, M. 83
Sperling, S. 110
Srivastava, A. 8
Staino, K. 2
Steele, H. 68
Steinbring, J. 7, 77
Stenbaek, M. 44-62, 278
Stewart, C. 12
Stewart H. 104
Strand, P. 259
Subervi-Vélez, F. 4, 256-259, 270, 276

Taboury, E. 243
Taboury, M. 243
Tanizaki, J. 282
Tanner, A. 110
Tatar, E. 156
Tealdo, A. 128
Thomas, W. 219, 241
Thompson, D. 87-88
Tienda, M. 257
Tonkin, E. 2
Trask, H. 154, 159
Tuckman, G. 121
Tudesq, A. 170-171, 176, 248

Tyler, E. 106

Ugalde, A. 261

Valaskakis, G. 9-10, 63-81, 103, 278
Vallee, F. 66
Van Dijk, T. 3, 9, 104, 121, 282
Veciana-Suarez, A. 15
Vecsey, C. 105-106, 118
Vega, B. 261
Velasco, N. 128
Venner, M. 95, 97
Vibe, C. 49

Wallerstein, I. 24
Walp, R. 40
Walsh, M. 83
Watson, S. 83
Weinfeld, M. 9
Wenzel, G. 110
White, J. 159
White, N. 3
White, P. 3
White, R. 12
Wilcox, R. 151
Wilford, N. 69
Wilkin, A. 244
Williams, R. 30
Williams, T. 241
Willmot, E. 84, 91, 96-97
Willshire-Carrera, J. 273
Wilson, C. 3-4, 89, 160
Wilson, T. 73, 77-78, 103
Winner, C. 106
Winstedt, O. 57
Wollacott, J. 121
Woodrow, K. 260
Worth, S. 84
Wüest, J. 188

Young, B. 153

Zipes, J. 271
Zubrzycki, J. 4, 102

Subject Index

Aboriginalism, 88

Aborigines, 1, 6, 82-101, 280

Advertising, 14-15, 56, 94, 121, 157, 172, 176-177, 182-184, 188, 191, 193, 220, 236, 239, 257, 259, 271-272, 284

African-Americans, 61, 83, 257

Algeria, 10, 243-255, 280

Animation, 233

Animism, 106, 119

Arabization, 10, 244-247, 252-253

Araucans, 129-130

Argentina, 266, 271

Arrentes, 92, 94

Assimilation, 2, 4, 9, 13, 17, 23, 51-52, 59-60, 69, 76-78, 102, 117, 119, 258, 276-284, 287

Athabascan Indians, 31

Audience, 14-15, 55, 86, 108, 144, 146-147, 158-159, 173, 175-177, 189, 191-193, 203, 205, 213-216, 232, 248-249, 251-252, 263, 265-269, 272, 281

Australia, 1, 6, 9, 82-101, 160, 280

Basques, 1, 5, 165-195

Berbers, 243-255, 280

Blood Indians, 113

Brazil, 270-271

Broadcasting, 12, 23-43, 63-81, 82-101, 217-242

Canada, 1, 9-10, 39, 51, 59, 63-81, 102-126, 278-279

Catholic church, 11, 116, 128, 132-134, 139, 171, 186, 189, 219, 265, 279

Chile, 1, 11, 127-148, 271, 279

Class, 13, 17, 260-263

Colombians, 261, 264, 268, 271

Communication, 27-28, 30-31

Communication ethics, 12

Congregational church, 150

Contact agent, 65-66

Content, 15, 29, 34-35, 39, 47, 50-51, 55, 58, 76-77, 83-89, 94, 98-99, 106-122, 140-141, 158-159, 173-174, 177, 180-181, 183, 185-187, 189, 204-216, 230-234, 236-239, 249-251, 264-272, 276-288

Continuity, 207-211, 281

Cosmopolitanism, 207-209, 211-212, 281

Counterideology, 277-278, 282-283

Cree Indians, 7, 77, 120

Creoles, 130

Crow Indians, 104

Cubans, 257, 260-261, 265, 267-268, 273

Cultural preservation, 13, 73, 102, 140, 276

Culture, 13, 75, 84, 133, 215, 259

Deep ecology, 103, 118

Democracy, 27, 36, 40

Denmark, 44-62

Diffusion of innovations, 24

Discourse analysis, 104

Divisive model, 10

Dominant ideology, 277-280

Dominicans, 261, 264, 266, 269, 271

Dual role, 4, 276

Economic model, 9-10

Ecuadoreans, 261

Elitism, 285

Empowerment, 16-17, 258, 260, 272, 278

Environment, 40, 85, 102-123, 143

Environmental philosophy, 102, 104-108, 143, 279

Ethnicity defined, 1-2

Fiction, 88
France, 11, 13, 165-195, 208, 247-248
Funding, 14-15, 48, 50, 56, 74, 95, 98, 121,
    172-173, 176, 178-179, 182, 184, 193,
    239

Genre, 280
Germans, 130
Great Britain, 217-242, 278
Greenland, 1, 7, 14, 44-62, 278

Haida Indians, 115-116
Hilali tribes, 244-247, 254
Hiring, 14-15, 159-160, 176, 191, 279, 287
Hispanics, 1, 5, 13-14, 256-275, 279
Huilliches, 127, 129-130

Ideology, 15-16, 25-27, 102, 106-108, 119,
    122, 170-171, 185-186, 190-191, 201-
    202, 204-207, 214-215, 265-267, 273,
    277-280, 282-283
Immigrants, 1, 5
Integrationist model, 8-9
Intellectual ghettoization, 280-281, 285
Inuit, 1, 41, 44-62, 63-81, 278
Inupiats, 23
Irish, 1, 5, 13, 74, 217-242, 278
Islam, 245-247, 254-255
Israel, 5, 196-216, 281

Japan, 282

Kabyles, 1, 5, 10, 243-255, 280
Koories, 83
Koyukon Indians, 111
Kwakiutl Indians, 104

Language, 12-13, 46-47, 54, 57, 59, 67, 78-
    79, 83, 92, 94, 140, 152-153, 155, 165-
    195, 217-242, 243-247, 249, 256-275,
    281, 283
Latinization, 259
Libertarian model, 119-121
Localism, 207, 209-213, 281
Lutheran church, 45

Magazines, 196-198, 203-216
Mapuches, 1, 11, 127-148, 279
Media impact, 3, 77-79, 277
Media imperative, 3
Media packages, 106, 121
Medium theory, 6
Metis, 130
Mexicans, 257, 259-261, 264, 269-270
Milingimbis, 99
Modernization, 5-6, 24-25, 45-46, 51-53, 64-
    68, 77, 86, 104-108, 128-131, 153, 285
Moroccan Jews, 202-203, 207
Multiculturalism, 8-11
Music, 92, 156-157, 168, 176-177, 185, 249-
    251, 268-269, 282

Native Americans, 1, 7, 23-43, 84, 111
Native Canadians, 1, 7, 63-81, 102-126, 278-
    279
Navajo Indians, 84
New muckraking, 121
Newness, 207, 211-213, 281
News, 3, 76, 157-158, 186-187, 231-232,
    234, 249, 251, 270-271, 286
News agenda, 283
Newspapers, 10, 46-51, 60, 102-126, 149-
    156, 256, 263-267, 279
Nicaraguans, 265, 267, 273

Occitans, 1, 5, 165-195
Ojibway Indians, 120
Oral culture, 5-7, 84-89
Organizational sponsor, 15, 127-128
Organizational structure, 13-15, 119, 172,
    228, 238, 285-287

Papua New Guinea, 92
Parisianism, 188
Participatory journalism, 12
Peigan Indians, 115
Peru, 271
Picunches, 129
Pitjantjatjaras, 92, 94, 96
Polish Jews, 200-201
Preemptive model, 10-11
Professionalism, 12

Proselytism model, 11
Puerto Ricans, 256-257, 261, 263-264, 266, 269-271

Race, 83
Racism, 9, 83
Radio, 6, 10-11, 51-57, 68-69, 72, 89-93, 95, 97-99, 127-128, 132-148, 157-158, 165-195, 217-242, 248-255, 267-269, 282
"Radio libre", 170-172
"Radio périphérique", 170
"Radio vision", 137-139
Romanian Jews, 1, 196-216, 279, 281
Russian Jews, 202-204, 207

Satellite communications, 27-41, 70-74, 79, 83-84, 93-97
Secrecy, 86-87
Shallow environmentalism, 104-108, 118-119
Social movements, 11-13, 52-53, 168-170, 174, 185-186, 190-191, 222-225, 227, 284
Social responsibility model, 119-121
Spain, 128-130, 166, 168-169, 171, 182-183, 185, 194, 246, 255

State policies, 8-11, 16, 169-170, 172, 176, 193-194, 247, 252-253, 276-277

Technology, 25-27, 36, 64-72, 282
Technopessimism, 7, 60
"Telenovelas", 269-272
Television, 3, 6-7, 9-10, 23-43, 56-61, 69, 77, 85-86, 88-91, 93, 95, 158-159, 217-242, 269-272
Tlingit Indians, 31
Torres Strait Islanders, 89-91, 95, 98-99
Traditional culture, 4-7, 75-77, 86, 88-89, 104-108, 110, 119
Trail radio, 72

Unification church, 265-266, 280
United States, 1, 9-10, 13-14, 23-43, 51, 61, 83-84, 111, 149-161, 208, 256-275, 279

Venezuela, 270-271
Voluntary minorities, 1, 5

Wall journalism, 141
Warlpiris, 85-87, 92, 94, 96
Welsh, 1, 13, 5, 217-242, 278

Yolngus, 88

About the Editor

Stephen Harold Riggins (Ph.D., University of Toronto) is Associate Professor of Sociology at Memorial University of Newfoundland, St. John's. His research interests concern the sociology of culture and mass media, Midwestern social history, and the study of material artifacts. He is the editor of *Beyond Goffman* and has published articles in *Current Perspectives in Social Theory, Semiotica, Semiotic Inquiry, Anthropologica, Midwestern Folklore,* and the *Indiana Magazine of History.* He has worked as a reporter for Canadian native newspapers and edited a special issue of *Anthropologica* on native journalism in North America.

About the Contributors

Gabriel Bar-Haïm is a member of the Sociology Department at the University of Winnipeg, Manitoba, Canada

Jean-Jacques Cheval is Assistant Professor at the Department of Social Communication at the University "Michel de Montaigne" of Bordeaux III, Talence, France.

Raymond Colle is associated with the Pontificia Universidad Catolica de Chile, San Bernardo, Chile.

Patrick J. Daley teaches in the Department of Communication at the University of New Hampshire, Durham.

John D. H. Downing is John T. Jones, Jr., Centennial Professor in the Department of Radio-Television-Film at the University of Texas, Austin.

John Henningham is Professor of Journalism at the University of Queensland, St. Lucia, Queensland, Australia.

W. J. Howell, Jr., is Professor of Communication Studies at Canisius College, Buffalo, New York.

Zahir Ihaddaden is a Professor at the Institut des Sciences de l'Information, University of Algiers, Algeria.

Beverly James teaches in the Department of Communication at the University of New Hampshire, Durham.

Michael Meadows teaches in the Department of Communication at the University of Queensland, St. Lucia, Queensland, Australia.

Marianne A. Stenbaek is the Director of the Centre for Northern Studies and Research, McGill University, Montreal, Quebec, Canada.

Gail Valaskakis is Professor of Journalism at Concordia University, Montreal, Quebec, Canada.